OFFICIAL PROCEEDINGS

OF THE

NATIONAL DEMOCRATIC CONVENTION,

Held in St. Louis, Mo., June 27th, 28th and 29th, 1876.

WITH AN APPENDIX

CONTAINING THE LETTERS OF ACCEPTANCE OF GOV. TILDEN AND GOV. HENDRICKS.

REPORTED FOR THE CONVENTION.

ST. LOUIS:
WOODWARD, TIERNAN & HALE, PRINTERS AND BINDERS.
1876.

MERCHANTS' EXCHANGE, ST. LOUIS, 1876.

Introduction.

The National Democratic Convention, to nominate candidates for President and Vice-President of the United States, which assembled in St. Louis June 27th, 1876, was the first Convention of the kind in the history of the country that met west of the Mississippi River. The sitting of such a Convention has always been an event of deep National interest, but the political condition of the country at the opening of the present campaign, and the encouraging prospects of the success of the Democratic ticket, gave an extraordinary prominence to the St. Louis Convention, and drew together an immense concourse of visitors from all parts of the United States. The citizens of St. Louis, appreciating the honor of entertaining a National political body, for which all the great cities of the country had been aspirants, joined with enthusiasm, and without distinction of party, in the work of arrangement, desirous only that the historical occasion should properly represent the spirit and hospitality of the city. The grand hall of the new Exchange building, one of the finest chambers in the world, was offered for the Convention by the merchants of St. Louis, and the funds necessary for its decoration and arrangement, and all other preparations, were subscribed by the citizens generally. The Resident Committee, appointed at Washington by the National Democratic Committee, had charge of the work of preparation, and every possible effort was made to render it complete in every detail.

The grand hall was arranged for seating six thousand people, its seventy windows were curtained with crimson, and upon its walls were displayed the shields and coats-of-arms of the States, encircled with laurel-leaves and budding cereals, and the platform and President's stand were magnificently ornamented with living shrubs and flowers. The seats allotted to the respective delegations were designated by blue silk banners, with silver fringe, mounted on spear-heads, and bearing the names of the States, and all the aisles and passage-ways were richly carpeted. The tasteful blending of colors in the work of ornamentation, and the vivid tints of the ceiling frescoes, made the appearance of the immense chamber extremely beautiful, and when the floor and galleries were filled by an audience of nearly eight thousand people, during the sitting of the Convention, the spectacle was one of extraordinary animation and impressiveness.

Ample accommodations were also provided in the Exchange building for committee-rooms, and the elegantly furnished reading-room was placed at the disposal of the National Democratic Committee, as their headquarters during the continuance of the Convention. The business office of the Committee was in the Drug Exchange room, the use of which was also gratuitously tendered for the purpose.

A Reception Committee of one hundred and seventy-five members, subdivided in proportion to the numbers of the different delegations, extended all appropriate courtesies and hospitality to the members of the Convention. A grand procession of the Fire and Police Departments, displays of fire-works from the dome of the Court-House, receptions at private residences, excursions to the parks and suburbs, and other incidents, added variety and interest to the occasion, and gave the visitors to St. Louis during the Convention an impression of its hospitality, and metropolitan and progressive spirit, that cannot readily be forgotten. The whole expense of the Convention, in every particular, was borne by the city of St. Louis.

During their stay in the city, the members of the National Committee were the guests of the Resident Committee on Arrangements, and it may be added that the hotel proprietors of the city entered into an agreement that nothing but ordinary rates should be charged to delegates and all other persons during the sitting of the Convention.

NATIONAL DEMOCRATIC CONVENTION.

EXCHANGE HALL, ST. LOUIS, JUNE, 1876.

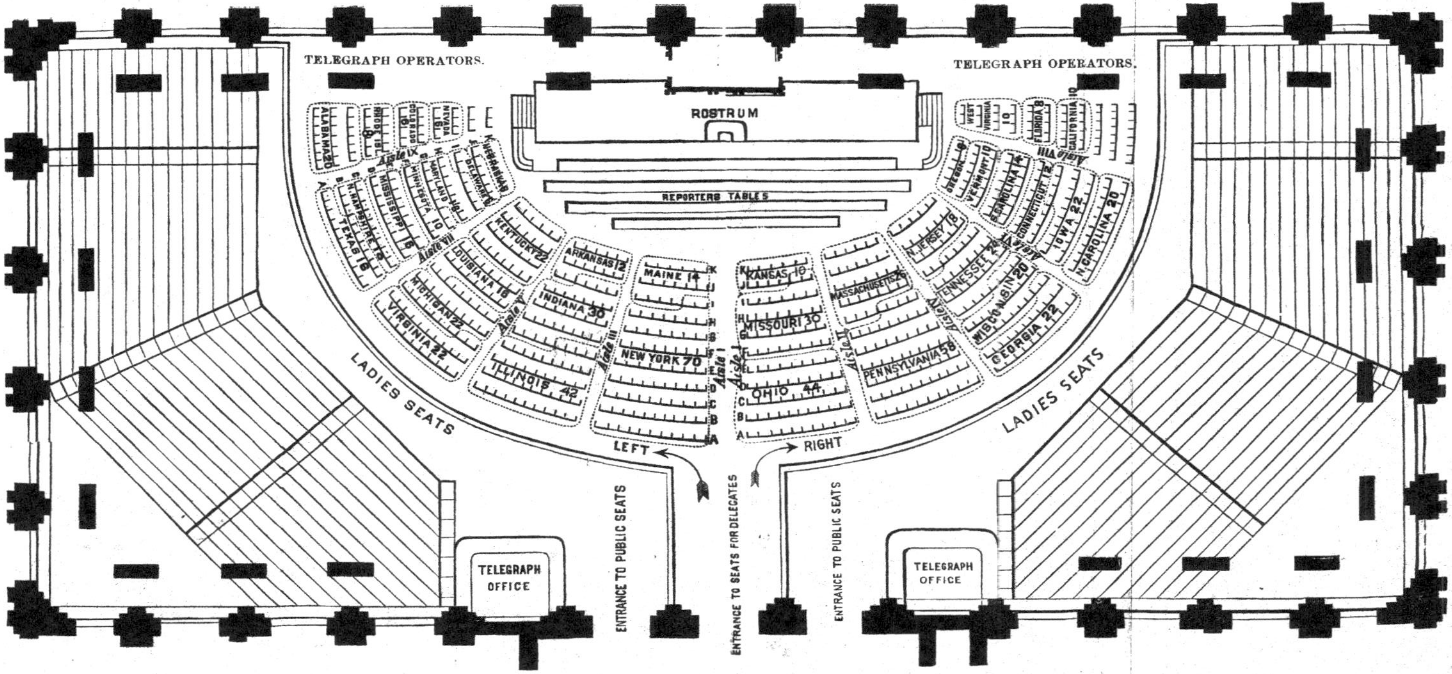

TELEGRAPH OPERATORS.

TELEGRAPH OPERATORS.

ROSTRUM

REPORTERS TABLES

ALABAMA 20 · RHODE ISL. 8 · COLORADO 6 · NEVADA 6 · N. HAMPSHIRE 10 · TEXAS 16 · MISSISSIPPI 16 · MINNESOTA 10 · MARYLAND 16 · DELAWARE 6 · NEBRASKA 6 · KENTUCKY 22 · LOUISIANA 16 · MICHIGAN 22 · VIRGINIA 22 · ARKANSAS 12 · INDIANA 30 · ILLINOIS 42 · MAINE 14 · NEW YORK 70

KANSAS 10 · MISSOURI 30 · OHIO 44 · MASSACHUSETTS 26 · PENNSYLVANIA 58 · N. JERSEY 18 · TENNESSEE 24 · WISCONSIN 20 · GEORGIA 22 · OREGON 6 · VERMONT 10 · S. CAROLINA 14 · CONNECTICUT 12 · IOWA 22 · N. CAROLINA 20 · WEST VIRGINIA 10 · FLORIDA 8 · CALIFORNIA 10

Aisle I · Aisle I · Aisle II · Aisle III · Aisle IV · Aisle V · Aisle VI · Aisle VII · Aisle VIII · Aisle IX

LADIES SEATS

LADIES SEATS

LEFT

RIGHT

TELEGRAPH OFFICE

TELEGRAPH OFFICE

ENTRANCE TO PUBLIC SEATS

ENTRANCE TO SEATS FOR DELEGATES

ENTRANCE TO PUBLIC SEATS

DIAGRAM OF EXCHANGE HALL DURING THE CONVENTION.

Preliminary Proceedings.

The National Democratic Committee met at Willard's Hotel, Washington, D. C., at 12 o'clock M., February 22d, 1876, pursuant to call, and for the purpose of determining the time and place for the holding of the National Democratic Convention, and promulgating the official call therefor.

Augustus Schell, of New York, Chairman of the Committee, occupied the chair. All the members present, with the exception of a few, who were represented by proxies.

On motion of Senator Randolph, T. M. Patterson, of Colorado, was admitted to represent that Territory.

A brief debate took place on the question whether the time or place of the National Democratic Convention should first be fixed, and it was determined that the time should first be agreed upon.

Mr. John G. Thompson, of Ohio, moved that Tuesday, the 27th of June, 1876, be the day fixed for the assembling of the Convention.

Mr. Eaton, of Kansas, moved, as an amendment, the first Tuesday in May. This question was discussed in all its bearings, when the Committee rejected Mr. Eaton's amendment, and agreed to the motion of Mr. Thompson, fixing the 27th of June as the time for holding the National Democratic Nominating Convention.

On motion of Mr. Goode, of Virginia, it was resolved that the delegations now here, desiring the Convention to be held in their respective cities, be heard through one of the members of each delegation, the remarks to be restricted to fifteen minutes.

On motion of Mr. Thompson, it was resolved that the different States, as here represented, desiring the Convention to be held in certain cities, now make nominations.

Accordingly, Mr. McCormick, of Illinois, named Chicago.

Mr. McHenry, of Kentucky, named Louisville.

Mr. Banks, of Mississippi, by request, named Washington.

Mr. Priest, of Missouri, named St. Louis.

Mr. Thompson, of Ohio, named Cincinnati.

Mr. Barr, of Pennsylvania, named Philadelphia.

A recess of fifteen minutes was taken, after which a motion was made and carried that the Chairman prepare the call for the National Convention, to be submitted to the Committee before being signed by the members.

Representatives of Chicago, Louisville, Washington, St. Louis, Cincinnati and Philadelphia then addressed the Committee in advocacy of the claims and advantages of their respective cities, after which the Committee adjourned until evening.

EVENING SESSION.

The Committee, on reassembling, proceeded to ballot on the place for holding the National Convention, with the following result:

FIRST BALLOT.

Number of votes cast........ 38
Necessary to a choice........ 20

St. Louis	14	Cincinnati	4
Chicago	8	Philadelphia	4
Louisville	7	Washington	1

SECOND BALLOT.

There being no choice, the Committee voted again, as follows:

St. Louis	15	Louisville	5
Chicago	9	Philadelphia	1
Cincinnati	8		

THIRD BALLOT.

On the third ballot the vote stood:

St. Louis	17	Louisville	3
Chicago	10	Cincinnati	8

No votes were cast for Philadelphia.

FOURTH BALLOT.

The fourth ballot resulted as follows:

St. Louis	19	Cincinnati	6
Chicago	12	Louisville	1

LAST BALLOT.

The fifth ballot resulted as follows:

St. Louis	21	Cincinnati	2
Chicago	15		

St. Louis having received the majority of votes cast, the Chairman declared that city as the place for holding the Convention.

Mr. Priest, of St. Louis, expressed his thanks to the Committee for the selection they had made. He would tell the Committee they had made no mistake, and that the reception that would be extended to the delegates would vindicate the selection made. They would be received with warm hearts and open hands to hospitable homes. He hoped the same good feeling and good judgment would be shown in every step in the campaign.

Mr. Thompson, of Ohio, moved that the vote be declared unanimous, which was seconded by Mr. McCormick, of Illinois.

Mr. McHenry expressed himself much gratified at the prevalent good feeling. Next to Louisville he preferred St. Louis, where he was sure all would meet with an enthusiastic welcome.

The vote selecting St. Louis was then declared unanimous, amid applause.

On motion of Mr. Walker, of Virginia, proxy for Nevada, it was resolved that in view of Colorado as a State in July next, that Territory be invited to send a delegate to the National Democratic Convention.

A resolution was adopted instructing the Executive Committee and Hon. John G. Priest, of Missouri, to make all necessary arrangements for the holding of the National Convention.

APPOINTMENT OF COMMITTEES.

The following is the official record of the action of the Executive Committee of the National Democratic Committee on the subject of the arrangements for the Convention on the 27th of June:

At a meeting of the Executive Committee of the National Democratic Committee, held at Washington, D. C., February 23d, 1876, the following resolution was adopted:

Resolved, That a committee, consisting of the member from Missouri, the Secretary of the Committee and three other members, be authorized to make all necessary arrangements for holding the Convention.

The following were appointed as such committee:

JOHN G. PRIEST, of Mo., Chairman.
FREDERICK O. PRINCE, of Mass.
ISAAC E. EATON, of Kansas.
WM. B. BATE, of Tennessee.
JOHN G. THOMPSON, of Ohio.

At a meeting of the Executive Committee of the National Democratic Committee, held at Washington, D. C., February 24th, 1876, the following resolution was adopted:

Resolved, That D. H. Armstrong, Web. M. Samuel, H. J. Spaunhorst, J. Fred. Thornton, Francis D. Lee, D. H. MacAdam, Joseph

Brown, Geo. W. Ford, D. P. Rowland, Julius S. Walsh, and John M. Gilkeson, be and they are hereby constituted the Resident Committee of the city of St. Louis, under the Sub-Committee of the National Executive Committee, and are authorized to make all needful local provisions and such necessary arrangements as shall be demanded for the convenience of the Convention to be held in that city on June 27th, 1876.

Arrangements in St. Louis.

The Resident Committee on Arrangements of St. Louis held their first meeting at the Southern Hotel, March 8th, 1876, pursuant to a call issued by John G. Priest, representative from Missouri in the National Democratic Convention, and the following organization was effected: David H. Armstrong, Chairman of Committee; Joseph Brown, Treasurer; D. H. MacAdam, Secretary.

The earlier meetings were held at the Southern Hotel until the office and headquarters of the Committee were established in the Exchange Building, Rooms Nos. 130 and 132, which apartments were handsomely furnished for the purpose. With the approval of the Committee the Secretary appointed Mr. F. A. McGarahan Assistant Secretary, and this gentleman had charge of the office until the final adjournment of the Committee.

Immediately succeeding organization the Resident Committee appointed the following gentlemen a

FINANCE COMMITTEE.

CHARLES SPECK,
ISAAC COOK,
THEOPHILE PAPIN,
J. FRED THORNTON,
WM. M. SENTER,
A. A. MELLIER,
LESLIE A. MOFFETT,
JOSEPH T. McCULLOUGH,
C. BENT CARR,
S. H. LAFLIN,
CHARLES L. HUNT,
THEO. HUNT,
CHARLES GREEN,
MILES SELLS,
DAN'L G. TAYLOR,
GEO. E. FINCH,
WM. LEIGH WICKHAM,
BENJAMIN STICKNEY, Jr.,
R. S. McDONALD,
H. C. CLEMENT,
S. M. DODD,
ALEXANDER CLEMENS,
JNO. B. MAUDE,
JNO. B. GRAY,
E. A. MANNY,
JNO. W. O'CONNELL,
JULIUS S. WALSH,
EDWARD WILKERSON,
FRANK CARTER,
CHAUNCEY F. SHULTZ,
A. W. SLAYBACK,
WILLIAM MITCHELL,
D. P. ROWLAND,
JNO. G. PRATHER,
ALF. W. HENRY,
J. C. KIRKBRIDE,
T. A. ENNIS,
M. M. BUCK,
JAMES E. SHORB.

Hon. Chas. Speck was elected Chairman of the Finance Committee, J. Fred Thornton, Secretary, and Leslie A. Moffett, Treasurer.

COMMITTEE ON TRANSPORTATION.

The following gentlemen were appointed a Committee on Transportation, to arrange for securing reduced rates to delegates and all other persons visiting St. Louis to attend the Convention:

R. P. TANSEY,
CHAS. E. FOLLETT,
D. H. ARMSTRONG,
R. T. BRYDON,
W. R. ALLEN,
E. A. FORD,
C. K. LORD,
J. CHARLTON,
J. W. MASS,
D. H. MACADAM,
JAMES D. BROWN,
J. MEREDITH DAVIES,
H. S. DEPEW,
W. L. MALCOLM,
D. WISHART.

R. P. Tansey was elected Chairman of the Committee, and D. H. MacAdam, Secretary. The Committee succeeded in obtaining half-fare rates from about one hundred and thirty railroad and steamboat companies, including all the leading lines in the country.

RECEPTION COMMITTEE.

The Resident Committee also appointed a Reception Committee of about one hundred and seventy-five members, of which Hon. James H. Britton was Chairman, and Walter C. Katte, Secretary. This Committee was subdivided among the different delegations, so that the representatives of each State received the attention and courtesies of a separate committee.

ARRANGEMENT OF THE HALL.

The arrangement of the Exchange Hall for the Convention was placed in the hands of a sub-committee of the Resident Committee, composed of the following gentlemen:

FRANCIS D. LEE, Chairman.
JOSEPH BROWN,
GEORGE W. FORD.

The design adopted in the arrangement of the hall is illustrated by a diagram accompanying this report, and afforded accommodation, including the standing-room on the floor and galleries, for an audience of over eight thousand people.

The following facts respecting the Exchange building and hall are presented as a matter of general interest in connection with the occasion:

The building fronts 233 feet on Third street, and 187 feet on Pine and Chestnut streets, and, while externally a unit, is in reality divided into two distinct structures, one fronting on Third street, designed for banks and offices, and the other occupying the western portion of the site, and separated from the first by courts 27 feet wide, with open arcades along the Pine and Chestnut street fronts, the portion occupied by the Grand Exchange Hall. The hall is 221 feet 10 inches long by 92 feet 6 inches wide, and 68 feet to the ceiling, lit on all sides by seventy windows, arranged in two tiers, the lower ones 26 by 10, and the upper 23 by 10. A light gallery, supported by enriched brackets and consoles, extends around the hall and between the two lines of windows. Not a column or other obstruction exists in the hall, and the roof has a clear span from wall to wall. The entire wood-work of the hall is of solid walnut, mahogany, and other hard woods, and is finished in the highest style of art. The ceiling is a marvel of beauty, being frescoed in three large panels.

In preparing this grand chamber for the Convention a tasteful and elaborate ornamentation, wrought out with flowers and evergreens, intermingled with banners, shields bearing the coats-of-arms of States, and rich drapings of national colors, added to the brilliancy and beauty of the general effect.

During the sessions of the Convention music was supplied at appropriate intervals by Postlewaite's band, which occupied an elevated stand behind the rostrum.

In response to the communication from the merchants of St. Louis, addressed to the National Democratic Committee, offering the Exchange hall for the sessions of the Convention, the following reply was received:

ST. LOUIS, MO., March 27th, 1876.

Hon. NATHAN COLE, President Merchants' Exchange:

DEAR SIR:—Your communication of January 12th, 1876, tendering, on behalf of the merchants of St. Louis, to the National Democratic Committee, the hall of the New Chamber of Commerce for the sessions of the National Convention to be held in St. Louis, June 27th, 1876, was duly submitted to the Committee, and the invitation therein conveyed was accepted with the warmest expressions of appreciation for the public spirit and courtesy that suggested it.

It is my duty, on behalf of the Committee, to transmit this formal notification of the acceptance of the invitation (although the press had informed you at the time of the action taken), and I will avail myself of the opportunity to add that the prospective use of your magnificent Chamber greatly facilitates the arrangements for the Convention, and will enable us to prepare a reception for that body and the large number of distinguished citizens from all parts of the Union who will participate in its deliberations, corresponding in character with the commercial and political influence and importance of this city.

Without reference to any question of political opinion, I think the merchants of St. Louis in this matter have adopted a course in accordance with the hospitality and progressive spirit of our citizens, and which will exercise a beneficial influence in extending our municipal reputation.

Respectfully,

JOHN G. PRIEST,

Member from Missouri of National Committee.

OFFICIAL CALL

FOR THE

National Democratic Convention.

The National Democratic Committee, to whom is delegated the power of fixing the time and place of holding the National Democratic Convention of 1876, have appointed Tuesday, the 27th day of June next, noon, and selected St. Louis as the place of holding such Convention. Each State will be entitled to a representation equal to double the number of its Senators and Representatives in the Congress of the United States, and the Territory of Colorado, whose admission in July as a State will give it a vote in the next Electoral College, is also invited to send delegates to the Convention.

Democratic, Conservative and other citizens of the United States, irrespective of past political associations, desiring to co-operate with the Democratic party in its present efforts and objects, are cordially invited to join in sending delegates to the National Convention.

Co-operation is desired from all persons who would change an administration that has suffered the public credit to become and remain inferior to other and less favored nations, has permitted commerce to be taken away by foreign powers, has stifled trade by unequal and pernicious legislation, has imposed unusual taxation and rendered it most burdensome, has changed growing prosperity to wide-spread suffering and want, has squandered the public moneys recklessly and defiantly, and shamelessly used the power, that should have been swift to punish crime, to protect it.

For these and other reasons the National Democratic Party deems the public danger imminent, and earnestly desirous of securing to our country the blessing of an economical, pure and free government, cordially invite the co-operation of their fellow-citizens in the effort to attain this object.

THOMAS A. WALKER, Ala.
S. R. COCKRELL, Ark.
FRANK MCCAPPIN, Cal.
WILLIAM H. BARNUM, Conn.
CHARLES BEASTEN, Del.
CHARLES E. DYKE, Fla.
A. R. LAWTON, Ga.
CYRUS H. MCCORMICK, Ills.
THOMAS DOWLING, Ind.
M. M. HAM, Iowa.
ISAAC E. EATON, Kan.
HENRY D. MCHENRY, Ky.
HENRY D. OGDEN, La.
L. D. M. SWEAT, Maine.
A. LEO KNOTT, Md.
WILLIAM A. MOORE, Mich.
WILLIAM LOCHRANE, Minn.
J. H. SHARP, Miss.
JOHN G. PRIEST, Mo.
GEORGE L. MILLER, Neb.
THOMAS H. WILLIAMS, Nev.
M. V. B. EDGERLY, N. H.
THEO. F. RANDOLPH, N. J.
M. W. RANSOM, N. C.
JOHN G. THOMPSON, Ohio.
JAMES K. KELLY, Oregon.
JAMES P. BARR, Penn.
NICHOLAS VAN SLYCK, R. I.
THOMAS Y. SIMONS, S. C.
WILLIAM B. BATE, Tenn.
F. S. STOCKDALE, Texas.
B. B. SMALLEY, Vt.
JOHN GOODE, Jr., Va.
JOHN BLAIR HOGE, W. Va.
GEO. H. PAUL, Wis.
THOS. M. PATTERSON, Col.

AUGUSTUS SCHELL, N. Y., *Chairman.*

FREDERICK O. PRINCE, Mass., *Sec'y National Democratic Com.*

WASHINGTON, February 22, 1876.

Samuel J. Tilden

[illegible]
New York, D. Appleton & Co.

Thomas A Hendricks

Engraved by the Western Engraving Co. St Louis
for the Resident Committee of the St Louis Convention

NATIONAL DEMOCRATIC CONVENTION.

FIRST DAY.

ST. LOUIS, MO., June 27th, 1876.

The National Democratic Convention, to nominate candidates for the offices of President and Vice-President of the United States, assembled in the grand hall of the Merchants' Exchange, in the city of St. Louis, this day at 12 o'clock, M., pursuant to the call of the National Democratic Committee.

Hon. Augustus Schell, of New York, Chairman of the National Democratic Committee, appeared upon the platform and called the Convention to order.

ADDRESS BY AUGUSTUS SCHELL.

GENTLEMEN OF THE CONVENTION: As Chairman of the National Democratic Committee, the duty has been assigned me to call this Convention to order. According to the usages of the Democratic party, this large body of representative men, coming from every State of our Union, have assembled for the purpose of nominating candidates (for the Democratic party) for President and Vice-President of the United States, whose election shall change the administration of the government, and save it from the corruptions that are destroying it.

Fortunately the momentous issue in the ensuing Presidential election is outlined in clear and distinct form and proportions; it can not be underestimated, overlooked, avoided. Administrative reform is the inexorable demand of the American people of all classes and all parties. The admission is unqualified, that the government must be purified, elevated; and the question is, who shall cleanse and raise it? Can it be done by the unclean hands that have soiled it? And in this hour, when national honor and the moral sense of mankind demands a reform—a change that would work a revolution in any other country.

Will the people tolerate for one moment the idea that the thing to be reformed can or will reform itself? This idea of self-reformation may answer very well for an individual, who must answer for his sins to his own conscience and his God. But what becomes of official integrity, responsibility and purity, when the men you entrust with the conduct of your affairs abuse their power, betray their trusts, violate their obligations and oaths, and, when called to an account, turn around and with unblushing effrontery tell you, "To be sure we have done all this; give us another lease of power and we will undo it." No! The people are generous and confiding, they are honest always, and in the long run intelligent and sagacious; often slowly, but in the end unerringly, they comprehend their rights and interests. And those rights have been too persistently violated and those interests too constantly neglected for the people of this country ever again to intrust the Republican party with the administration of the government

There is also another issue which demands the consideration of the country, that is the question of the currency. The Democratic party has, from its origin and through all the time of its existence, and is now, the hard-money party of the country. The subtle and adroit efforts on the part of the Republican party to charge upon the Democratic party the present condition of affairs, and to insist that that party is now the soft-money party, is unjust; for let me ask on what page of the statute, in what act of public authority in which Democrats have had the power and the control, is there written one word, one line or one law which has produced or caused the present condition of things? All the acts of this government providing for the issue of paper money, authorizing its use as a legal tender, have been passed, the judgment of the Supreme Court in declaring said acts constitutional has been rendered, while the Republican party has had full control of every department of the government. What has been the effect of it? Commerce is paralyzed; the manufacturing interests almost destroyed; prosperity has disappeared and want has taken its place. How is it to be remedied? The Democratic party, with its instincts and its knowledge of public affairs, will see that the remedy is applied. It cannot be brought about by forced contraction. It should not be assisted by additional inflation, but we take the country as it stands. We are called upon to apply the remedy, and one remedy which commends itself to every honest man and every reasonable Democrat, is to demand the repeal of the "resumption act." Repeal that act; put the government in the power of the Democratic party and let them pursue the course which they will pursue, of an economical administration of that government and the diminution of taxation, and I assure you that the time is not far distant when specie payments will be resumed, the industries of the country revived, and the whole American people be once more prosperous and happy.

Gentlemen, the time is auspicious and the occasion suggestive. One hundred years ago the first Democratic assembly met in Philadelphia—representatives of colonies on the Atlantic shore of this country. They there, under the guidance of that sage, that patriot, and that man ever to be remembered, Thomas Jefferson, laid the foundation of that civil and religious liberty which our fathers established and which we now enjoy. On this occasion, in this centennial year, the Democratic party has assembled in Convention to do that which our fathers did; that is to say, proclaim the course and suggest the means which shall once more give prosperity and happiness to our people.

During all the time that the power of the government has been in the hands of the Democratic party, our country has been prosperous and our people have been happy; but whenever its flag has drooped by the advance to power of the Republican party, sorrow and shame has been our condition. May we not hope now, after sixteen years of Republican rule, that the Democratic party—that grand old party which has never betrayed its trust or dishonored its name—be once more restored to power and assume its rightful position before the country?

It is not for me to forecast the action of this Convention, either in the selection of candidates or the adoption of its platform. We are bound by rules that prohibit the possibility of the nomination of any candidate who is not only the undoubted choice of the delegates here, but of the people they represent. And this Convention will present as candidates for President and Vice-President, men whose public record is pure and patriotic, whose personal characters are stainless, and whose statesmanship has been tried and proved by large experience in high official positions. The most of this people yearn not only for a great reformer but for a ripe and pure statesman as its chief executive.

In announcing its platform, this Convention will act wisely. It is a Democratic doctrine that the best government is the one that governs the least. Acting upon this principle, that may be the wisest policy that will seek to restore our former prosperity by leaving most to the economy and recuperative energies of the people, and the least to the positive legislation of the Federal government.

TEMPORARY CHAIRMAN.

Mr. Watterson was unanimously elected Temporary Chairman, and Senator Barnum, of Connecticut, and Senator Ransom, of North Carolina, were appointed a committee to conduct him to the chair.

Mr. Watterson assumed the chair, and was received with cheers. Upon the subsidence of the applause, Mr. Watterson addressed the Convention as follows:

SPEECH OF HENRY M. WATTERSON.

GENTLEMEN OF THE CONVENTION: We are called together to determine by our wisdom whether honest government, administered by honest men, shall be restored to the American people, or to decide by our folly that it is the destiny of this country to pursue an endless, ever-revolving circle of partisan passion and corruption, until with the loss of our material well-being, we shall lose the poor man's last best hope—civil liberty itself. Every citizen of the Republic, be he of the one party or the other, feels, and has felt for many a year, the depressing influence of what are called hard times. We look about us and we see neglected fields and vacant houses. The factory is closed, the furnace-door is shut. There are myriads of idle hands. The happy activity of prosperous life is nowhere to be found.

> "Loyalists fatten while honest men starve;
> Empty the mart, and shipless the bay."

What is it? What has wrought so great a change in a land that, ruled by an intelligent, progressive, constitutional party, advanced within half a century from the condition of a huddle of petty and squalid provincial sovereignties to a foremost place among the nations of the earth?

The reason of men must answer—partisan misrule and sectional misdirection. The Republicans, my friends, are not alone responsible. With them rests the disgrace; with us the folly. These twin agents of national mischance, working under the miserable rule of contraries, have kept the people of the North and South asunder, and have supplied sustenance to corruption. They have disturbed values. They have unsettled prices. They have made our whole financial system a cheat and a snare. They have driven the best elements of political society into exile, and have organized charlatanism into a sort of public polity, enabling the knave to take advantage of the dupe, and sacrificing every popular interest to the lust of that oligarchy which has become so encrusted in power as to believe itself entitled to rule by the sheer force of its own wrong-doing.

So much let us set down to the convenient pretext of war. So much to the long account of damages between the North and the South. It is for you to say whether the same conflict, with consequences multiplied and magnified, shall be inaugurated between the East and the West.

I shall not undertake on an occasion of this kind, and in a presence so imposing, to enforce the familiar lesson of mutual forbearance. Nobody doubts our capacity to make battle among ourselves. I ask your indulgence only on my own behalf. You have called me to a place not merely of distinction but of difficulty, to a place requiring the best training of a better man than I am. In taking it, I trust to your confidence and good nature, and to a heart incapable of an unmanly or unfair act. The work before us should relate to ideas rather than to individuals. It is the issue, not the man, that should engage us. We have come here to make the people's fight, not our fight; for free, no less than honest government; for the reform of the public service and the regeneration of the public morals; for administrative relief from administrative ritualism, embraced in the simple creed of home rule, reduced taxes, and a living chance for the South as well as the North, for both the East and the West. If anything comes from our proceedings it must spring from the spirit of aspiration or fellowship which warmed the followers of Andrew Jackson and Silas Wright, of Henry Clay and Daniel Webster, whose political descendants meet together on common ground at last to wrest the government of their fathers, federal, state and municipal, from the clutch of rings and robbers, and who mean to extirpate these wherever they are found, and whether they be Democratic or Republican. [Applause.]

At the close of Mr. Watterson's address, Bishop Marvin, of the M. E. Church, offered the following prayer:

PRAYER BY BISHOP MARVIN.

O God, we worship Thee. Thou art the Sovereign of Nations and of Worlds. Thy name is above every place and Thy authority ruleth over all. With Thee the nations are a very little thing. Thou takest up the isles as the dust of the earth. But Thou condescendest, in infinite goodness, to charge Thyself with the interests and affairs of all men. Thou art not unconcerned with regard to the happiness of the creatures whom Thou hast made. We give Thee praise for Thy mercy to us, for Thy goodness to our nation. Thou didst preserve the American colonies in their incipiency, in the presence of hostile savages, and Thou hast raised them into the power of great states and into a vast government, and hast been merciful to us in all the past history of our lives. We have sinned. We have done wickedly before Thee. Private crime and vice have run riot in our country, and public corruption has brought dishonor and reproach upon our name; and yet Thou hast been merciful to us in the midst of all and notwithstanding all. An ample agriculture, the basis of all prosperity, has fed all, sustained all, and enriched all; mineral wealth emboweled in our mountains and opening ample resources for the present and the future. Labor is in constant demand at reasonable reward. Our factories, our workshops are crowded with intelligent, industrious, ingenious, skilful artisans, and supply our homes with every demand of civilized life. Our commerce governs the whole earth and levies contribution upon all climes and all nations, to our comforts and our luxuries, and to the refinement of domestic and of social life. Our art has touched our civilization with its refinement and its elegance; and, O Lord, we give Thee praise that schools and colleges abound, and religion hallows all by the purity of its doctrine, the elevation of its spirit, and the prevalence of its rights.

Blessed be Thy name, O God, for Thy mercy, for Thou hast distinguished us with Thy goodness, Thou hast made us conspicuous among the nations of the earth. Thou hast nourished us in peace and hast been our panoply in war. The manifestations of Thy displeasure have been few and occasional. Our history has been a history of development and growth. Our national boundaries encompass a vast domain that lies upon two oceans and touches upon tropical and arctic extremes.

O God, Thou hast brought us through the first century of our independent existence, and looked down to-day upon the festivities and rejoicings of a mighty people. The future is with God. Visit not our sins upon us, but grant us Thy blessing in all our borders.

Gracious God, look upon this Convention. Guide it in its deliberations, and put Thy blessing upon all the results of its labors. May these contribute to national and sectional harmony, and to restore the cordial good-fellowship that must be the basis of all right government and permanent prosperity in our nation. May the results of this Convention tend to public purity and national integrity in every department of the administration, and in all time to come may a good government and free institutions, faithfully administered, secure a prosperous commerce and the growing industries in all our land, and may public virtue distinguish us as our material resources distinguish us amongst the nations of the earth; and when the last catastrophe and final stroke of time shall sound, may this nation be found prosperous and happy, united and peaceful; and all these mercies we ask through Jesus Christ, our Creator and Redeemer. Amen.

TEMPORARY ORGANIZATION.

The CHAIRMAN: The Chair is directed by the Democratic National Committee to announce as Temporary Secretary of the Convention, Mr. Frederick O. Prince, of Massachusetts, and as Assistant Secretaries, Mr. T. O. Walker, of Iowa, and Mr. S. K. Doniphan, of Ohio.

Before the Convention proceeds to business the Chair would ask, as a matter of convenience to the reporters and the Convention, that the gentlemen who are recognized by the Chair will call their name and State. The Convention is now ready for business, and the Chair desires to know its pleasure.

Mr. ABBOTT, of Massachusetts: I desire to offer a resolution.

The CHAIR: The Chair is further directed by the National Democratic Committee to state that Mr. Dan. Able, of Missouri, has been selected as Sergeant-at-Arms.

The gentleman from Massachusetts (Mr. Abbott) offers the following resolution:

Resolved, That the rules of the last National Democratic Convention govern this body until otherwise ordered.

The CHAIR: The question is upon the adoption of the resolution.

A DELEGATE from Kentucky: I move that the resolution be referred to the Committee on Organization.

The CHAIR: The gentleman from Kentucky moves that this resolution be referred to the Committee on Organization. The gentleman from Massachusetts (Mr. Abbott) has the floor.

Mr. ABBOTT: My only purpose in rising is to withdraw the motion.

The CHAIR: The question, then, is upon the resolution.

Mr. LITTLEJOHN, of New York: I desire to inquire if those rules include what is known as the two-third rule? [Cries of "Yes, yes."]

The CHAIRMAN: The Chair would state that the resolution does include the two-thirds rule. [Cries of "Bully!"]

The resolution was adopted amidst vociferous applause.

CALLING THE ROLL FOR COMMITTEE ON CREDENTIALS.

Mr. SMALLEY, of Vermont: I desire to offer the following resolution:

Resolved, That the States be called in their order, and that the chairman of each delegation present the credentials from his State.

Mr. FILLEY, of New York: I move that the Hon. E. O. Perrin, Reading Secretary of the last National Convention, be nominated for that position to this Convention.

The CHAIRMAN: The gentleman is out of order. A resolution is pending.

The resolution of Mr. Smalley, of Vermont, was adopted.

The CHAIRMAN: The Secretary will call the roll of States in accordance with the resolution just passed.

SEVERAL VOICES: Mr. President—

The CHAIRMAN: No other business will be in order while the roll is being called.

Mr. WALLACE, of Pennsylvania: As chairman of the Pennsylvania delegation, I arise in my place and demand to be heard; I rise to move to reconsider the resolution, in order that we may have the Democratic precedents observed upon this floor. [Applause.]

A DELEGATE from New York: I move to lay that motion on the table.

Mr. WALLACE, of Pennsylvania: Mr. President, I have the floor. I have a right to the time allowed in the rules of the House of Representatives, which give me an hour, if I see fit to demand it.

Mr. WALLACE: Now, Mr. President, I know, sir, that all the past—

A DELEGATE from New York: Mr. Chairman, a point of order.

The CHAIR: The gentleman will state his point of order.

The DELEGATE from New York: The point of order is that the Convention has just ordered that the roll of States be called, and the chairmen of the different delegations present their credentials.

The CHAIR: The point of order is not well taken. The Secretary of the Convention had not begun to read the roll of the States. The gentleman from Pennsylvania has the floor.

A DELEGATE from New York: The point of order is that the Chairman of the Convention announced the Temporary Secretaries, but he did not put the question to the Convention; that is my point of order.

The CHAIR: The point of order is too late; another question is pending. The gentleman from Pennsylvania has the floor.

Mr. WALLACE, of Pennsylvania: Mr. Chairman, I rise to say that in all past Democratic Conventions a Committee on Credentials and a Committee on Permanent Organization have been appointed. The resolution of the gentleman is an innovation. The first business in order is to call the States, in order that they present their Committee on Credentials and upon Organization. I insist that the history of our party proves that this is the practice of National Conventions, and I trust that this Convention will not permit this innovation upon Democratic precedents. I am entitled to one hour; if any gentleman desires to occupy a part of my time he is—

A DELEGATE from New York: Do we understand that each gentleman, under the rulings of the last National Convention, is entitled to one hour, or is not the gentleman claiming the privilege under the rules of the National Congress?

The CHAIR: The Chair would state that the gentleman from Pennsylvania has not exhausted his one hour and still has the floor.

The DELEGATE from New York: Under the ruling of the last National Convention, is a member of the Convention entitled to an hour?

The CHAIR: The Chair will decide that point when occasion requires. The gentleman from Pennsylvania has the floor.

Mr. WALLACE: I insist upon the motion to reconsider the resolution passed by the Convention.

Mr. WADE, of New York: Mr. Chairman, the resolution offered by the gentleman from Vermont is the ordinary resolution offered in every Democratic National Convention for the last twenty years. It simply calls for the call of the roll of States, and that the chairmen selected by the several delegations present their credentials to the Secretary of this Convention. It will be the duty of the Secretary, when those credentials are presented, to turn them over to the Committee upon Credentials which undoubtedly will hereafter be formed. It is the ordinary resolution, so that the Chair and the gentlemen here may know whether or no there are contested delegations from any State. And I think if the gentleman from Pennsylvania will reflect a moment he will see it is the ordinary way and the ordinary resolution.

Mr. WALLACE, of Pennsylvania: In answer to the argument of the gentleman, I hold in my hand the proceedings—

The CHAIR: The gentleman from Iowa—will the gentleman from Pennsylvania yield to the gentleman from Iowa?

Mr. WALLACE, of Pennsylvania: I will.

Mr. FINCH, of Iowa: What is the question before the house?

The CHAIR: The question before the house is the motion of the gentleman from Pennsylvania to reconsider the vote just passed. In order to give the Convention a clear understanding of the question, the Secretary will read the resolution which the gentleman from Pennsylvania moves to reconsider.

Mr. WALLACE: Now, Mr. President—

The SECRETARY [reading]: *Resolved,* That the States be called in their order, and that the chairman of each delegation present the credentials from his State.

The CHAIR: That resolution was passed by the Convention. The gentleman from Pennsylvania moves that that vote be reconsidered. The gentleman from Pennsylvania has the floor.

Mr. WALLACE, of Pennsylvania: I now read, in answer to the gentleman from New York, the resolution adopted in the Convention of 1868. It is in these words: "That there shall be now two committees appointed, each committee to consist of one delegate from each State, to be selected by the respective delegates thereof; one committee to act as a Committee on Permanent Organization, and the other as a Committee on Credentials." I therefore submit that it is in order to call the States for the report of a committee-man on credentials, and a committee-man on organization. It belongs to the States to name them.

The CHAIR: The Chair will state that the Secretary of the Convention has been directed to call the roll by the Convention. The gentleman from Pennsylvania moves that the vote by which the resolution was adopted be reconsidered.

Mr. DOOLITTLE, of Wisconsin: Mr. President, I believe what the gentleman from Pennsylvania desires and suggests will expedite all this business, and probably prevent any recurrence of it in the future. It is that we have a Reading Secretary temporarily appointed, so that the resolutions read from the Chair may be heard all over the house. Our excellent Secretary fails in that respect to be heard in all parts of the chamber. I have heard the name of Mr. Harrington suggested.

The CHAIR: The gentleman is out of order. The election of a Secretary is not in order. A Secretary has been elected, and the gentleman is not in order.

Mr. DOOLITTLE: By leave of the gentleman from Pennsylvania, I made the suggestion.

The CHAIR: The question is on the motion of the gentleman from Pennsylvania to reconsider the vote just passed.

The motion was lost.

The CHAIR: The Secretary will call the roll.

The Secretary then proceeded with the call of the roll for the appointment of the Committee on Credentials, with the following result:

COMMITTEE ON CREDENTIALS.

ALABAMA—E. H. Moran.
CALIFORNIA—James L. English.
COLORADO—Adair Wilson.
CONNECTICUT—Richard S. Hicks.
DELAWARE—Chas. H. Richards.
FLORIDA—C. W. Yule.
GEORGIA—P. M. B. Young.
ILLINOIS—John Forsythe.
INDIANA—Gen. M. D. Manson.
IOWA—Geo. C. Wright.
KANSAS—G. W. Burchard.
KENTUCKY—Jas. M. Bigger.
LOUISIANA—J. J. Mellon.
MAINE—Wm. McLellan.
MARYLAND—Andrew G. Chapman.
MASSACHUSETTS—Nich. Hathaway.
MICHIGAN—M. V. Montgomery.
MINNESOTA—Geo. E. Skinner.
MISSISSIPPI—I. C. Prewell.
MISSOURI—A. P. Morehouse.
NEBRASKA—F. A. Harmon.
NEVADA—J. S. Kaneen.
NEW HAMPSHIRE—W. H. Cummings.
NEW JERSEY—John P. Stockton.
NEW YORK—Rufus W. Peckham.
NORTH CAROLINA—Chas. Latham.
OHIO—W. W. Armstrong.
OREGON—J. C. Brady.
PENNSYLVANIA—A. G. Broadhead.
RHODE ISLAND—Alpheus F. Angell.
SOUTH CAROLINA—Jno. C. Sheppard.
TENNESSEE—John A. Gardner.
TEXAS—Thomas H. Murray.
VERMONT—John Caim.
VIRGINIA—Fitzhugh Lee.
WEST VIRGINIA—Leroy Cofram.
WISCONSIN—Wm. Wilson.

READING SECRETARY.

Mr. BINNEY, of Illinois: Mr. Chairman, I now move you, sir, that the Hon. E. O. Perrin, the Reading Secretary of the last National Convention—

The CHAIR: The gentleman is not in order. The roll-call of the States has not yet been completed. The Secretary will continue with the roll-call.

Mr. BINNEY: The roll-call of the States has been finished, as I understand.

The CHAIR: The Chair was mistaken. The gentleman has the floor. The Chair will entertain his motion.

Mr. BINNEY: I move you that Mr. Perrin, who was the Reading Secretary of the last National Convention, be elected as Assistant Secretary of this Convention. [Applause.]

Mr. FINCH, of Iowa: Mr. Chairman, I move that the officers of this Convention be selected through the medium of the Committee on Permanent Organization. [Applause.] Mr. Perrin has not an inheritance from the Democratic party. [Applause.] The Democratic party in its National Conventions may have one man for one occasion, and another for another. [Applause.] We have no royal descent. I might suggest a name from my own State who has as good a voice as Mr. Perrin, and I think it would be proper to leave this thing to the Committee on Permanent Organization, and not forestall the action of this Convention. [Applause.]

Mr. EATON, of Kansas: I rise to a point of order. The ordinary course that has been pursued has been for the National Committee to select the Temporary Secretaries. They have already selected them, and it is not competent now for any member of this Convention to move that a Temporary Secretary shall be appointed.

The CHAIR: The gentleman from Kansas rises to a point of order that the gentleman has not the right at this late hour to raise the issue of the selection of an Assistant Secretary after the Temporary Secretary has already been selected by the National Democratic Committee, according to Democratic usages. The Chair decides that the point of order is well taken. [Applause.]

ORGANIZATION.

Mr. Buck, of Minnesota, offered the following resolution, which was unanimously adopted:

Resolved, That there now shall be two committees appointed. Each committee to consist of one delegate from each State, to be selected by the respective delegates thereof. One committee to act as a Committee on Credentials, and the other on Permanent Organization; and that the roll of States be called, and that the chairman of the delegation of each State announces the name of the delegates selected for such committees.

In accordance with the foregoing resolution, the Secretary proceeded to call the roll of States for the appointment of a Committee on Organization.

COMMITTEE ON ORGANIZATION.

ALABAMA—C. C. Langdon.
ARKANSAS—J. W. Butler.
CONNECTICUT—F. T. Baldwin.
CALIFORNIA—A. J. Williams.
COLORADO—Gen. Dwight Morris.
DELAWARE—Wm. G. Whitely.
FLORIDA—J. V. Harris.
GEORGIA—J. J. Jones.
ILLINOIS—Charles Dunham.
INDIANA—B. W. Hanna.
IOWA—L. G. Kinne.
KANSAS—M. V. B. Bennett.
KENTUCKY—Jas. B. Garnell.
LOUISIANA—E. E. Kid.
MAINE—Jno. S. Ricker.
MARYLAND—Fred C. Tabatt.
MASSACHUSETTS—Geo. W. Gill.
MICHIGAN—J. D. Norton.
MINNESOTA—C. F. Buck.
MISSISSIPPI—H. L. Jarnigan.
MISSOURI—R. S. Anderson.
NEBRASKA—Tobias Castor.
NEVADA—J. M. Dorsey.
NEW HAMPSHIRE—Henry H. Metcalf.
NEW JERSEY—John McGregor.
NEW YORK—John C. Jacobs.
NORTH CAROLINA—J. S. Battle.
OHIO—Gen. J. B Steadman.
OREGON—J. H. Turner.
PENNSYLVANIA—W. V. McGrath.
RHODE ISLAND—John P. Cooney.
SOUTH CAROLINA—John H. Evins.
TENNESSEE—Jno. M. Fleming.
TEXAS—M. D. R. Taylor.
VERMONT—Geo. M. Fisk.
VIRGINIA—Wm. H. Hinton.
WEST VIRGINIA—Jacob B. Jackson.
WISCONSIN—Jos. Rankin.

THE REPORTS OF COMMITTEES.

Mr. CARROLL, of Tennessee: I desire to offer the following resolution:

Resolved, That the committees just named be instructed to report at five o'clock this evening, and that when this Convention adjourn it be to that hour.

The resolution was adopted.

Mr. SMITH, of Illinois: I offer the following resolution:

Resolved, That a committee of one delegate from each State, to be selected by the delegations thereof, be appointed to report resolutions, and that all resolutions in relation to the platform of the Democratic party be referred to said committee without debate.

Adopted.

Mr. WEED, of New York: I move, Mr. President, that the chairmen of the respective delegations be instructed to hand to the Secretary of this Convention the names of all persons elected by them to act upon the Committee on Resolutions just authorized.

The CHAIRMAN: Without objection, the course suggested by the gentleman from New York will be adopted.

A DELEGATION OF LADIES.

Mr. WEED, of New York: Mr. Chairman, I move that this Convention do now adjourn to five o'clock.

The CHAIRMAN: Will the gentleman from New York be good enough to withdraw his motion until the Chair makes an announcement?

Mr. WEED: I will, sir.

The CHAIRMAN: The Chair is requested to announce that the Committee on Organization will meet at 3:30 o'clock this afternoon, in the rooms of the National Democratic Committee, at the Lindell hotel. The Chair desires to state that he is requested by delegates from the Women's Rights National Convention to state that representatives of that organization are here, and desire about ten minutes to make a statement to the Convention. [Cries of "Hear them! hear them!"]

The CHAIRMAN: Without objection, they will now be heard.

The CHAIR: The Chair will appoint Mr. Weed, of New York, and Mr. Smalley, of Vermont, a committee to escort the ladies to the platform. [Applause and laughter.]

A DELEGATE: Mr. President—

The CHAIR: No motion is in order; a lady has the floor. [Laughter.]

SEVERAL VOICES: Mr. President—

The CHAIR: Gentlemen will take their seats; the Chair has stated that a lady has the floor. The Chair has the honor to present to the Convention Miss Phœbe Couzins, of St. Louis. [Applause.]

A DELEGATE: I rise to a point of order.

The CHAIR: The gentleman is out of order, and will take his seat immediately.

The same DELEGATE: Can't I make a point of order?

The CHAIR: No, sir, a lady has the floor, and no point of order is in order. [Cries of "Hurrah for the Chair!")

Miss Couzins then stepped forward and delivered the following address:

ADDRESS OF MISS PHŒBE COUZINS.

MR. PRESIDENT AND GENTLEMEN OF THE DEMOCRATIC CONVENTION: The Centennial anniversary of our nation's birth-day is also, happily, a Centennial leap-year. [Applause.] It is in order, then, I take it, to not only receive proposals at the hands of fair women, but also to accept them. [Applause.] Taking advantage, then, of this right and your courtesy, I am here as a delegated authority from the fair sex not only to reaffirm the principles of liberty and equality for them, but also to sue for the hands of those here assembled in national convention.

And, Mr. President, I take it the hand must be neither larger nor smaller than a man's hand. In the good old days of our ancestors it was deemed an unpardonable offence if the leap-year privileges accorded to women were not unhesitatingly acquiesced in, and he who did not respond unhesitatingly a "yes" to the coy maiden's fair wooing was consigned to single blessedness.

And now, gentlemen, if the Democratic party deserves to live long, be prosperous and happy, give heed to the warning from out the gates of Paradise, "It is not good for man to be alone," and accept as a companion in your political household she who blends all the discordant elements into one harmonious whole. [Applause.] Thomas Jefferson has said: "Let it be remembered that it has ever been the pride of woman that the rights for which she contended were the rights of human nature;" and, gentlemen, we ask this recognition, not as women, but as human beings, and we sue to-day for our Magna Charta, not by force of might and power, but by the more potent voice of truth and justice, speaking to every thinking man in tones far more persuasive than those which appealed to King John on the field of Runnymede. [Applause.]

Gentlemen, we cannot assert this right by a resort to the sword. We confess our inability to thunder forth our claim at the cannon's mouth, or to fire a shot that can be heard around the world.

But in this grand Centennial year when all others are free, and when our souls too are responding to the music of the utterances of Jefferson and Hancock, of Adams and of Patrick Henry, and with minds expanding to a realization of their grandeur, with pulses beating for the freedom they proclaimed, we would fain pluck a live coal from off the altar of our liberties that shall kindle in your souls a zeal for the rights of the individual calling for universal humanity, such as our fathers uttered when they addressed the hearts of the people with the cry "Taxation without representation is tyranny," and write the burning thoughts and noble utterances they read by the camp-fires of the revolution, that immortal truth, "All humanity is created free and equal."

Gentlemen, we appeal to your sense of justice and of right, using but the grand old truths of our fathers to support our claim.

And here we rest our case, commending only to you that glorious truth, that sense of justice is the sovereign power of the human mind, the most unyielding of any, which rewards with a higher sanction, which punishes with a deeper agony than any earthly tribunal, which never slumbers, never dies, which constantly utters and demands justice by the eternal rule of honesty, truth and equity; and on this eternal foundation, honesty, truth and equity, we stand. We offer and present to you the "Memorial of the National Woman's Suffrage Association, to the National Democratic Convention, to be held at St. Louis, June 27, 1876."

ADDRESS OF THE NATIONAL WOMAN SUFFRAGE ASSOCIATION TO THE NATIONAL CONVENTION.

PHILADELPHIA, JUNE 20, 1876.

To the President and Members of the National Democratic Convention, assembled at St. Louis, June 27th, 1876.

GENTLEMEN: In reading the call for your Convention, the "National Woman Suffrage Association" were gratified to find that your invitation was not limited to voters, but cordially extended to all citizens of the United States.

We accordingly send delegates from our association asking for them a voice in your proceedings, and also a plank in your platform, declaring the political rights of women.

Women are the only class of citizens still wholly unrepresented in the government, and yet we possess every qualification requisite for voters in the several States. Women possess property and education; we take out naturalization papers and passports; we pre-empt lands, pay taxes, and suffer for our own violation of the laws; we are neither idiots, lunatics nor criminals; and, according to your State constitutions, lack but one qualification for voters, which is an insurmountable qualification, and therefore equivalent to a bill of attainder against one-half the people; a power no State nor Congress can legally exercise, being forbidden in article 1, sections 9 and 10 of the Constitution.

Our rulers may have the right to regulate the suffrage, but they cannot abolish it altogether for any class of citizens, as has been done in the case of the women of this republic, without a direct violation of the fundamental law of the land.

As you hold the Constitution of the fathers to be a sacred legacy to us and our children forever, we ask you to so interpret that Magna Charta of human rights as to secure justice and equality of all United States citizens, irrespective of sex.

We desire to call your attention to the violation of the essential principle of self-government in the disfranchisement of the women of the several States, and we appeal to you, not only because as a minority you are in a position to consider principles, but because you were the party first to extend suffrage, by removing the property qualification from all white men, and thus making the political status of the richest and poorest citizen the same. That act of justice to the laboring masses insured your power, with but few interruptions, until the war.

When the District of Columbia suffrage bill was under discussion in 1866, it was a Democratic Senator, Mr. Cowan, of Pennsylvania, who proposed an amendment to strike out the word "male," and thus extend the right of suffrage to the women, as well as the black men of the District. That amendment gave us a splendid discussion on woman suffrage, that lasted three days in the Senate of the United States.

It was a Democratic Legislature that secured the right of suffrage to the women of Wyoming, and we now ask you, in national convention, to pledge the Democratic party to extend this act of justice to the women throughout the nation, and thus call to your side a new political force that will restore and perpetuate your power for years to come.

The Republican party gave us a plank in their platform in 1872, pledging themselves to a "respectful consideration" of our demands. But by their constitutional interpretations, legislative enactments and judicial decisions, so far from redeeming their pledge, they have buried our petitions and appeals under laws in direct opposition to their high-sounding promises and professions.

And now, in 1876, they give us another plank in their platform, approving "the substantial advance made towards the establishment of equal rights for women," cunningly reminding us that the privileges and immunities we now enjoy are all due to Republican legislation; although under a Republican dynasty inspectors of elections have been arrested and imprisoned for taking the votes of women; temperance women arrested and imprisoned for praying in the streets; houses, lands, bonds, and stock of women seized and sold for their refusal to pay unjust taxation; and more than all, we have this singular spectacle: A Republican woman, who had spoken for the Republican party throughout the last presidential campaign, arrested by a Republican officer for voting the Republican ticket, denied the right of trial by jury by a Republican judge, convicted and sentenced to a fine of $100 and cost of prosecution, and all this for asserting at the polls the most sacred of all the rights of American citizenship, the right of suffrage, specifically secured by recent Republican amendments to the Federal Constitution.

Again: The Supreme Court of the United States, by its recent decision in the Minor vs. Happersatt case, has stultified its own interpretation of constitutional law.

A negro, by virtue of his United States citizenship, is declared, under recent amendments, a voter in every State in the Union; but when a woman, by virtue of her United States citizenship, applies to the Supreme Court of the United States for protection in the exercise of this same right, she is remanded to the State by the unanimous decision of the nine judges on the bench, that "the Constitution of the United States does not confer the right of suffrage upon any one."

All concessions of privileges or redress of grievances are mockery for any class that has no voice in the laws and law-makers, hence we demand the ballot, that sceptre of power, in our own hands, as the only sure protection for our rights of person and property under all conditions. If the few may grant or withhold rights at their pleasure, the many cannot be said to enjoy the blessings of self-government. Jefferson said, "The God who gave us life gave us liberty at the same time; the hand of force may destroy but cannot disjoin them."

While the first and highest motive we would urge on you is the recognition, in all your action, of the great principles of justice and equality that underlie our form of government, it is not unworthy to remind you that the party that takes this onward step will reap its just reward.

Had you heeded our appeals made to you at Tammany Hall, New York, in 1868, and again in Baltimore in 1872, your party might now have been in power, as you would have had, what neither party can boast to-day, a live issue, on which to rouse the enthusiasm of the people.

Reform is the watchword of the hour; but how can we hope for honor and honesty in either party in minor matters, so long as both consent to rob one-half the people—their own mothers, sisters, wives and daughters—of their most sacred rights?

As a party you defended the right of self-government in Louisiana ably and eloquently during the last session in Congress. Are the rights of women in all the Southern States, whose slaves are now their rulers, less sacred than those of the men of Louisiana? "The whole art of government," says Jefferson, "consists in being honest."

It needs but little observation to see that the tide of progress, in all countries, is setting toward the emancipation and enfranchisement of women; and this step in civilization is to be taken in our own day and generation.

Whether the Democratic party will take the initiative in this reform, and reap the glory of crowning fifteen million women with the rights of American citizenship, and thereby vindicate our theory of self-government, is the momentous question we ask you to decide in this eventful hour, as we round out the first century of our national life.

ELIZABETH CADY STANTON, *Prest.*
MATILDA JOSLYN GAGE, *Ch. Ex. Com.*
SUSAN B. ANTHONY, *Cor. Sec.*
CENTENNIAL HEADQUARTERS, 1431 Chestnut St., Philadelphia, Pa.

PLANK FOR THE DEMOCRATIC PLATFORM.

WHEREAS, The Democratic party was the first to abolish the property qualification, and extend the right of suffrage to all white men in some of the older States; and

WHEREAS, It was a Democratic Legislature which extended the right of suffrage to the women of Wyoming; therefore,

Resolved, That we pledge ourselves to secure the right of suffrage to the women of the United States on equal terms with men.

The CHAIR: The Convention has heard the memorial, and the Chair will entertain a motion as to what disposition it will make of it.

Mr. MCCLERNAND, of Illinois: I move that the memorial be referred to the Committee on Resolutions, for their respectful consideration.

The CHAIR: Without objection, the resolution will be referred under the rule, as moved by the gentleman from Illinois.

Mr. DAVIS: I ask that the roll of the States be called, and that the chairman of each State delegation announce the name of the Committee on Resolutions, so that we may know who compose the committee.

The CHAIR: Without objection, the roll will be called, as moved by the gentleman from Kansas.

Mr. BIRCH, of Tennessee: I rise to a point of order. When the motion was made by the gentleman at my left for a Committee on Resolutions—the point is this, that we were still in a temporary state of organization. We are not yet organized. We have no report from the Committee on Credentials. We have no permanent organization, and it is therefore out of order to have a Committee upon Resolutions until that permanent organization is effected.

The CHAIR: The Chair will decide that this Convention has the right to determine what it will do at any stage of its organization.

Mr. SMITH, of Wisconsin: This Convention has not determined to have a Committee on Resolutions yet at all.

The CHAIR: The Chair would state that this Convention has passed a resolution to raise a Committee on Resolutions. The roll of States has not been called upon that resolution. The Secretary of the Convention will call the roll of the States, and as each State is called the chairman of its delegation will send the name of the delegate appointed by his delegation upon the Committee on Resolutions to the Secretary.

COMMITTEE ON RESOLUTIONS.

The Secretary then called the roll of States for the appointment of a Committee on Resolutions, with the following result:

ALABAMA—Leroy P. Walker.
ARKANSAS—L. H. Mangum.
CALIFORNIA—John S. Hagar.
COLORADO—F. J. Marshall.
CONNECTICUT—R. D. Hubbard.
DELAWARE—George Gray.
FLORIDA—John Westcott.
GEORGIA—E. B. Howell.
ILLINOIS—John A. McClernand.
INDIANA—D. W. Voorhies.
IOWA—H. H. Trimble.
KANSAS—Thomas L. Dorris.
KENTUCKY—Oliver Duvall.
LOUISIANA—R. H. Mann.
MAINE—D. R. Hastings.
MARYLAND—George Freaner.

MASSACHUSETTS—Edward Avery.
MICHIGAN—Wm. L. Bancroft.
MINNESOTA—Daniel Bucks.
MISSISSIPPI—A. H. Clayton.
MISSOURI—C. H. Hardin.
NEBRASKA—Geo. L. Mellen.
NEVADA—A. C. Ellis.
NEW HAMPSHIRE—E. C. Bailey.
NEW JERSEY—Joseph N. Gates.
NEW YORK—Wm. Dorsheimer.
NORTH CAROLINA—T. D. Clingham.
OHIO—Gen. Tom Ewing.
OREGON—M. V. Brown.
PENNSYLVANIA—Malcolm Hay.
RHODE ISLAND—Wm. B. Beach.
SOUTH CAROLINA—Sam'l McGowan.
TENNESSEE—John C. Brown.
TEXAS—Ashbell Smith.
VERMONT—James H. Williams.
VIRGINIA—John A. Meredith.
WEST VIRGINIA—John J. Davis.
WISCONSIN—Alexander Mitchell.

The following resolution, offered by S. S. Hayes, of Illinois, was referred to the Committee on Resolutions without being read to the Convention:

With the frankness and candor to be expected of a great party coeval with the republic, and founded on the eternal principles of truth and justice, we declare our opposition—

First—To a further increase of the public debt and of the demand notes of the government, which should be restrained by constitutional amendments.

Second—The interference with the operation of the laws of trade by legislative favors to any class, or by reckless changes in the measures of value.

Third—To the resumption clause of the act of 1875, which subjects the country to years of paralysis and depression without the hope of any good result, and threatens the destruction of our industries and the ruin of our people. Its immediate repeal is demanded by every consideration of sound policy.

We also declare in favor of—

First—The strict maintenance of the public faith, and the payment of all our obligations according to law and the pledges we have made to our creditors.

Second—An early return to the specie standard, by providing for the redemption in coin, or coin bonds, of our demand notes, with proper provisions for their reissue.

Third—The continuance of our legal-tender laws, and of the volume of our national currency without inflation or contraction, leaving our merchants, manufacturers and laborers free to prosecute their lawful enterprises without fear of injury from the government, and thereby to hasten our recovery from the effects of misrule and bad legislation, restore the general prosperity, and secure to labor its just reward.

The following petition was offered by Mr. Miller, of Nebraska:

OMAHA, June 22, 1876.—The undersigned citizens of Nebraska, being deeply impressed with the belief that a change in the constitution of the United States, extending the presidential term to six years, and making the incumbent ineligible to a re-election, is indispensable to effectual civil-service reform and pure and honorable administration of the general government, respectfully and urgently request that this proposition be placed before the people as a plank in the platform. And, furthermore, that numerous offices, created on account of the emergency of the war, be abolished, and all salaries be regulated in accordance with the reduction in money circulation, the shrinkage in values, and the inevitable financial distress that is upon the entire country.

Lorin Miller, E. Wakeley, Enos Lowe, W. H. Remington, E. Kimball, W. M. Warden, Chas. P. Deuel, J. C. Thomas, Geo. Thrall, W. B. Loring, O. D. Richardson, Geo. D. Medlock, C. S. Goodrich, Harry P. Deuel, W. P. Wilcox, M. W. Clair, Jas. K. Ish, C. B. Rustin, D. F. Stephens, E. W. Nash, Samuel Burns, J. J. Sutphen, Jno. McCormick, F. C. Morgan, M. Hillman, Ben. Gallagher, A. S. Brown, Wm. G. Maul, Aaron Cahn, J. W. Paddock, Albert O. Norein, E. Cavanaugh, Michael Donovan.

The Secretary then, upon request, re-announced the times and places of meeting of the various committees, and the Convention took a recess until 5 o'clock P. M.

AFTERNOON SESSION.

The Convention reassembled at 5:20 o'clock.

The CHAIRMAN: The Convention will please come to order. The first business before the Convention will be the report of the Committee on Credentials. The gentleman from California, Mr. English, has the floor.

Mr. ENGLISH, of California: I will send the report to the Secretary's desk.

The CHAIRMAN: The Secretary of the Convention will read the report of the Committee on Credentials.

The Secretary read as follows:

Your Committee on Credentials would respectfully report that there are no contested seats [applause]; that the States are fully represented [renewed applause], and that the delegates reported by the chairmen of the respective delegations as delegates to this Convention, are entitled to seats in the Convention as delegates from their respective States.

Respectfully submitted,

JAS. LAWRENCE ENGLISH,
Chairman of Committee on Credentials.

[Applause.]

The CHAIRMAN: The Convention has heard the report of the Committee on Credentials; the question is, shall the report be adopted?

Mr. FINCH, of Iowa: Mr. Chairman, I desire that there be added to the report the resolution which I now send to the Secretary. I will state that the object of it is to allow the Territories representation upon the same basis as all the States. [Applause.]

The CHAIRMAN: The question is upon the adoption of the report of the Committee on Credentials. No resolution can be entertained while that question is pending. What is the pleasure of the Convention?

Mr. MANSON, of Indiana: I wish to say that the committee adjourned before 3:30 o'clock; the delegation was not full at all, and as I learned from the records there were only eight States represented, and there are sufficient here from the District of Columbia asking to be admitted as delegates upon this floor, I wish to refer this to the Convention.

Mr. TODD, of Maryland: Mr. Chairman, I hold in my hand a petition in regard to the matter of the delegates from the District of Columbia. I would like to ask for information if they are entitled to seats.

The CHAIRMAN: The Chair is unable to furnish the gentleman with the information, and refers him to the Committee on Credentials.

Mr. TODD: I ask that the petition be read.

The CHAIRMAN: There being no objection, the petition will be read.

The Secretary read as follows:

To the National Democratic Convention:

The delegates from the District of Columbia respectfully represent that said District, with a population of 150,000 inhabitants, is taxed without representation and robbed by the rings of the Radical administration, and for many other causes of complaint against the misrule of Radicals in national and local politics, and acts done in violation of law and justice in said District, humbly pray that the Democracy of said District may be represented and allowed a voice in this Convention. Our people are sincere adherents of Democratic principles, and most deeply interested in the impending campaign.

Respectfully submitted,

COLUMBUS ALEXANDER,
ROBERT POWELL,
Delegates.

The CHAIRMAN: The petition will be referred to the Committee on Credentials under the rules.

Mr. TODD: I move that the gentlemen have seats on this floor without the privilege of voting.

The CHAIR: The gentleman is out of order. The petition goes to the Committee on Credentials without debate. The question is on the adoption of the report of the Committee on Credentials.

Mr. MCLANE, of Maryland: I move an amendment to the report of the committee, to allow these gentlemen seats upon the floor without the privilege of voting.

The CHAIR: The Chair will entertain the motion of the gentleman after the present question is disposed of. The question is on the adoption of the report of the Committee on Credentials.

Mr. MCLANE: It is impossible for the Chair to entertain the proposition after the report has been voted upon.

The CHAIR: The Chair has stated it will entertain the motion after the house has disposed of the report of the Committee on Credentials.

Mr. DESHA, of Kentucky: With all due deference to the Chair, it does seem to me now is the proper time to entertain a proposition to amend the report of the committee. After the report is adopted it will be out of order to move any amendment to it.

The CHAIR: The Chair did not understand an amendment was offered to the report of the committee. The Chair refers to the petition of the delegation from the District of Columbia. Does the Chair understand the gentleman from Maryland to offer an amendment to the report of the Committee on Credentials?

Mr. MCLANE: Yes, sir.

The CHAIR: Will the gentleman reduce his amendment to writing?

Mr. MCLANE: I will do it.

Mr. FINCH, of Iowa: I moved that the report of the Committee on Credentials be amended by the adoption of these additional delegations, and I heard a second.

The CHAIR: The Chair did not understand the gentleman to make a motion.

Mr. FINCH: The Chair made a mistake.

The CHAIR: The Chair rules the gentleman out of order. The gentleman has his remedy before the Convention.

Mr. FINCH: I appeal to the house from the decision of the Chair.

The CHAIR: The gentleman appeals from the decision of the Chair. As many as are in favor of sustaining the decision of the Chair will say aye.

The response was a unanimous aye, which was the signal for tremendous applause.

The CHAIR: The gentleman from Maryland has the floor. He has been asked to reduce his amendment to writing. The Chair will entertain the motion when it is handed up.

Pending the writing out of the amendment by the gentleman from Maryland, Gen. Williams, of Indiana, came upon the platform, and being recognized by the delegates, was saluted with a cheer.

The Secretary then read the resolution of Mr. Todd as follows:

Resolved, That the report of the Committee on Credentials be amended so as to admit delegates claiming seats in this Convention from the District of Columbia, without the privilege of voting. [Cries of "That's right."]

Mr. WHITELEY, of Delaware: I rise to a point of order. I have no objection to the delegates from the District of Columbia, but I ask if it is proper for this body to amend the report of the Committee on Credentials? These credentials should be sent to that committee for them to report upon.

The CHAIR: The report is in the possession of the Convention. The question before the house is the acceptance or rejection of the report, and amendments are in order.

Mr. HEISTER CLYMER, of Pennsylvania: I move to amend by inserting the words "and the delegates from the Territories," and on that amendment I demand the previous question.

The previous question was carried, and amendments of Mr. Todd and Mr. Clymer were adopted.

The question being upon the adoption of the report as amended, it was carried with cheers.

THE LIST OF DELEGATES.

The following is the official list of the Delegates to the Convention reported by the Committee:

ALABAMA—20.

AT LARGE.

	L. P. Walker	Huntsville.
	C. C. Langdon	Mobile.
	Eli S. Shorter	Eufaula.
	John T. Morgan	Selma.
First District.—	John Maguire	Mobile.
" "	F. S. Lyons	Demopolis.
Second "	H. M. Caldwell	Greenville.
" "	W. W. Screws	Montgomery.
Third "	J. N. Arrington	Union Springs.
" "	F. Watkins	Opelika.
Fourth "	E. W. Pettus	Selma.
" "	C. L. Scott	Camden.
Fifth "	E. H. Moren	Centreville.
" "	U. U. Armstrong	Notasulga.
Sixth "	M. L. Stansel	Carrollton.
" "	N. N. Clements	Tuscaloosa.
Seventh "	R. B. Kyle	Gadsden.
" "	W. A. Handley	Roanoke.
Eighth "	John D. Snodgrass	Scottsboro.
" "	A. H. Keller	Tuscumbia.

ARKANSAS—12.

AT LARGE.

	F. Doswell	
	N. M. Rose	
	M. L. Jones	
	N. N. Reynolds	
First District.—	L. H. Mangum	
" "	J. N. Butler	
Second "	B. D. Williams	
" "	L. G. Garrett	
Third "	Jesse Turner	
" "	J. P. Mitchell	
Fourth "	J. M. Loughborough	
" "	M. M. McGuire	

CALIFORNIA—12.

AT LARGE.

	Joseph P. Hoge	San Francisco.
	Clay W. Taylor	Shasta.
	John S. Hager	San Francisco.
	James L. English	Sacramento.

First District.—George H. Rogers............................San Francisco.
" " William Dunphy............................San Francisco.
Second " J. Hays....................................Oakland.
" " F. T. Baldwin..............................Stockton.
Third " Harmen Bay...............................Chico.
" " George M. Cornwall.........................Napa.
Fourth " J. A. Moultrie...............................San Jose.
" " T. D. Mott..................................Los Angeles.

CONNECTICUT—12.

AT LARGE.

W. H. Barnum..Salisbury.
W. B. Franklin..Hartford.
Colin M. Ingersoll....................................New Haven.
Geo. D. Whittlesey....................................New London.

First District.—R. D. Hubbard..............................Hartford.
" " R. S. Hicks...................................Stafford Springs.
Second " Isaac Arnold..............................Haddam.
" " Thomas Elms................................Birmingham.
Third " John L. Hunter............................Willimantic.
" " Edward Hunter..............................Norwich.
Fourth " Dwight Morris............................Bridgeport.
" " Henry Sherwood............................Sherman.

DELAWARE—6.

Gov. Saulsbury..Dover.
John W. Hall..Frederica.
William G. Whitely....................................Wilmington.
Geo. Gray...New Castle.
Edward L. Martin......................................Seaford.
Chas. H. Richards.....................................Georgetown.

FLORIDA—8.

S. G. M. Gary..
G. A. Stanley..
John Westcott..
A. Doggett...
J. H. McKinne..
T. J. Harris...
C. W. Yulee..
J. E. Hartridge......................................

GEORGIA—22.

AT LARGE.

James M. Smith.......................................Atlanta.
George T. Barnes.....................................Augusta.
Rufus E. Lester......................................Savannah.
John W. Wofford......................................Cartersville.

First District.—John C. Nichols.............................Blackshear.
" " J. J. Jones.............................Waynesboro.
Second " H. G. Turner.............................Quitman.
" " E. C. Bower.............................Bleakley.
Third " Allen Fort.............................Americus.
" " Walter T. McArthur.............................Lumber City.
Fourth " Obadiah Warner.............................Greeneville.
" " Mark H. Blanford.............................Columbus.
Fifth " John J. Hall.............................Griffin.
" " E. P. Howell.............................Atlanta.
Sixth " J. W. Preston.............................Monticello.
" " J. M. Pace.............................Covington.
Seventh " W. M. Payne.............................Ringgold.
" " P. M. B. Young.............................Carterville.
Eighth " W. G. Johnson.............................Lexington.
" " C. S. Dubose.............................Warrenton.
Ninth " H. H. Carleton.............................Athens.
" " H. P. Bell.............................Cumming.

ILLINOIS—42.

AT LARGE.

William J. Allen.............................Cairo.
Fred. H. Winston.............................Chicago.
Chauncey L. Higbee.............................Pittsfield, Pike Co.
Charles Dunham.............................Geneseo.

First District.—Melville W. Fuller.............................Chicago.
" " John Forsythe.............................Chicago.
Second " Snowdon S. Hays.............................Chicago.
" " John C. Richberg.............................Chicago.
Third " Perry H. Smith.............................Chicago.
" " Herman Lieb.............................Chicago.
Fourth " Thos. Butterworth.............................Rockford.
" " Augustus M. Herrington.............................Gendra.
Fifth " W. H. Mitchell.............................Freeport.
" " M. D. Hathaway.............................Rochelle.
Sixth " Wm. H. Messenkop.............................Princeton.
" " J. S. Drake.............................Rock Island.
Seventh " Wm. Reddick.............................La Salle.
" " D. H. Pinney.............................Joliet.
Eighth " Jonathan Duff.............................Pontiac.
" " J. E. Ong.............................Lacon.
Ninth " John S. Lee.............................Peoria.
" " Samuel P. Cummings.............................Astoria.
Tenth " David Ellis.............................Carthage.
" " Chas. H. Whittaker.............................Macomb.
Eleventh " Louis E. Worcester.............................Whitehall.
" " Samuel R. Chittenden.............................Mendon.
Twelfth " John A. McClernand.............................Springfield.
" " James M. Epler.............................Jacksonville.
Thirteenth " James S. Ewing.............................Bloomington.
" " James L. Hoblit.............................Lincoln, Logan Co.
Fourteenth " E. S. Terry.............................Danville.
" " Thos. H. Macoughtry.............................Auscola.

Fifteenth	*Dist.*—	Wm. M. Garrard	Lawrenceville.
"	"	Wm. S. O'Hair	Paris.
Sixteenth	"	Thos. B. Murray	Fayette.
"	"	G. Van Hoornbeke	Carlisle.
Seventeenth	"	Wm. R. Welsh	Carlinville.
"	"	Gus. A. Koerner	Belleville.
Eighteenth	"	Geo. W. Wall	Du Quoin.
"	"	Monroe C. Crawford	Jonesboro.
Nineteenth	"	Willis Duff Green	Mt. Vernon.
"	"	Samuel L. Chaney	Harrisburg.

INDIANA—30.

AT LARGE.

Bayles W. Hanna	Terre Haute.
Mahlon D. Manson	Crawfordsville.
Chas. Denby	Evansville.
Joseph E. McDonald	Indianapolis.

First	*District.*—	Thos. E. Garvin	Evansville.
"	"	O. M. Welborn	Princeton.
Second	"	Sam'l H. Taylor	Washington.
"	"	Thos. R. Cobb	Vincennes.
Third	"	Sam'l B. Voyles	Salem.
"	"	Francis I. Hord	Columbus.
Fourth	"	Cortez Ewing	Greensburgh.
"	"	Thos. Armstrong	Florence.
Fifth	"	Omar H. Roberts	Lawrenceburgh.
"	"	James Elder	Richmond.
Sixth	"	James W. Sansbury	Anderson.
"	"	J. F. McDowell	Marion.
Seventh	"	W. G. Neff	Greencastle.
"	"	James B. Ryan	Indianapolis.
Eighth	"	Daniel W. Voorhees	Terre Haute.
"	"	Elijah Newland	Bedford.
Ninth	"	John S. Williams	Lafayette.
"	"	David P. Barnard	Frankfort.
Tenth	"	J. H. Winterbotham	Michigan City.
"	"	B. B. Dailey	Delphi.
Eleventh	"	John Mitchell	Peru.
"	"	A. F. Armstrong	Kokomo.
Twelfth	"	Sam'l McGaughey	Huntington.
"	"	M. B. Spencer	Fort Wayne.
Thirteenth	"	John B. Stoll	Ligonier.
"	"	Daniel McDonald	Plymouth.

IOWA—22.

AT LARGE.

H. H. Trimble	Bloomfield.
B. F. Montgomery	Council Bluffs.
D. O. Finch	Des Moines.
M. M. Ham	Dubuque.

First	*District.*—	Edmund Jaeger	Keokuk.
"	"	E. McKitterick	Burlington.
Second	"	A. J. Monroe	Monticello.
"	"	E. H. Thayer	Clinton.

Third District—S. G. Van Anda..............................Manchester.
" " C. M. Durham..............................Independence.
Fourth " G. R. Miller..............................Mason City.
" " G. C. Wright..............................Waverly.
Fifth " Peter A. Dey..............................Iowa City.
" " L. G. Kinne..............................Toledo.
Sixth " H. B. Hendershott..............................Ottumwa.
" " T. J. Anderson..............................Knoxville.
Seventh " D. M. Baker..............................Chariton.
" " V. Wanewright..............................Winterset.
Eighth " Jacob Williams..............................Council Bluffs.
" " W. A. Stow..............................Hamburg.
Ninth " John P. Allison..............................Sioux City.
" " T. L. Bowman..............................Carroll.

KANSAS—10.

AT LARGE.

Charles W. Blair..............................Fort Scott.
Wilson Shannon..............................Lawrence.
Joseph W. Taylor..............................Leavenworth.
Isaac E. Eaton..............................Leavenworth.

First District.—S. M. Palmer..............................Salina, Saline Co.
" " J. G. Lowe..............................Washington.
Second " M. V. B. Bennett..............................Columbus.
" " G. W. Burchard..............................Independence.
Third " S. M. Donelson..............................Elgin.
" " T. L. Davis..............................Eureka.

KENTUCKY—24.

AT LARGE.

W. C. P. Breckenridge..............................Lexington.
Henry Watterson..............................Louisville.
Willis B. Machen..............................Eddyville.
John M. Rice..............................Louisa.

First District.—J. M. Bigger..............................Paducah.
" " J. B. Garnett..............................Cadiz.
Second " Malcolm Yeaman..............................Henderson.
" " Eugene Eaves..............................Greenville.
Third " W. W. Bush..............................Franklin.
" " B. T. Perkins..............................Elkton.
Fourth " R. A. Burton..............................Lebanon.
" " A. M. Brown..............................Elizabethtown.
Fifth " W. B. Hoke..............................Louisville.
" " G. P. Doern..............................Louisville.
Sixth " Lucius Desha..............................Cynthiana.
" " R. Perry..............................Warsaw.
Seventh " W. A. Cunningham..............................Paris.
" " Alvin Duvall..............................Frankfort.
Eighth " A. T. Chenault..............................White Hall.
" " N. Gaither..............................Harrodsburg.
Ninth " A. L. Martin..............................Prestonburg.
" " John Dishman..............................Barbourville.
Tenth " James Shackelford..............................Maysville.
" " A. J. Markley..............................Foster, Bracken Co.

LOUISIANA—16.

AT LARGE.

R. C. Wickliffe..Bayou Sara.
Thomas C. Manning.................................Alexandria.
Robert H. Marr.......................................New Orleans.
E. E. Kidd...Vernon.

First District.—Louis St. Martin...........................New Orleans.
" " John Tobin.................................New Orleans.
Second " John J. Mellon.............................New Orleans.
" " James McConnell..........................New Orleans.
Third " F. S. Goode...............................Houma.
" " Joseph L. Brent...........................New River.
Fourth " James Jefferies............................Alexandria.
" " John C. Moncure..........................Shreveport.
Fifth " H. C. Mitchell.............................Homer.
" " J. B. Cockren..............................Delta.
Sixth " W. H. Pipes.................................Clinton.
" " Henry L. Garland..........................Opelousas.

MAINE—14.

AT LARGE.

Samuel J. Anderson.................................Portland.
Samuel Watts...Thomaston.
Francis W. Hill.......................................Exeter.
Sam. D. Leavitt......................................Eastport.

First District.—Timothy Shaw...........................Biddeford.
" " R. M. Richardson..........................Portland.
Second " David R. Hastings..........................Fryeburg.
" " Arthur Sewell...............................Bath.
Third " V. D. Pinkham..............................Augusta.
" " Sam'l E. Smith.............................Wiscassett.
Fourth " J. S. Ricker ....Bangor.
" " A. M. Robinson, Jr.........................Bangor.
Fifth " Wm. H. McLellan..........................Belfast.
" " James R. Redman..........................Ellsworth.

MARYLAND—16.

AT LARGE.

Robert M. McLane...................................Baltimore.
R. B. Carmichael.....................................Queenstown.
E. K. Wilson...Snow Hill.
Outerbridge Horsey..................................Burkitsville.

First District.—Wm. H. Gale...............................Princess Ann.
" " James Alfred Pierce.......................Chestertown.
Second " Stevenson Archer..........................Belair.
" " J. Fred. C. Talbot...........................Towsontown.
Third " Joshua I. Turner...........................Baltimore.
" " Robert J. Slater............................Baltimore.
Fourth " Wm. T. Markland..........................Baltimore.
" " Robert T. Banks............................Baltimore.
Fifth " Andrew G. Chapman.......................Port Tobacco.
" " Sprigg Harwood.............................Annapolis.
Sixth " Richard D. Johnson.........................Cumberland.
" " George Freaner..............................Hagerstown.

MASSACHUSETTS—26.

AT LARGE.

Josiah G. Abbott..........Boston.
Edward Avery..........Boston.
Patrick A. Collins..........Boston.
George W. Gill..........Worcester.

First District.—Nicholas Hathaway..........Fall River.
" " Philander Cobb..........Kingston.
Second " Francis W. Bird..........E. Walpole.
" " Edward P. Reed..........Abington.
Third " Michael Doherty..........Boston.
" " James Power..........Boston.
Fourth " Leopold Morse..........Boston.
" " Timothy J. Daley..........Boston.
Fifth " Richard Frothingham..........Charlestown.
" " Charles G. Clark..........Lynn.
Sixth " Charles A. Ropes..........Salem.
" " James H. Carleton..........Haverhill.
Seventh " Patrick Murphy..........Lawrence.
" " Albert A. Haggett..........Lowell.
Eighth " Fred'k W. Clapp..........Framingham.
" " Michael Norton..........Boston.
Ninth " Geo. F. Verry..........Worcester.
" " James E. Estabrook..........Worcester.
Tenth " Wm. M. Gaylord..........Northampton.
" " Nahum Harwood..........Leominster.
Eleventh " Hugh Donelly..........Springfield.
" " Cebra Quackenbush..........Pittsfield.

MICHIGAN—22.

AT LARGE.

William L. Webber..........East Saginaw.
Peter White..........Marquette.
Merrill I. Mills..........Detroit.
Henry Chamberlain..........Three Oaks.

First District.—A. W. Copland..........Detroit.
" " Edward Kanter..........Detroit.
Second " Herman J. Redfield..........Monroe.
" " G. C. Munroe..........Jonesville.
Third " Michael Shoemaker..........Jackson.
" " A. J. Boyne..........Hastings.
Fourth " George B. Turner..........Cassopolis.
" " E. O. Briggs..........Paw Paw.
Fifth " James Blair..........Grand Rapids.
" " Fred. A. Nims..........Muskegon.
Sixth " Martin V. Montgomery..........Lansing.
" " John D. Norton..........Pontiac.
Seventh " Wm. L. Bancroft..........Port Huron.
" " John M. Wattles..........Lapeer.
Eighth " George L. Burrows..........Saginaw.
" " A. G. Maxwell..........Bay City.
Ninth " T. D. Stimson..........Big Rapids.
" " Edward Ryan..........Hancock.

MINNESOTA—10.

AT LARGE.

Eugene M. Wilson.......................Minneapolis.
Daniel Buck.......................Mankato.
J. H. McKenny.......................Chatfield.
C. F. Buck.......................Winona.

First District.—Michael Doran.......................Le Seuer.
" " John F. Norrish.......................Hastings.
Second " George E. Skinner.......................Faribault.
" " William Lee.......................St. Paul.
Third " J. N. Castle.......................Stillwater.
" " T. G. Mealey.......................Monticello.

MISSISSIPPI—16.

AT LARGE.

E. C. Walthall.......................Grenada.
W. S. Featherston.......................Holly.
Locke E. Houston.......................Aberdeen.
Felix Labauve.......................Hernando.

First District.—James O. Banks.......................Columbus.
" " R. H. Allen.......................Baldwin.
Second " A. M. Clayton.......................Lamar.
" " T. W. White.......................Hernando.
Third " W. R. Barksdale.......................Grenada.
" " H. L. Jarnigan.......................Macon.
Fourth " J. C. Prewett.......................Yazoo City.
" " J. C. Smith.......................
Fifth " Frank Johnson.......................Jackson.
" " R. C. Saffoid.......................Handsboro.
Sixth " L. N. Baldwin.......................Port Gibson.
" " Wade Hampton, Jr.......................Duncansby Landing.

MISSOURI—30.

AT LARGE.

C. H. Hardin.......................Jefferson City.
Stilson Hutchins.......................St. Louis.
Silas Woodson.......................St. Joseph.
H. J. Spaunhorst.......................St. Louis.

First District.—John G. Priest.......................St. Louis.
" " Abe McHose.......................St. Louis.
Second " A. W. Slayback.......................St. Louis.
" " R. D. Lancaster.......................St. Louis.
Third " Michael J. Cullen.......................St. Louis.
" " James C. Edwards.......................St. Louis.
Fourth " Joseph C. Moore.......................Charleston.
" " L. D. Walker.......................Farmington.
Fifth " R. S. Anderson.......................Leesburg.
" " David Newman.......................Rolla.
Sixth " Jos. Wisby.......................Marshfield.
" " R. H. Rose.......................Carthage.
Seventh " A. W. Anthony.......................Versailles.
" " E. A. Nickerson.......................Warrensburg.
Eighth " M. Munford.......................Kansas.
" " N. A. Wade.......................Butler.

Ninth District.—Jno. N. McMichael........................Plattsburg.
" " A. P. Morehouse........................Maryville.
Tenth " T. B. Yates........................Gallatin.
" " J. E. Nelson........................Milan.
Eleventh " A. W. Doniphan........................Richmond.
" " E. C. Moore........................Columbia.
Twelfth " J. B. Alverson........................La Grange.
" " A. W. Lamb........................Hannibal.
Thirteenth " T. G. Hutt........................Troy.
" " A. M. Alexander........................Paris.

NEBRASKA—6.

AT LARGE.

George L. Miller........................Omaha.
Tobias Castor........................Wiebre.
Alexander Bear........................Norfolk.
Gilbert B. Scofield........................Nebraska City.

First District.—F. A. Harman........................Bloomington.
" " Chas. McDonald........................North Platte.

NEVADA—6.

AT LARGE.

R. P. Keating........................Gold Hill.
J. S. Kaneen........................Virginia City.
R. E. Kelly........................Ormsby County.
A. C. Ellis........................Carson City.

First District.—J. C. Fall........................Unionsville.
" " John H. Dennis........................Eureka.

NEW HAMPSHIRE—10.

AT LARGE.

Henry H. Metcalf........................Dover.
Lafayette Hall........................New Market.
Edwin C. Bailey........................Hopkinton.
Geo. W. Goffe........................Bedford.

First District.—Jno. C. Moulton........................Laconia.
" " Alvah W. Sulloway........................Franklin.
Second " Fred. A. Parker........................Keene.
" " Gustavus Lucke........................Walpole.
Third " G. F. Putnam........................Warren.
" " W. H. Cummings........................Lisbon.

NEW JERSEY—18.

AT LARGE.

John P. Stockton........................Trenton.
Leon Abbett........................Jersey City.
John McGregor........................Newark.
Miles Ross........................New Brunswick.

First District.—Ebenezer Westcott........................Camden.
" " James R. Hoagland........................Bridgeton.
Second " Andrew J. Smith........................Heightston.
" " Garrett D. W. Vroom........................Trenton.
Third " Joseph W. Yates........................Plainfield.
" " Geo. C. Beekman........................Freehold.

Fourth *Dist.*—Calvin Corle..............................Somerville.
" " Thos. Kays..............................Newton.
Fifth " John Hopper..............................Patterson.
" " Garrett Ackerson, Jr..............................Hackensack.
Sixth " David Dodd..............................Orange.
" " Patrick Doyle..............................Newark.
Seventh " Rudolph F. Rabe..............................Hoboken.
" " P. H. Laverty..............................Jersey City.

NEW YORK—70.

AT LARGE.

Francis Kernan..............................Utica.
William Dorsheimer..............................Buffalo.
Abraham S. Hewitt..............................Utica.
Henry C. Murphy..............................Brooklyn.

First *District.*—James M. Oakley..............................Jamaica.
" " Gilbert C. Dean..............................Pattenville.
Second " Thos. Kinsella..............................Brooklyn.
" " Roger A. Pryor..............................Brooklyn.
Third " Wm. C. Kingsley..............................Brooklyn.
" " James F. Pierce..............................Brooklyn.
Fourth " John C. Jacobs..............................Brooklyn.
" " Archibald M. Bliss..............................Brooklyn.
Fifth " John Kelly..............................New York.
" " Wm. R. Roberts..............................New York.
Sixth " Sam'l S. Cox..............................New York.
" " John Fox..............................New York.
Seventh " August Belmont..............................New York.
" " H. F. Dunmock..............................New York.
Eighth " Edward L. Donnelly..............................New York.
" " Peter B. Olney..............................New York.
Ninth " Wm. C. Whitney..............................New York.
" " Frederick Smythe..............................New York.
Tenth " Edward Cooper..............................New York.
" " Manton Marble..............................New York.
Eleventh " Augustus Schell..............................New York.
" " Wm. H. Wickham..............................New York.
Twelfth " Geo. W. Davis..............................New Rochelle.
" " Casper C. Childs..............................Sing Sing.
Thirteenth " James Mackin..............................Fishkill on Hudson.
" " Robert E. Andrews..............................Hudson.
Fourteenth " Daniel B. St. John..............................Newburgh.
" " Geo. M. Beebe..............................Monticello.
Fifteenth " Wm. F. Russell..............................Saugerties.
" " John A. Griswold..............................Catskill.
Sixteenth " D. Manning..............................Albany.
" " Rufus W. Peckham..............................Albany.
Seventeenth " J. Russell Parsons..............................Hoosick Falls
" " Solomon W. Russell..............................Troy.
Eighteenth " Smith M. Weed..............................Plattsburgh.
" " Artemus B. Waldo..............................Plattsburgh.
Nineteenth " Daniel Magone, Jr..............................Ogdensburgh.
" " Wm. H. Sawyer..............................Canton
Twentieth " James Shanahan..............................Tribes Hill.
" " Samuel F. Benedict..............................Schenectady.

Twenty-first District.—O. M. Allaben..........................Margarettsville.
" " Gilbert H. Manning..................Norwich.
Twenty-second " Allen C. Beach........................Watertown.
" " Dewitt C. West.......................Lowville.
Twenty-third " James Stevens........................Rome.
" " J. K. Brown..........................Holland Patent.
Twenty-fourth " Dewitt C. Littlejohn..................Oswego.
" " Christopher A. Wolrath..............Oneida.
Twenty-fifth " Benton B. Jones.......................Courtland.
" " Alfred Wilkinson.....................Syracuse.
Twenty-sixth " Chas. Ross...........................Auburn.
" " Geo. W. Cuyler.......................Palmyra.
Twenty-seventh " G. H. Lapham.........................Penn Yan.
" " S. H. Hammond.......................Geneva.
Twenty-eighth " Sam'l D. Halliday.....................Ithaca.
" " D. T. Easton..........................Owego.
Twenty-ninth " E. W. Chamberlain...................Belmont.
" " Wm. B. Ruggles.......................Bath.
Thirtieth " Frederick Cook.......................Rochester.
" " Wm. Purcell..........................Rochester.
Thirty-first " W. S. Wright.........................Lockport.
" " H. J. Glowackie......................Batavia.
Thirty-second " Albert P. Laning.....................Buffalo.
" " Cyrenus C. Torrance.................Gowanda.
Thirty-third " Chas. S. Cary.........................Olean.
" " Wm. Bookstaver.....................Dunkirk.

NORTH CAROLINA—20.

AT LARGE.

T. L. Clingman......................................Asheville.
P. C. Cameron.......................................Hillsboro.
W. J. Green..Warrenton.
H. B. Short...Flemington.

First District.—Charles Latham...........................Plymouth.
" " Thos. G. Skinner..........................Hertford.
Second " Wm. T. Dortch............................Goldsboro.
" " H. E. T. Manning.........................Weldon.
Third " F. W. Kertchner..........................Wilmington.
" " J. H. Myrover.............................Fayetteville.
Fourth " James S. Battle...........................Rocky Mount.
" " Thomas Webb.............................Hillsboro.
Fifth " J. N. Staples..............................Greensboro.
" " E. B. Withers..............................Yanceyville.
Sixth " John D. Shaw.............................Lincolnton.
" " B. F. Little.................................Little's Mills.
Seventh " F. E. Shober...............................Salisbury.
" " G. M. Mathes.............................Winston.
Eighth " S. McD. Tate..............................Morganton.
" " W. M. Hardy..............................Asheville.

OHIO—44.

AT LARGE.

Geo. W. Morgan....................................
W. L. O'Brien.......................................
Thos. Ewing, Jr.....................................
Henry Bohl..

First	*District.*—	Isaac C. Collins
"	"	Wm. J. O'Neil
Second	"	Thos. B. Paxton
"	"	Silas W. Hoffman
Third	"	Wm. Howard
"	"	Isaac Glaze
Fourth	"	Jacob Baker
"	"	Geo. W Houk
Fifth	"	F. C. LeBond
"	"	Wm. Carter
Sixth	"	J. B. Steadman
"	"	Wm. Sheridan
Seventh	"	John A. Nipgen
"	"	T. W. Higgins
Eighth	"	Geo. Lincoln
"	"	W. V. Marquis
Ninth	"	John D. Thompson
"	"	James M. White
Tenth	"	Geo. E. Seney
"	"	C. S. Parker
Eleventh	"	R. E. Reese
"	"	H. L. Chapman
Twelfth	"	E. F. Bingham
"	"	Chas. F. Rainey
Thirteenth	"	Geo. Atherton
"	"	Chas. H. Mathews
Fourteenth	"	James A. Estell
"	"	John B. Netcher
Fifteenth	"	F. A. Davis
"	"	P. B. Buell
Sixteenth	"	J. M. Estep
"	"	B. F. Spriggs
Seventeenth	"	Wm. L. Brown
"	"	R. S. Shields
Eighteenth	"	A. H. Comins
"	"	M. W. Axtell
Nineteenth	"	S. L. Hunt
"	"	Eusebius Lee
Twentieth	"	W. W. Armstrong
"	"	Waldemier Otis

OREGON—6.

H. H. Gilfry	Salem.
J. C. Braly	McMinnville.
Thos. Milliorn	Junction City.
M. V. Brown	Albany.
R. R. Thompson	Portland.
James H. Turner	Pendleton.

PENNSYLVANIA—58.

AT LARGE.

Wm. A. Wallace	Clearfield.
Heister Clymer	Reading.
Andrew H. Hill	Lewisburg.
Hugh M. North	Columbia.

First	*District.*—	Geo. McGowan	Philadelphia.
"	"	W. M. Reilly	Philadelphia.
Second	"	John R. Reed	Philadelphia.
"	"	Thos. D. Pierce	Philadelphia.
Third	"	R. E. Randall	Philadelphia.
"	"	Wm. McMullen	Philadelphia.
Fourth	"	W. V. McGrath	Philadelphia.
"	"	H. Donohue	Philadelphia.
Fifth	"	John Fullerton	Philadelphia.
"	"	F. Gerger	Philadelphia.
Sixth	"	Robert E. Monaghan	West Chester.
"	"	J. B. Rhodes	Leni.
Seventh	"	Geo. Ross	Doylestown.
"	"	J. V. Gotwalts	Norristown.
Eighth	"	A. B. Warner	Reading.
"	"	Evan Mishler	Reading.
Ninth	"	J. L. Steinmets	Lancaster.
"	"	W. H. Grier	Columbus.
Tenth	"	Wm. Mutchler	Easton.
"	"	T. B. Metzger	Allentown.
Eleventh	"	D. Lowenburg	Bloomsburg.
"	"	A. G. Broadhead, Jr	Mauch Chunk.
Twelfth	"	H. B. Wright	Wilkesbarre.
"	"	James Corbett	Scranton.
Thirteenth	"	Wm. N. Randall	Schuylkill Haven.
"	"	W. J. Matz	Pottsville.
Fourteenth	"	Geo. W. Ryon	Schamokin.
"	"	Geo. H. Spang	Lebanon.
Fifteenth	"	R. A. Packer	Wysox.
"	"	J. M. Piollet	Wysox.
Sixteenth	"	Jno. B. Beck	Williamsport.
"	"	Geo. D. Jackson	Dushore.
Seventeenth	"	R. L. Johnston	Evensburg.
"	"	E. F. Kerr	Bedford.
Eighteenth	"	A. J. Fisher	McAllisterville.
"	"	John A. Magee	New Bloomfield.
Nineteenth	"	F. E. Beltzhover	Carlisle.
"	"	T. G. Neely	Gettysburg.
Twentieth	"	A. C. Noyes	Westport.
"	"	Thos. M. Uttley	Lewistown.
Twenty-first	"	Chas. E. Boyle	Uniontown.
"	"	Alex. Patton	Rice's Landing.
Twenty-second	"	A. F. Keating	Pittsburg.
"	"	W. J. Brennan	Pittsburg.
Twenty-third	"	Malcolm Hay	Pittsburg.
"	"	A. G. Cochrane	Pittsburg.
Twenty-fourth	"	W. B. Dunlap	Rochester.
"	"	I. Bentley	Washington.
Twenty-fifth	"	S. M. Clarke	Indiana.
"	"	John Gilpin	Kittaning.
Twenty-sixth	"	J. A. Stranahan	Mercer.
"	"	J. T. Bard	Slippery Rock.
Twenty-seventh	"	J. R. Thompson	Erie.
"	"	R. L. Cochran	Franklin.

RHODE ISLAND—8.

Nicholas Van Slyck........Providence.
William B. Beach........Providence.
John P. Cooney........Providence.
Jno. M. Studley........Providence.
W. T. C. Wardwell........Bristol.
Henry D. DeBlois........Newport.
Alphius F. Angell........Reevepoint.
John B. Pierce........Wickford.

SOUTH CAROLINA—14.

AT LARGE.

John Bratton........Winnsboro.
D. Wyatt Aiken........Cokesbury.
J. D. Kennedy........Camden.
J. A. Hoyt........Anderson.

First District.—J. S. Richardson........Sumter.
" " J. D. McLucas........Marion.
Second " M. P. O'Conner........Charleston.
" " J. F. Ficken........Charleston.
Third " Sam'l McGowan........Abbeville.
" " W. B. Stanley........Columbia.
Fourth " J. H. Evins........Spartanburg.
" " B. F. Perry........Greenville.
Fifth " J. C. Sheppard........Edgefield.
" " Wm. Elliott........Beaufort.

TENNESSEE—24.

AT LARGE.

John M. Fleming........Knoxville.
John C. Brown........Pulaski.
John C. Birch........Nashville.
John H. Gardener........Gardener's Station.

First District.—S. Kirkpatrick........Jonesboro.
" " John E. Helms........Morristown.
Second " Alfred Caldwell........Knoxville.
" " Thos. O'Connor........Knoxville.
Third " P. H. Coffee........McMinnville.
" " M. H. Clift........Chattanooga.
Fourth " John P. Murray........Gainesboro.
" " W. R. Saddler........Saddlersville.
Fifth " James D. Richardson........Murfreesboro.
" " James W. Newman........Fayetteville.
Sixth " Samuel Donelson........Nashville.
" " W. G. Ewin........Waverly.
Seventh " W. C. Whitthorne........Columbia.
" " T. F. P. Allison........College Grove.
Eighth " A. W. Campbell........Jackson.
" " Wm. M. Wright........Huntington.
Ninth " S. W. Cochran........Troy.
" " P. J. Smith........Covington.
Tenth " W. H. Carroll........Memphis.
" " M. T. Polk........Bolivar.

TEXAS—20.

AT LARGE.

F. B. Sexton..Marshall.
W. S. Herndon......................................Tyler.
E. G. Bower..Dallas.
T. B. Wheeler......................................Austin.
M. D. K. Taylor....................................Jefferson.
Joseph Bates.......................................Brazoria.
J. M. Williams.....................................Independence.
N. Holland...Belleville.

First District.—D. A. Nunn.......................Crockett.
" " W. H. Tucker...................................Palestine.
Second " H. W. Lightfoot.........................Paris.
" " J. A. Weaver...................................Sulphur Springs.
Third " J. C. McCoy..............................Dallas.
" " T. H. Murray...................................McKinney.
Fourth " Asbel Smith.............................Evergreen.
" " Geo. Clark.....................................Waco.
Fifth " F. C. Stockdale..........................Indianola.
" " Jos. E. Dwyer..................................San Antonio.
Sixth " J. D. Giddings...........................Brenham.
" " W. L. Moody....................................Galveston.

VERMONT—10.

AT LARGE.

Marcus D. Gilman...................................Montpelier.
Bradley B. Smalley.................................Burlington.
Jasper Rand..St. Albans.
P. S. Benjamin.....................................Wolcott.

First District.—James H. Williams................Bellows Falls.
" " Joseph W. Bliss................................Bradford.
Second " C. W. Chase.............................Lyndon.
" " Thos. B. Kennedy...............................Fairfield.
Third " Geo. M. Fisk.............................Northfield.
" " John Cain......................................Rutland.

VIRGINIA—22.

AT LARGE.

James A. Walker....................................Newbern.
R. A. Coghill......................................New Glasgow.
D. J. Goodwin......................................Portsmouth.
Fitzhugh Lee.......................................Richland Mills.

First District.—Ben. T. Gunter...................Accomac C. H.
" " C. F. Sinclair.................................Manassas.
Second " Wm. Lamb................................Norfolk.
" " J. B. Prince...................................Jerusalem.
Third " John A. Meredith.........................Richmond.
" " T. O'Brien.....................................Midlothian.
Fourth " W. E. Hinton, Jr........................Petersburg.
" " W. H. Mann.....................................Nottoway C. H.
Fifth " Thos. S. Flournoy........................Danville.
" " W. H. Sutherlin................................Hillsville.
Sixth " Thos. S. Bocock..........................Lynchburg.
" " Wm. P. Johnson.................................Lexington.

Seventh Dist.—S. V. Southall....Charlottesville.
" " M. G. Harman....Staunton.
Eighth " H. E. Peyton....Waterford.
" " S. C. Neale....Alexandria.
Ninth " Wm. Watts....Big Lick.
" " Wm. B. Astor....Lebanon.

WEST VIRGINIA—10.

AT LARGE.

J. N. Camden....Parkersburg.
J. J. Davis....Clarksburg.
Alfred Beckley....Raleigh C. H.
L. R. Cofran....Grafton.

First District.—G. D. Camden....Clarksburg.
" " Wilson Beall....Wellsburg.
Second " C. J. P. Cresap....Beverly.
" " A. B. Jackson....Parkersburg.
Third " Henry C. Simms....Huntington.
" " James W. Kelly....Hartford City.

WISCONSIN—20.

AT LARGE.

Geo. B. Smith....Madison.
James R. Doolittle....Racine.
Alexander Mitchell....Milwaukee.
Theodore Rodolf....La Crosse.

First District.—N. D. Fratt....Racine.
" " Geo. H. Daubner....Brookfield Centre.
Second " W. F. Vilas....Madison.
" " G. W. Bird....Jefferson.
Third " J. H. Earnest....Shullsburg.
" " I. T. Carr....Monroe.
Fourth " J. A. Hinsey....Milwaukee.
" " A. Semler....West Bend.
Fifth " E. C. Lewis....Juneau.
" " Joseph Rankin....Manitowoc.
Sixth " James Robinson....Chilton.
" " Myron Reed....Waupaca.
Seventh " H. H. Hayden....Eau Claire.
" " S. H. Dickinson....Sparta.
Eighth " W. Wilson....Menomonee.
" " J. C. Clark....Wausau.

ARIZONA.

COLORADO—6.

Thomas M. Patterson....Denver.
Adair Wilson....Del Norte.
A. J. Williams....Denver.
Frank J. Marshall....Georgetown.
D. J. Martin....Colorado Springs.
Samuel McBride....Pueblo.

DAKOTA—2.

M. W. Sheafe, Jr....Elk Point.
L. D. Parmer....Yankton.

IDAHO.

MONTANA—2.

Martin Maginnis..................................Helena.
Samuel T. Hauser..................................Helena.

UTAH—2.

R. C. Chambers..................................Park City.
J. P. Page..................................

WASHINGTON.

WYOMING—1.

E. L. Pease..................................

DISTRICT OF COLUMBIA—2.

Columbus Alexander..................................
Robert Ball..................................

The CHAIR: The next thing in order is the report from the Committee on Organization. Mr. Hanna, of Indiana, has the floor.

Mr. Hanna, of Indiana, from the Committee on Permanent Organization, made the following report:

Mr. CHAIRMAN: In behalf of the Committee on Permanent Organization, I have the honor to submit the following report of officers for this Convention:

PERMANENT OFFICERS.

For Permanent President, Gen. JOHN A. MCCLERNAND, of Illinois. [Cheers.]

VICE-PRESIDENTS AND SECRETARIES.

Alabama—Vice-President, S. S. LYON; Secretary, W. W. SCREWS.
Arkansas—Vice-President, G. D. ROYSTON; Secretary, W. H. CATE.
California—Vice-President, Col. JACK HAYES; Secretary, GEO. M. CORNWELL.
Colorado—Vice-President, D. J. MARTIN; Secretary, SAMUEL MCBRIDE.
Connecticut—Vice-President, COLIN M. INGERSOLL; Secretary, THOS. ELEMUS.
Delaware—Vice-President, J. W. HALL; Secretary, E. L. MARTIN.
Florida—Vice-President, G. A. STANLEY; Secretary, JOHN C. HARTRIDGE.
Georgia—Vice-President, RUFUS E. LESTER; Secretary, H. H. CARLTON.
Illinois—Vice-President, E. S. TERRY; Secretary, A. C. STOREY.
Indiana—Vice-President, JOHN B. STOLL; Secretary, THOS. E. GARVIN.
Iowa—Vice-President, D. F. ELLSWORTH; Secretary, E. H. THAYER.
Kansas—Vice-President, WILSON SHANNON; Secretary, SAMUEL DONALDSON.
Kentucky—Vice-President, W. B. MATCHEN; Secretary, J. M. DODD.
Louisiana—Vice-President, T. C. MANNING; Secretary, F. S. GOODE.
Maine—Vice-President, F. W. Hill; Secretary, L. D. LEAVITT.
Maryland—Vice-President, R. R. CARMICHAEL; Secretary, R. D. JOHNSON.
Massachusetts—Vice-President, CHAS. G. CLARK; Secretary, MICHAEL NORTON.
Michigan—Vice-President, PETER WHITE; Secretary, F. A. NIMS.

Minnesota—Vice-President, T. G. MEALEY; Secretary, J. F. NORRISH.
Mississippi—Vice-President, ——; Secretary, ——.
Missouri—Vice-President, A. W. LAMB; Secretary, N. A. WADE.
Nebraska—Vice-President, ALEX. BEAR; Secretary, CHAS. MCDONALD.
Nevada—Vice-President, JOHN C. FALL; Secretary, R. C. KELLY.
New Hampshire—Vice-President, JOHN C. MOULTON; Secretary, F. A. BARKER.
New Jersey—Vice-President, JOHN HOPPER; Secretary, RUDOLPH RABE.
New York—Vice-President, W. H. WICKHAM; Secretary, GEO. W. DANIELS.
North Carolina—Vice-President, F. E. SHOBER; Secretary, H. T. MANNING.
Ohio—Vice-President, WM. CARTER; Secretary, W. W. ARMSTRONG.
Pennsylvania—Vice-President, T. E. MONAGHAN; Secretary, CHAS. E. BOYLE.
Rhode Island—Vice-President, JOHN B. PIERCE; Secretary, JOHN M. STUDLEY.
South Carolina—Vice-President, B. F. PERRY; Secretary, J. A. HOYT.
Tennessee—Vice-President, J. D. RICHARDSON; Secretary, M. T. POLK.
Texas—Vice-President, W. S. HERNDON; Secretary, H. W. LIGHTFORD.
Vermont—Vice-President, P. S. BENJAMIN; Secretary, C. H. CHASE.
Virginia—Vice-President, J. A. WALKER; Secretary, W. H. MANN.
West Virginia—Vice-President, ALFRED BECHLEY; Secretary, H. C. SIMMS.
Wisconsin—Vice-President, THEODORE RODOLF; Secretary, H. H. HAYDEN.

READING SECRETARIES AND SERGEANT-AT-ARMS.

The following-named gentlemen are recommended as Reading Secretaries of the Convention:

S. K. DONOVAN, T. O. WALKER, of Iowa, N. M. BELL, SAM. C. REID and A. T. WHITTLESEY.

Sergeant-at-Arms: DAN ABLE, of St. Louis.

The Committee also recommend that the rules and regulations of the National Democratic Convention of 1872 be adopted by this Convention for the government of its proceedings.

The CHAIRMAN: The Convention has heard the report of the Committee on Organization. The question is, shall the report be adopted? The Chair is ready to hear the pleasure of the Convention.

A DIGRESSION.

Mr. SMITH, of Wisconsin: I wish to correct the name of the Vice-President for Wisconsin. It should be Theodore Rodolf.

Mr. WILLIAMS, of——: I move to insert the name of E. O. Perrin, of New York, as one of the Reading Secretaries.

The motion was put and the motion lost.

Mr. WILLIAMS: I call for a standing vote on the question.

The CHAIRMAN: The Chairman has decided the question. The question is on the adoption of the report on organization.

The question was put and the report adopted.

The CHAIRMAN: The Chairman will appoint the Hon. Dan. W. Voorhees, of Indiana [applause], Gen. Fitzhugh Lee, of Virginia [applause], and Gov. Wm. Dorsheimer, of New York, to escort Gen. McClernand to the chair.

After waiting for a few moments it appeared the gentlemen named were not present, and

The CHAIRMAN said: Gen. Fitzhugh Lee being out of the hall, the Hon. Thos. S. Bocock will please act in his place. The Chair would ask the New York delegation if Gov. Dorsheimer is in his place?

A DELEGATE: He is not here.

The CHAIRMAN: The Chair will ask Mr. Manton Marble, of New York, to take the place of Gov. Dorsheimer. [Applause.]

Gen. McClernand was then escorted to the platform amid loud applause and spoke as follows:

SPEECH OF GEN. M'CLERNAND.

GENTLEMEN OF THE CONVENTION: In choosing me to preside over your deliberations, you have conferred on me a high and unexpected honor, which I gratefully acknowledge. This honor carries with it a duty both delicate and responsible, which it will be my aim and effort to discharge with all proper dispatch, but above all with fairness and impartiality. [Applause.]

Seconded by your hearty co-operation and guided by the rules you have been pleased to adopt, my task will be much facilitated. I hope the manner of its performance may prove satisfactory. To extend my remarks, I must do so almost without any previous preparation and upon the spur of the occasion. I trust, therefore, you will be pleased to hear me indulgently.

You are here, gentlemen, the delegates of the National Democracy, and come from every portion of our common country. The occasion is an interesting and important one. A great and solemn duty awaits you. Let us pause for a moment to consider it. The land is in the hands of partisan spoilers. It is infected and blighted by spreading and cankering misrule. Passing to particulars, the Constitution is trampled under foot, and the Republic practically converted into a party despotism. [Applause.] Governors of States, chosen by the people, have been deposed by the sword, and legislative assemblies dispersed by the same means. [Applause.] Discriminate and invidious laws have been enacted in the interest of favored classes and pursuits to the injury and ruin of others, and thus is upheld the dogma of protection — a relic of barbarism. [Applause.] The centralization of power, political and monetary, has become a threatening and marked phenomenon of these disjointed times. [Applause.] A depreciated and debased paper currency, substituting the use of coin, has unsettled values and paralyzed enterprise and industry. [Applause.] Malversations in office, high and low, have become the order of the day. Even a Minister of State, a cabinet officer, and the President's Private Secretary have not escaped judicial inculpation. The work of detection and exposure is still going on. The Democratic majority in the popular branch of Congress has unearthed many fraudulent and corrupt transactions, but these, with the rest, are too numerous for present notice. [Applause.] It is enough to say, generally, that the civil service, in almost all its extent, is reeking with rottenness. The Augean stable urgently needs to be cleansed, and the Democracy are the Hercules, all-competent and ready for the task. [Applause.]

Hastening on with a few further desultory remarks, I have to repeat, gentlemen, you are here the representatives of the Democracy of the whole Union — that Union formed by our fathers and then numbering thirteen States; now thirty-eight States, members of one family, with the same heritage of liberty and equal laws, and heirs of one destiny — that Union, for a time, unnaturally divided against itself, but now restored under the genial influence of a growing concord and harmony amongst its members. [Applause.]

What is the part of patriotism? If your deliberations to-day shall be wise, if your perception of the necessities of our time, our country and our politics shall be just and sagacious, if the hearts of the people shall quicken yours, then, beyond all peradventure, your work will survive as a priceless blessing to your children and your children's children. The States will be restored to their proper federal relations and to their rightful local authority. Local self-government will be re-established to protect and assure the rights of person and property. The Republic will be preserved and perpetuated, and greater than the founders of republics are the preservers of republics. [Loud applause.]

There are to-day, gentlemen, no enemies to the nation on this continent, except, in a certain sense, the authors and abettors of administrative centralism — that centralism which is congesting at the capital those vital currents which, unloosed, would and ought to flow out to every part, giving life and energy to the body politic in all its members and extremes — except that corruption which is the curse of centralism and has never failed, in any age or country, to bring ruin in its train. [Applause.] What do we see? Centralism and corruption have already imposed upon the States the rapacious tyrannies of *carpet-bag* rule, illustrated by the addition of two hundred millions of public debt.

Centralism and corruption have also invaded our Northern States and cities and infected them with the same disease of extravagance and fraud. They have debauched the Federal Government itself, and made the names of scores of its high officers and public men a public scandal and shame. The record is horrible — it is one of incapacity, venality and waste. The party responsible for these abominations, powerless to repress them, now, with stupendous effrontery, pledges itself to this task. Reform is impracticable to it. Reform of itself implies the amputation of its own members, to which parties are no more disposed than are individuals to maim themselves. [Applause.]

The party in power pledged itself to restore specie payments, yet, from year to year, it takes us further from that consummation. It pledged itself to civil service reform, yet, by its action, mocks all reform. So it pledged itself to protect American labor, yet, by its customs levies, it has robbed and oppressed labor. A few score monopolists, a few thousand corruptionists have been enriched, but capital in the hands of those who earned it by industry and saved it by frugality is everywhere distrustful and rusts unused. Such are the unvarnished facts—such a faithful picture. Lo! is this the final outcome of essential republican self-government? Gracious God, forbid it! [Applause.]

Yes, gentlemen, we have wandered far from the right path. We must hasten to return to the ark of the Constitution, to frugal expenditures, to the administrative purity of the founders of the Republic. [Applause.] All must be lost without it. The Government is dissolving in its own corruptions. Now is the time to make our election sure. The golden moment neglected, is gone to make no return. Reform! reform! reform! is the supreme commanding issue of the day. All others are inferior — all others are trivial to it. [Applause.] In its name and authority we appeal to our fellow-citizens of every former political affiliation to rush to the rescue. [Loud applause.] Country above party—everything for the cause. [Continued applause.] Now, gentlemen, in conclusion, recognizing this imperious necessity, guaranteeing in your platform the work of national regeneration, selecting standard-bearers true and devoted to the sacred mission, victory in November — victory in the October elections—is already yours. [Applause.] Incarnating the vital issue of *reform* in candidate and platform, and battling for it to the end, the States that honored Douglas and Lincoln — the States that to-day honor Hendricks and Thurman, Hancock and Parker, Bayard and Tilden — these States, with their thronging populations, like the woods and winds that rose and followed the fluting Orpheus, will rise and follow you to final triumph. [Loud applause.]

Gentlemen, I again return you my thanks for the distinguished honor you have been pleased to confer upon me, which, taking me by surprise, as I have said, must excuse the waywardness and want of method of my remarks. [Loud applause.]

Mr. WILLIAMS, of Indiana: I understand the Committee on Resolutions are not ready to report. They have only informally organized and have not taken any action upon their doings. I therefore move that we adjourn until to-morrow morning at 11 o'clock. At the request of my friends about here, I make it 10 o'clock.

At the request of Mr. Belmont, I withdraw the motion and yield the floor to him.

At this juncture Mr. AUGUST BELMONT, of New York, got the floor and addressed the Convention as follows:

The struggle upon which we are entering to-day will in its consequences be of as vital importance as that of any Presidential election in which the destinies of the American people have heretofore been at stake. It will decide whether the corrupt and sectional party, which by its misrule has caused a prostration of trade and industry more ruinous and more wide-spread than any this country has ever suffered, is to be fastened upon us for four years more, or whether the Democratic party will be able to regain the reins of government in order to guide us back to peace, union and prosperity. [Applause.]

The Republican leaders, reckless, selfish, and aggressive as ever, have by their speeches in Congress, by the inflammatory teachings of an unprincipled partisan press, and finally by the platforms of their State and National Conventions, tried to divert the attention of the electors from their misdeeds and the real issues of the coming campaign.

In order to escape the just indignation of an outraged people, whose confidence they have so shamefully betrayed, they appeal to sectional and sectarian prejudices in order to sow the seeds of discord between North and South, Protestant and Catholic.

In this Centennial year of a nation's rejoicings, when the hallowed memories of the past admonish us to draw closer and stronger the bonds of fraternity and union; when we have seen the soldiers of South Carolina linked arm and arm at the foot of Bunker Hill with their brethren of Massachusetts; when the veterans of New England adorn with flowers the graves of Confederate soldiers—a tribute from the brave to the brave—the politicians of the Administration party, bent only upon their own selfish ends, attempt to stir up the worst passions of human nature, and, not satisfied with the miseries of the day, are willing to leave to our children an inheritance of suspicion, prejudice and hatred. [Applause.]

They have played this same nefarious game before, and encouraged by the timorous policy of our leaders in former Conventions, they hope to achieve another victory through our fears, which made us resort to expediencies and injudicious nominations outside of the Democratic party. [Applause.] Experience has shown the fallacy of such policy. For every Republican vote which we gained, or hoped to gain, we lost the votes of thousands of our own people.

Let the lessons of the past serve as warnings at this juncture. This is a struggle between Democracy, representing union, progress and prosperity, and Republicanism, representing sectional strife, religious intolerance, and a continuation of financial and industrial prostration. [Applause.] In such a contest victory must be ours, if we adopt a strong and unequivocal platform on all the cardinal questions which agitate the people, and place upon it a National Democrat, whose private character and public record will infuse that enthusiasm and that confidence into our ranks which alone can insure success. [Cheers.] The Republicans have once more unfurled the "bloody shirt," that piratical flag, with which they hope to capture the liberties of the people. Let us march against them under the broad banner of the Union—that flag which has never known and will never know defeat, either from domestic or foreign foes. [Applause.]

Mr. Chairman, I offer the following resolutions, which, with the consent of this Convention, I move to be referred to the Committee on Resolutions:

RESOLUTIONS OFFERED BY MR. BELMONT, OF NEW YORK.

We appeal to the honor and manhood of the American people to begin this second century of American Union and Independence by trampling under foot and extinguishing forever the smouldering ashes of distrust, rancor and animosity between the two great sections of our common country.

We denounce with indignation the calculated malignity with which the leaders of the Republican party have labored to keep alive, through eleven years of peace, the worst passions of civil war. The Macchiavellian motto of the Republican party has been and is, "*divide the people and we shall rule them.*" For the Democratic party we reply: "Unite the people and make them free." We denounce the Republican party, on this great issue, as a party of false pretences. It is a false pretence to assume the character of a national party, and at the same time to exist only by sectional divisions; it is a false pretence to assume the name of a union party, and at the same time to be an obstacle to national unity; it is a false pretence to assume the name of a liberal party, and at the same time to appeal to the religious prejudices of the people; it is a false pretence to claim the title of a progressive party, and at the same time to turn the people back from peace and the future to war and the past.

THE ADJOURNMENT.

Mr. WILLIAMS, of Indiana: I suppose, under the order adopted this morning, these resolutions of Mr. Belmont will go to the Committee on Resolutions?

The CHAIR: Of course; of course.

Mr. WILLIAMS: I now renew my motion that this Convention adjourn until to-morrow morning at 11 o'clock.

Cries, "Ten! Ten!"

Mr. WILLIAMS: I desire to say, sir, that it is very doubtful, from information that has come to my knowledge from one of the Committee on Resolutions standing here at my right, whether it will be possible for the Committee on Resolutions to report before that hour; and if we come here at 10 o'clock and the Committee on Resolutions are not ready to report, we shall be here in our seats with nothing to do. I have received information that by 11 o'clock the Committee on Resolutions will be ready to report, and I therefore move that it is much better for us to adjourn to 11 o'clock instead of 10, and I therefore insist on my motion that we adjourn until 11 o'clock.

Mr. WALRATH, of New York: Mr. Chairman, I second the motion, for the reason that the delegation from the State of New York have a meeting at 10 o'clock to-morrow morning, and it will require some time to get our tickets and do other business. I hope that the gentleman's motion will prevail.

Mr. Williams' motion was carried, and the Convention adjourned until to-morrow morning at 11 o'clock.

SPEECHES.

After the adjournment of the Convention there were loud calls all over the hall for "Voorhees," who in response thereto made the following remarks:

SPEECH OF HON. DAN. W. VOORHEES, OF INDIANA.

MY FELLOW-CITIZENS OF THIS CONVENTION: I am overwhelmed with gratitude to so many of my fellow-citizens of distinguished character from every part of the United States, who have done me the singular honor of calling for my presence on this occasion and under these circumstances. I cannot attribute it to anything in my humble career; I know not what to attribute it to, and I may say that at least for once in my life I am at a loss as to the manner in which I shall respond to such an overwhelming compliment as has been paid to me. I feel abashed in the presence of this mighty congregation of people who expect to hear my humble words. I am here with you, fellow-Democrats of the United States, for the exalted and patriotic purpose of endeavoring to redeem and wrench our country from the hands of the despoilers and the public plunderers. [Applause.] I am here with you for the purpose of trying to better unite the scattered, shattered, broken bands of our Union by gathering together in one mighty brotherhood, looking in each other's faces, renewing ancient friendship, steadying the column, turning its head towards victory and glory in the future as we have done in the past. [Applause.]

We are entering upon a new century. Portions of the last century were full of glory. The closing years of our last century, however, have had tears and blood commingled, sorrow and gloom. The cypress of mourning has been in thousands of households, but with the coming of this new century there comes a new dispensation, the dawn of a revelation of glory such as shall eclipse the past years of the century that has gone by. [Applause.] Standing, as I do, one of the humble representatives of the great valley of the Mississippi, we stand in a central point to invoke union, to invoke harmony, to invoke a compromise of conflicting opinions in the Democratic ranks. [Applause.] There is nothing, my friends, in the differences and divergences of opinion in the Democratic party that cannot be honorably, easily, smoothly and harmoniously adjusted, so that when the lines of battle are formed there shall be no heart-burnings, no divisions, no collisions of thought. [Applause.] There is no reason why we should not thus adjust our differences, if differences we have; and standing, as I do, one of the representatives of the great Mississippi valley, we appeal to the people of the far East. We say to them: "What is for your prosperity is likewise for ours." [Applause.] You all rest upon the prosperity of the agricultural interests of the mighty Mississippi valley. [Applause.] The foundation of commercial glory and greatness is the farmer's plow and the sickle and the rich harvest. [Applause.] We freight your ships, we make your cities prosper. You, in turn, benefit us in a thousand ways. We interlace and interchange and bind our interests together, when we properly consider it. We appeal to you now. Give us a living chance in this Convention and in this contest, and we will make a glorious return in October for your final charge upon the enemy. [Loud and continued cheers.]

I stand in your presence neither arrogant nor suppliant; stand for absolute justice, willing to concede everything that is just to everybody else, only asking the same mete to ourselves. Let us not be extreme to each other; let us not seek to be distasteful. Man's talent to be disagreeable to his fellow-man is quite sufficient without cultivating it at all. [Applause.] We should cultivate amiability and friendship rather. I make these remarks to our brethren of the East. We have fought a thousand battles with you for the Democracy, and never one against you. Our scores of political conflict are upon our breasts and none upon our backs. [Applause.]

To our old-time brethren of the South, a word or two to you. I am one of the men surely that need no apology to look my Southern brother in the eye and expect him to believe that I speak to him with no forked tongue. [Cheers.] No political battle was ever so hot; the clouds of obloquy and storm and danger never ran so low or black over the heads of the Democracy, with whom I have worked and toiled for years, as to deter us from standing by all the constitutional rights and guarantees of our oppressed Southern brothers. [Loud cheers.] I ask my Southern brethren who know me, and whom I know, do not in this hour of national counsel, this hour of national preparation for the great conflict against the Radical foe—led, as was well said by the distinguished gentleman from New York, by the pirate's flag of bloody shirt — arrayed against you, do not in this hour leave us in the Northwest, wounded, helpless, to be scalped and murdered upon the field of battle. We have no personal animosities to gratify, we have no personal aims to subserve. If there is one man who can get more votes than another, were my own brother a candidate I would be for that other man. The times are too serious, the issues too mighty, for a personal thought to intervene.

Three times in the last twelve years we in the Northwest have charged the enemy's lines under the head of the gallant Democracy of New York. If it has to be so again we will dress in parade, and even if it is a forlorn hope, we will fight it like men. [Loud cheers.] I say there are no heart-burnings, there are no animosities to gratify. Men of this Convention, it was no purpose of mine to speak here. I feel like apologizing for it, but your voice sent me here. I did not desire to speak, but I belong to that class of men who cannot speak and say nothing. I must say something. [Applause.] And what I say is the utterance of a sincere heart. In the counsel of old, tried, cherished and beloved friends, let us purify our hearts for this great work that is before us. Let us look narrowly to our motives Let us look narrowly to our duties, and when the sun goes down upon the finished work of this Convention, I pray Almighty God that it may be as ordered, that in November your country will stand redeemed, disenthralled and re-enfranchised in all the rights of a free people, from the tyrannical bond that has crushed and oppressed us so long. That is my prayer. [Cheers.]

My fellow-citizens of the Convention, thanking you with a grateful heart, over and over again, I will not detain you any longer. ["Go on, go on!"]

It would be unseemly and improper for me to hold this body of men any longer together, and thanking you with a heartfelt gratitude for this demonstration, I take my leave. [Loud and continued applause.]

Loud calls were made for "Sunset" Cox, and in response that gentleman advanced to the rostrum, where his appearance was greeted with enthusiastic cheers.

SPEECH OF HON. S. S. COX, OF NEW YORK.

Mr. Cox addressed the assemblage as follows:

GENTLEMEN: It is very hard to follow Daniel W. Voorhees in a speech without you have his size and his voice. [Laughter.] I come fresh from Washington. I have been sent here by my constituents in New York City to represent their thought and view to some extent in this Convention. It was urgent in many ways that I should be at my post of duty. [Cries of "Louder."] I will work up directly if you will only wait. [Laughter.] If you ever made a pump you all know very well you can't make the water come out of the spout until you pour down a little beforehand now and then. [Laughter.]

When I left Washington there was an attempt on the part of the Senate to bring the House into a collision. That collision concerned the money bills of the Government. It is a matter that this Convention must meet, and I desire to speak about that most emphatically; if I cannot before the Convention, at least before some of the delegates. We have passed our twelve appropriation bills. They were before the Senate on last Saturday—all of them. We have cut down the Republican estimates sixty-four millions of dollars. [Cheers, and cries of "Stick to it!"] Aye, we will stick to it. [Laughter and applause.] Let the thunder of this Convention follow the electric telegraph, and let this Convention say to Congress, "Be firm, and stand by it," and the sixty-four millions of excess of Republican estimates will be reduced forty millions above the appropriations of last year, to which we have reduced the twelve appropriation bills; and they will thus be cut down, and the people will see why it is that profligacy, robbery, ringdom, and all the rake-helly brood of ragged rascaldom has been let loose in this country since the war. [Cheers.] They complain of us, that we have made investigations. Well, we have investigated everything and everywhere. It is a careful, studious and industrious Congress. But they say it is an ex-Confederate Congress! [laughter] and therefore it should not be honest, and find out rogues, because, perchance, one of those gallant men fought at Chancellorsville, or some other place, on the Confederate side during the long trouble. They say that such men should not persecute the post-trader on our border. [Laughter and applause.] They say that because of their inordinate expenditures we will cut down the army. Well, we might do without the army until after the November election. [Laughter.] Well, we might make an appropriation for the army in the next December session. They say we will break up the navy. Well, what does our navy do? Protect our commerce?—a commerce ruined by bad taxation and worse tariffs, out of existence. [Applause.] I think the navy might rest a little while. ["Good."] But what else would we stop? The Indian Bureau [laughter and applause]; Spotted Tail and Crazy Horse—they might be let loose on the plains. Let them, if they would stop those raids, turn the border-men loose, and they would end these contractors' wars very soon. [Applause.] But we might stop the internal revenue system awhile! Well, I would like to make the crooked paths straight. [Laughter.] Right here in St. Louis, I think, you have had some experience in relation to crooked whisky at least. [Laughter.] And the word went out, "Let no guilty man escape!" [laughter and applause] and the result is a discarded ex-Secretary of the Treasury, and guilt roams now all through that department. I think it might have a rest for a while. [Laughter and cheers.] There are those rings in Washington. God knows I would like to have the Washington ring and all of the rings exiled as far as the rings of Saturn itself. [Cheers.] No harm would be done by such honesty—exile. What the people in this Convention should say to their representatives is: be firm to your trust; stand by your bills; go on with your investigations. Unearth all the frauds connected with administration in the past, and then we can begin to build up the high places—we can prepare for the Centennial year.

O, these men that are now being prosecuted and investigated! How they have learned to love their country since Hayes and Wheeler have been nominated! [Laughter.] They think to conceal under their rap-rascality and hypocrisy the crimes of the past. They cannot hide under such respectable names. There is an alias to it, and it means Grantism, and Babcockism, and Belknapism, and Washingtonism, and every other ringism, and the people of this country are tired to death of the everlasting malfeasance in office. [Cries of "That's so."] It is the dominant question of this country, and it will override your question of currency with honest people; and in the work of purification and the work of pacification let us all unite, and let us invite all honest men of all parties to join. Let the colored man come, and let all liberal and independent men join us in that work. What we want is not only purification, not merely pacification North, South, East, and West, in our Convention and elsewhere, but we want credit to be established. Our government can get cash by having credit. Good money will come with credit. Good money will come with economy. [Cheers.]

I am not so particular about this money question as I once was, and I will tell you the reason. I don't care so much what kind of clothes I have got on, or what kind of a pocket I have in them, or what kind of a pocket-book I have, or whether the money is fifteen cents above or fifteen below gold, when I know that under those clothes and around that money and pocket I have a vital, dangerous, corrupting disease. [Cheers.] Cure the disease, cure the body politic from all its cancers, and our credit will come to us from abroad and at home; and then specie may be once more the standard of charges and prices; and until that time comes, until we are patient with it, we cannot have the old chink of gold and silver. [Cheers.]

Now, one word more. I voted in the committee to which I belong for the repeal of the resumption law. [Loud applause and "Bully!"] I voted for it because it did not provide for the resumption of specie payments. It provided for silver, and they called on Congress, and we passed silver bills for change. They were afraid to take the responsibility and we remonetized silver, but it is a different thing as to gold and resumption. No provision has been made, no proposition acceptable either to the Senate or House, for 1879; and I do not speak illy, or from a lack of confidence, when I say that the best bankers East and the best business men West join in the general expression that the resumption of specie payment cannot be accomplished in 1879 [loud applause] by any financiering. I think, therefore, this Convention would be wise, and I have no doubt they will be wise, to repeal that act; for how can you build on a solid foundation until you clean out the rubbish and the debris, among which I count the resumption act for 1879 a delusion and a snare? Its repeal may not be a panacea, but it may lead us in the future to a better and more truthful fiscal policy. So much for that. These Republicans have conducted their fiscal policy and their patriotism a good deal as that banker did, I think down in Arkansas. A report was made upon his bank. Somebody said, "Why find fault with such a good, pious banker as he! Has he not done well? Think of him. True it is that his accounts were all bad; they were not well kept. He was largely in default; but he has a good heart, and oh, how he loved the stars and stripes of his country!" [Loud laughter and applause.]

But, my fellow-citizens, we are to enter on a campaign; we are entering on a campaign. We ought to honor the centennial year. It is not on these mere fiscal or temporary questions that we are to win this contest altogether. We have fundamental principles of government as old as the revolution, which have marked parties from the beginning; the idea of home rule, self-government, express and granted powers. Stand by them. Aye, and stand by pacification and purification. [Applause.]

Now, who shall be your standard-bearers? [Loud cries of "Tilden," "Hendricks," and great confusion.] Now, my fellow-citizens, when I asked that question of you I intended to answer it myself. [Laughter.] I know the distinguished statesman of New York as a reformer in his State, and know him well. I know the objections that are made and well made, and well taken by my friend from Indiana, Mr. Voorhees, as to the fact that New York has had this great honor conferred upon her; but I will not remark upon that I know the gallant Gen. Hancock, who has always been true to the great seminal Democratic doctrine, that of placing the civil above the military power. [Loud applause.] I have known long and served in the national councils with Thomas A. Hendricks, of Indiana. [Loud applause.] No man could bear our banner with a whiter or purer record. [Great applause, continued for several seconds, followed by a single shout.] I was about to say (before chanticleer gave forth that clarion sound) I was about to say that I knew the Great Unknown [laughter], but I do not intend to tell you who he is at this time. [Renewed laughter.] Wait, and in a few days we will let you know. But one thing I will tell you. Whoever he may be, wherever he may come from, East or West, one thing must be said of him, and said of him in response to the great question of the great Psalmist of Israel: Who shall stand in the holy places? Who shall stand as our great chief executive in this great centennial year? [Cries of "Tilden," "Hancock," "Hendricks," &c., followed by a solo of "Uncle Sam."] If the Great Unknown will just make my speech I will yield to him. I was about to say this, with all earnestness, that the people this year demand, above all other things, a response to that question of the great Psalmist, for when he spoke of it he had in view the priest who would stand between the sins of the people and their God; would represent the majesty, the greatness, the glory of that ancient priesthood who shall stand to offer the sacrifice. [Cries of "Tilden," "Hancock."] Well, my fellow-citizens, I will give you the answer in the language of scripture. [Laughter and a voice, "In the language of Democracy it is 'Tilden.' "] I want to tell you one thing, and I shall not detain you but for one more sentence. It is not for this meeting altogether to name a man, whatever you may say. It is not for me, individually or otherwise, to name a man, for I am in a minority, I am told, in my delegation. It is for the good and lawful heart—the old motherly gumption of the Convention—to be in no haste to name him. For we have no ordinary name to contend with as against Hayes and Wheeler. [A voice, "That's what's the matter."] None of your impulses; none of your passions; none of your sectional hates or asperities; no party cries; no sectional shibboleths. Stand by the whole country, and then when the Fourth of July shall dawn in a few days, we can see the old Temple of Liberty, frith, architrave, column and dome, all redound with the good old Democratic government. [Prolonged applause.] The answer of the Psalmist is this (and it is my man for President), "He that hath a pure heart and clean hands." [Cries of "Tilden," "Hancock," &c.] Now one word more and I am done. If we have such a man—and such men are not scarce in the Democratic party, whatever they may be in the other—if we have the man to fill such qualifications, we should name him in this Convention. [Cries of "Tilden," "Hancock," "Hendricks," &c.]

At the conclusion of Mr. Cox's remarks the vast audience dispersed.

SECOND DAY.

ST. LOUIS, June 28th, 1876.

At 11 o'clock A. M., the Convention reassembled, pursuant to adjournment, in the Hall of the Exchange. The President called the Convention to order in the following words:

The Convention will please come to order. We must have order if we would proceed with our business intelligently and satisfactorily. I say we *must* have order, and I will employ all means and energies with which I am invested to secure it. [Applause.] Father Brady will open the proceedings of the day with prayer.

Father Brady, of the Annunciation Church, on Sixth and Chouteau avenue, then offered the following prayer:

In the name of the Father, and of the Son, and of the Holy Ghost. May the Almighty God, the God of Truth, of Wisdom and of Union, the Spirit that brings peace on earth to men and good will, descend unto the members of this Convention, that their labors may this day be conducted wisely and harmoniously. May the blessing of the Ruler of all nations come down upon you all, the members of all the delegations, those whom they represent, and upon all our people throughout the entire country; and may this blessing remain forever. This we pray, in the name of Him and through Him who has taught us how to pray.

Our Father who art in heaven, hallowed be Thy name, Thy kingdom come, Thy will be done on earth as it is in heaven. Give us this day our daily bread, and forgive us our trespasses as we forgive them who trespass against us, and lead us not into temptation, but deliver us from evil. Amen.

MINUTES DISPENSED WITH.

Gen. HAMMOND, of Tennessee: I move that the reading of the minutes of yesterday's proceedings of the Convention be dispensed with.

The motion was carried.

A DELEGATE from Georgia: I desire to offer a resolution, and ask that the rules be suspended and that it be placed upon its passage.

The CHAIR: Let me inquire of the gentleman if his resolution relates to the platform. If it does, it is not in order, but must go to the Committee on Resolutions without debate.

The DELEGATE from Georgia: Let the resolution be read and the Convention can judge of its merits.

The Secretary read as follows:

Resolved, That this Convention indorse the work of reform and economical government, being inaugurated by the House of Representatives of the United States, in their efforts to cut down the expenses of the Government.

A DELEGATE: I move to refer the resolution to the Committee on Resolutions. [Cries of "Read," "Read."]

The CHAIR: Delegates will take their seats and preserve order. [Applause.] The Secretary will proceed with the reading of the resolution.

The Secretary proceeded as follows:

And we cannot too firmly express our gratification at the efforts of the House of Representatives to discover and bring to light the frauds so long and so outrageously practiced upon the people by the present administration. We congratulate our country that the time has arrived when we may stop at least some of the criminals who have brought the country into disgrace at home and disrepute abroad, that they are to meet with the punishment due to their crimes.

Mr. YOUNG, of Georgia: I move to suspend the rules and pass the resolution.

The CHAIR: Under the rules adopted, the resolution must go to the Committee on Resolutions. The Chair so decides.

Mr. COX, of New York: I propose the following resolution, sir, for reference.

The CHAIR: The page will bring up the resolution.

The CHAIR: The resolution offered by the gentleman from New York will go to the Committee on Resolutions under the rule already adopted.

Mr. COX: I ask to have it read, sir, if it be in order.

The CHAIR: Let it be read.

The Secretary read the resolution as follows:

Resolved, That in the opinion of this Convention, the will of the people for retrenchment, as expressed in the preparation of the bills passed by the Democratic House of Representatives, and now before the Senate, should not be thwarted, and that we will sustain the Congressmen who are faithful to their trust in diminishing extravagance and repelling Senatorial dictation on our money bills.

The CHAIR: The resolution goes to the Committee on Resolu tions.

Mr. VILAS, of Wisconsin: I ask leave to offer the following resolution, and move its adoption:

Resolved, That in speaking on any question no delegate be allowed over five minutes, and that in presenting candidates no delegate be allowed over ten minutes.

The resolution was carried unanimously.

Mr. COX, of New York: I have to present to this Convention, on behalf of the Workingmen's Central Union of the State of New York, a memorial expressing their views. They are men who have votes, intelligence, strength, and unity; I would not ask to have their memorial read, for we have not time; I ask that it may be a part of our proceedings here to-day, and I send it to the clerk's desk for that purpose.

Mr. EATON, of Kansas: I move that the memorial from the workingmen of New York be embraced in the proceedings of this Convention.

Mr. COX: And referred to the Committee on Resolutions.

The motion, as amended, prevailed.

A GENERAL DISCUSSION.

Mr. KELLY, of New York: I have been requested by some of my colleagues on the New York delegation to present to the Convention the names of some gentlemen in New York who are opposed to the nomination of Gov. Tilden for the Presidency. [Hisses and cries of "Sit down."] And I ask that it be read, so that the Convention will understand the character of the men in that State who are opposed to Gov. Tilden's nomination. [Applause and hisses.]

Mr. JACOBS, of New York: I rise to a point of order. It is that this proposition at this time is out of order.

The CHAIR: I declare the point of order well taken by the gentleman from New York. [Applause.]

Mr. McLANE, of Maryland: I desire to hear from the Chair what is the order of business under the rule.

The CHAIR: The report of the Committee on Resolutions, and we are waiting for that.

Mr. McLANE: I desire, further, to inquire of the Chair whether the Committee on Resolutions have reported.

The CHAIR: Not yet.

Mr. McLANE: Then I ask the Chair to entertain a motion that the Convention now proceed to ballot [cheers], which is a motion of privilege.

The CHAIR: The motion is made that the Convention now proceed to ballot for candidates.

A DELEGATE: Mr. President—

The CHAIR: Wait till I announce the question—

Mr. McLANE, of Maryland: I submit this motion as a matter of privilege, which is always in order, and I would submit to the Chair and to the Convention—it being a debatable question—the reasons why I make that motion.

Senator KERNAN, of New York: Will the gentleman from Maryland yield to me for a question? I suggest first, and I move that a committee be duly appointed by the Chair to visit the Committee on Resolutions and to inquire if they are likely soon to present their report, and if they are not, then the gentleman from Maryland can put his motion.

Mr. McLANE: With great deference to the gentleman from New York (Senator Kernan), I do not think it expedient to yield to such a motion.

Senator KERNAN: It seems entirely satisfactory to me.

Mr. McLANE: The only practical result of such a motion would be to involve this Convention, through its committee, in a discussion with the Committee on Resolutions. It is not in the power of this Convention to interfere in any degree with the Committee already appointed upon Resolutions. They have the whole subject now before them. It cannot be the wish of any member of this Convention to hasten in any degree the deliberation of that committee, or to put any pressure upon that committee. They represent each one of the States, and it is to be supposed that they represent judiciously the sense of each and every delegation, and we on our side have our duty to perform. Our duty is to nominate without loss of time and without unnecessary discussion. [Cheers.] Without unnecessary debate, it is our duty to nominate our candidate. I make the motion, I am happy to say, without consultation with anybody in or out of my delegation. It is a purely individual suggestion, and I am convinced it is in the interest of the Democratic party and in the interest of the country that we should lose no time, and lose none of that fraternal spirit which brings us all together, and which now animates us.

I say it, Mr. Chairman, because I stand here ready to cast my ballot in this Convention, as at the polls, for any one of the various gentlemen that I have heard suggested. [Applause.] I make the motion because I am just as well content to have the nominee come from the West as from the East; and I would be too happy if it were possible to have him come from both the West and the East. [Applause.] My friend from Kentucky says that would be Delaware. I can tell him that if I had the choice, it should be from Delaware. [Applause.] From the East or the West [cries of "Time"], but it is not for me ["Time"] to indicate that choice. [Renewed cries of "Time."] I believe I have the floor. [Laughter.]

The CHAIR: The gentleman's time has not expired.

Mr. McLANE: If I had spoken ten minutes I would take my seat with pleasure, because I have said all I have to say. [Laughter.]

Mr. WOODSON, of Missouri: Mr. Chairman, I have a resolution I desire to offer in connection with the motion of the gentleman from Maryland (Mr. McLane), and I ask, Mr. President, that the resolution be read for the information of the Convention.

The CHAIR: It will be so read.

The resolution was read as follows:

Resolved, That this Convention will not ballot for a candidate for President or Vice-President of the United States until action is had on the report of the Committee on Resolutions. [Loud applause.]

Mr. WOODSON: I have but one word, Mr. President, to say upon that resolution. It occurs to me, sir, that we ought not to vote for candidates until we know what the action of this Convention is to be. It is hardly probable, Mr. President, that there will be a unanimous report from that committee. I hope, however, in this I am mistaken, because I suppose that every member of this Convention is anxious to see harmony, not only on the part of the Committee on Resolutions, but harmony in the action of this great body of delegates representing the Democracy of the United States. But, sir, we must have harmony upon principle, or we can have no harmony. I want them to see the report of the committee. If we can harmonize upon the report of the Committee on Resolutions, then, sir, we can answer the question propounded by the distinguished gentleman from New York (Mr. Cox), as to who will be the next President of the United States, and the answer will be, the man who is nominated by the Convention.

Mr. ABBOTT, of Massachusetts: I move to amend the motion of the gentleman from Missouri (Mr. Woodson), by striking out all after the word resolved, and inserting the following, which the Secretary will read.

While the amendment was being taken to the President's desk, Mr. Doolittle, of Wisconsin, said: "I suggest that the bouquet on the stand be removed, so that we can see the President on this side of the hall." [Laughter.]

The CHAIR: What does the gentleman mean by his statement? I am not aware that you claimed the attention of the Chair before.

Mr. DOOLITTLE: No, sir. The honorable gentleman from Massachusetts—

The CHAIR: Well, sir, he has been recognized.

Mr. DOOLITTLE: I understand so, sir.

The Secretary read the amendment of Mr. Abbott, as follows:

Resolved, That the roll of States be called in regular order, that each State be allowed to present the name of any candidate for the

Presidency, and that thereupon this Convention do proceed to vote by States, for a candidate for President of the United States and a candidate for Vice-President of the United States, and that in casting their vote for President and Vice-President, the chairman of each delegation shall rise in his place and name how the delegation votes, and his statement alone shall be considered the vote of the State. [Applause and cries of "No, no!"]

Mr. ABBOTT: I desire to state that my only motive in presenting the resolution was that we do not lose the day, but proceed immediately to vote for a candidate for President. I have no doubt that any man who is selected as candidate for President will stand upon the platform that is finally adopted by this Convention.

Mr. WALLACE, of Pennsylvania: I move to lay the resolution and amendment on the table, and upon that that the vote be taken by States.

Mr. CRAWFORD, of Illinois: I move, sir, a division of the question; that the vote be taken separately upon the original resolution and the amendment to the original proposition.

Mr. COX, of New York: I rise to a point of order. I make the point of order that you cannot call for a division while a motion to lay upon the table is pending.

The CHAIR: The point is sustained. Let the Clerk proceed with the roll-call. The question is to lay the motion on the table.

Mr. PUTNAM, of New Hampshire: No one in this part of the Convention understands the question at all. What is the question before us? We would like the Chair to state the question.

The CHAIR: The question is upon laying upon the table.

Mr. PUTNAM: What is it that is desired to be laid upon the table?

The CHAIR: The motion or resolution is that we shall proceed to the nomination of candidates for President and Vice-President.

Mr. PUTNAM: Will the Chair be so kind as to read the resolution and amendment?

The CHAIR: Let the resolution and amendment be read.

Mr. McLANE, of Maryland: I accept the amendment, as the author of the proposition. Therefore the Chair need only have read the proposed amendment. It becomes the question before the Convention.

The CHAIR: Then let the amendment to the amendment be read.

The Secretary read the amendments.

Mr. MCLANE: I accept the substitute, not the amendment, and ask that the substitute be read.

Mr. WEED, of New York: As I understood, the gentleman from Maryland accepted the amendment of the gentleman from Massachusetts.

The CHAIR: I so understood.

Mr. WEED: That makes, then, his motion the amendment to the resolution of the gentleman from Missouri.

The CHAIR: Certainly.

Mr. WEED: And if we vote to lay the whole subject upon the table, that disposes of the whole question for to-day. Am I correct?

Mr. MCLANE: If the motion be carried.

Mr. COX, of New York: I rise to a point of order.

The CHAIR: All we have to do is to proceed to vote upon the motion to lay on the table, which carries the whole subject with it.

Mr. COX: Do I understand the Chair to decide we could not vote for President to-day if we sustain the motion to lay on the table?

The CHAIR: The Chair said nothing on the subject whatever.

Mr. COX: Let me make a parliamentary inquiry. If we vote to lay this question on the table, can we not go into the nominations to-day?

The CHAIR: Let the original resolution be read and the subsequent amendments.

Mr. PUTNAM, of New Hampshire: Mr. President—

The CHAIR: The Secretary will proceed with the reading of the resolution and amendments.

The Secretary then read the original resolution and the following amendments:

By Mr. ABBOTT, of Massachusetts:

Resolved, That this Convention do proceed to vote by States for candidates for President and Vice-President of the United States, and that in casting their vote for President and Vice-President, the chairman of each delegation shall rise in his place and name how the delegation votes; and his statement alone shall be considered the vote of the State. [Cries of "No! no! no!" and hisses.]

The CHAIR: Order! order!

When order was restored, the Secretary read the amendment offered by ex-Gov. Woodson, of Missouri, as follows:

Resolved, That this Convention will not ballot for candidates for the Presidency and Vice-Presidency of the United States until the Committee on Resolutions have reported.

[Applause and cheers.]

The CHAIR: Now, gentlemen, the question is, shall these resolutions be laid on the table? The Clerk will proceed to the call of the roll.

As the Clerk called Alabama, Mr. Putnam, of New Hampshire, rose to his feet and said:

Mr. PRESIDENT: If you will hear me for a single moment, I desire to offer a single motion—that before we proceed with the roll-call, a reading clerk be stationed in this part of the hall [the south end], and another in the other part of the hall, and that the reading clerks repeat the statement of the clerk, as it is announced.

The CHAIR: The request of the gentleman from New Hampshire will be observed.

Mr. DOOLITTLE, of Wisconsin: I ask if, before the vote is taken on the main question, a motion to lay on the table will not prevail?

The CHAIR: Yes, sir.

Mr. WALLACE, of Pennsylvania: The amendment of the gentleman from Massachusetts (Mr. Abbott) is the first.

The CHAIR: The gentleman from Massachusetts offered a substitute.

The CHAIR: I am informed that the Committee on Resolutions are ready to report. [Cheers.] Shall we proceed with the roll-call? [Cries of "No! no!"]

Mr. ABBOTT, of Massachusetts: I withdraw my motion to take the vote by States, and agree on the motion that the vote be taken *viva voce*.

MR. KERNAN, of New York: I suggest now what I believe to be for the best interests of the country, our party and ourselves, and that is, that we hear from the Committee on Resolutions; and if, as I am informed, they expect to be ready to report by one or two o'clock, I suggest that we wait until we do hear from them, and let us get through with this wrangling at once.

The CHAIR: I have recognized the Chairman of the Committee on Resolutions (Mr. Meredith). [Cheers.]

THE COMMITTEE ON RESOLUTIONS.

MR. MEREDITH, of Virginia: Mr. President and gentlemen of the Convention, I am instructed by the Committee on Resolutions to inform the Convention that they have agreed upon a platform and resolutions [cheers]; that the resolutions have been referred to a committee of revision, and that the committee will reassemble at one o'clock and hear the report from the sub-committee on revision. I am instructed to ask leave of the Convention for the committee to sit longer for that purpose.

MR. KERNAN, of New York: In view of this report, by which I rejoice to hear that a platform has been agreed upon, and referred to a committee on revision, I move that this Convention take a recess until two o'clock to hear that report. [Cries of "No! no!"]

The motion was carried and the Convention took a recess until two o'clock.

SCENES DURING RECESS.

After the adjournment of the Convention the audience remained in the hall, and there were loud cries for Pryor, Doolittle and others. Meantime the band played several popular airs—Yankee Doodle, Dixie, &c., amid loud cheers. Finally, in response to repeated calls, ex-Senator Doolittle, of Wisconsin, came forward upon the platform, and amid loud applause spoke as follows:

SPEECH OF MR. DOOLITTLE.

FELLOW-CITIZENS AND MEMBERS OF THE CONVENTION: For one, I have been laboring since I came to St. Louis to keep myself cool, both inside as well as out. [Laughter and applause.] We have met on a great occasion, and I do not think it proper for me now, in the interval of the Convention having taken a recess, from this place and platform to speak to you at any considerable length, and certainly not, under any circumstances, to express to you any preference of my own on the great question upon which we shall come to act. [Applause.] I mean upon the great question of putting a candidate upon a platform after that platform is adopted. I feel as if it might be, perhaps, doing what would not be exactly proper on an occasion like this. I will refer, however, to two or three great questions in which I believe every heart is united.

I believe, as much as I believe in my existence, that if ever a great responsibility rested upon a Convention it rests upon this Convention now and here. That responsibility is to take such measures, to lay down such a platform, and to put upon it such candidates, as will make our success certain in the overthrow of the party in power. [Applause.]

This party in power is a great and powerful party. Do not let us deceive ourselves by supposing that it is weak. I know that party. I have known it long and well. I have fought with it and I have fought against it. [Applause.] I know it inside and out, through and through, and I tell you, gentlemen, that that party for the last fifteen years has been a war party, imbued with the spirit, accustomed to use the methods and practices which surround military encampments, not only during the war, but after the war had ended, in the reconstruction of the South. [Applause.] Guided by that spirit, this party in power, after the war had closed—three years after the war had closed, almost—I saw them take, in the Senate of the United States and in the House of Representatives, such action and such proceedings as could only be justified by military ideas, acting not as civilians in the administration of law, but as the leaders of military forces in the organization of the States of the South, in order to gain an unlimited control of both houses in Congress by a two-thirds majority, which could overrule the veto of the President. I saw in the Senate of the United States, by the domination and despotic exercise of this power, a gentleman upon the floor of this Convention was driven from the Senate—I refer to Mr. Stockton, of New Jersey—and in order to get the vote which was necessary to obtain that two-thirds majority and accomplish that purpose, I saw one Senator, who, from the committee, reported in favor of Mr. Stockton, break his pair with the colleague of the Senator from New Jersey, confined by sickness at home.

By that act of revolution against law and all the usages of the

Senate, they usurped that two-thirds majority which has ruled this country with military and despotic power from that day to the present moment. Having acquired this two-thirds majority in both houses, trampling under its feet all the pledges it made, and by which it obtained its lease of power, I saw that party trample the Constitution under its feet. I saw them pass military reconstruction acts, by which ten States in this Union and ten millions of people were robbed of every civil right of liberty and property, and I saw them subjected to the absolute unqualified domination of military dictators in time of peace. [Applause.]

You remember with what despotic and unrelenting power it undertook to depose the President and put in his place a man who would be more pliable to execute the behests of this despotic power at Washington. You know, too, how they persecuted those Senators who preferred to obey their oaths rather than obey the behests of this party. [Applause.] You saw, gentlemen, that same party, by telegraphic decrees, entering with the regular army State Legislatures and organizing them against the law of the people. [Applause.] But I will not dwell on these things. I have said this only for the purpose of making one further remark—that is, that if any man in this country supposes that because this party lately at Cincinnati, instead of putting forward its great recognized leaders, have put forward Mr. Hayes, of Ohio, and Mr. Wheeler, of New York—who are very respectable gentlemen in the States where they live, but are not much known elsewhere—that this party has changed its spirit, its genius, its ambitions, its despotic centralizing tendencies, you will be utterly mistaken. That party which could crush Trumbull and Schurz and Henderson, and even Sumner when he would not obey its behests [applause], will take Hayes and Wheeler in its hands like things of wax. [Applause.] They cannot resist nor refuse to obey what that party shall decree. Therefore the responsibility rests upon you, gentlemen, and upon me, in our action here, to put forward such a platform and such candidates that we can wrest this government from the hands of despotism and centralization and extravagance and corruption, such as makes the heart sick—corruption such as is our shame abroad and our disgrace and humiliation at home.

I say, gentlemen, if we would do it, we must act here wisely—not in the heat of passion. We must look beyond this chamber, and all the heat and excitement of the present hour; we must look beyond the excited crowds at the Lindell, the Southern, and other hotels in this city. We must look to the great field where the battle is to be fought [applause,] and lost or won. As I said in the beginning, gentlemen, I have been laboring hard to keep myself cool, both inside and out, in order that if I have any judgment to give, any opinion to express, or any advice to offer upon this great and important question, it may come as the opinion and advice and suggestion of a brain that is cool, and a breast that is excited with nothing but love for the Union and love for the country. [Cheers.] Gentlemen, let me say, in my brief period in public affairs—and not so very brief, either, for this is the tenth Presidential canvass in which I have taken and am to take an active part [applause], I have learned—and learned what I did not know in the beginning—that when conventions assemble in great numbers, and the friends of candidates are excited, they believe for the moment when the result is announced that the victory is already won. I have sadly found myself mistaken when we came to the field of battle. Four times, fellow-citizens, four times have I attended a convention since the close of the war—conventions which had the same purpose and spirit which we now have —I mean to restore the Union of the States upon the platform of fraternity, liberty and equality to all the States and to all the citizens of the States [applause], to restore that Union, not only the Union which we established by our conquering, but to establish that Union in our heart of hearts [applause], away down deep in all the affections and interests and aspirations of the whole people, North and South, black and white. [Applause.] Well do I remember the first at Philadelphia in 1866. I recognize here many familiar faces which met me there on that great occasion. They came together at Philadelphia ten years ago from all the States of the Union. It was the first reunion after the civil war. They came to shake hands together literally over the "bloody chasm," and when their united thanks went up to Almighty God that the war was over, that peace had come, that no more sons and fathers and brothers were to go down to battle and to death, that sweet peace had come, and come to stay [cheers], there was a joy in that Convention unutterable. Ten thousand men and women—strong men—in that Convention, filled with an exultation which words could not express, gave way to every demonstration of joy. They wept, they embraced, and then, recovering themselves, they cheered and shouted—such cheers and shouts as go up from conquering armies when great fields are won. [Cheers.] But, fellow-citizens, though the object with which we met, the ideas to which we gave utterance, the platform we adopted, and all that was done to restore the former—and let me say to you in a single word, we failed in my opinion because at the city of New York we did not properly organize the forces for the victory. [Applause.] So badly was the Democratic party beaten in 1868 that in 1872, as if by unanimous consent, they gave out their word to the Liberal Republicans—such Senators as Trumbull, Schurz and others—that if they would take the lead, if they would lay down a platform consistent with the constitutional views entertained by the great Democratic party and put candidates upon it, that party pledged its honor that, when assembled in convention, it would indorse and sustain them and aid them in the contest. You remember how well that pledge was kept, and I say to the Liberal Republicans, if there are any within the sound of my voice, or if anything that I say here shall reach them elsewhere; I say to the Liberal Republicans, and to all the Liberal Republicans, that they have been placed under a debt and obligation of gratitude to the Democratic party [cheers] that they ought never to forget, and which they can never so well repay as by uniting with the Democratic party now in the coming contest. [Cheers.]

But, fellow-citizens, you know and I know that with all our efforts we still failed to rescue this government from the hands of this powerful party, and I have only referred to these things, gentlemen, for the single purpose of giving you to understand the intensity of that responsibility which I feel as a member of this Convention in the action which is here to take place. I shall say not a word about candidates nor platform, for I feel it would in some measure be trespassing upon the courtesy which has been thus unanimously extended to me to address you upon the other subject. My only desire is, and my whole heart goes out in that, that we may be united shoulder to shoulder upon our platform of principles, and that when we come to nominate our candidates we can lay aside all personal interests, all personal ambitions, as far as human nature will allow it to be done [applause], and come together like a band of brothers, swearing, as our fathers in the Revolution did, that we would pledge our fortunes and our sacred honor to carry this election, and thus save republican institutions to ourselves and to our children.

SPEECH OF GEN. BRECKINRIDGE.

In response to loud calls, Gen. Breckinridge, of Kentucky, spoke as follows:

MY FELLOW-DEMOCRATS: I, of course, attribute the compliment of this kind call to no personal reasons emanating from myself, but as a compliment to that gallant and glorious old banner Democratic

State—the grand State of Kentucky [applause]; and it may be that the name which I bear has been somewhat interwoven with its history, and that therefore the call of myself, in honor of Kentucky, deserves that I should at least make my grateful acknowledgment for it. But I am not here simply as a Kentuckian. I love every foot of that dear old mother State with a passionate idolatry that knows no words to give it utterance. But my love is bounded by no State lines. [Applause.] I love this great country of which I am a son; I love all that is honorable in its past, and I look forward with unutterable joy to the glorious hopes of its future. [Applause.] I am here in part representing the State of Kentucky; to utter no voice of self-seeking, no voice of personal preference, but, putting all upon the altar of a common country, to unite with the Democrats of every section of this country in an honest, earnest, patriotic effort to turn from the government those who have despoiled it at home, and rendered it disgraceful abroad, and put it in the hands of honest, upright and grave men from any part of the country. [Applause.]

I do not like to hear so much in this Convention of the East, of the West, and of the South. We talk as if we were three separate governments, or three separate countries, under some unknown and intangible treaty of alliance, offensive and defensive. Where does the West and the East begin? Where is the South of which we hear so much? We are not here as Eastern men, or as Southern men, but we are here as Democrats and as Americans. [Applause.] Oh, my brethren, if I could but get into the heart of this Convention the sublime patriotism that we of Kentucky have, raise to the level of this great opportunity, and put behind us these sectional divisions and these State lines, and look at the country as one—one flag, one liberty, and one destiny—to be saved by this great one party of liberty, the great Democratic party, then personal dissensions would pass away, these offensive clamors would be silenced, and here, as brothers, we would gather around the same table, and come to a unanimous conclusion, and then act as one army under a chosen leader, in a victorious battle. [Applause.]

This is all that I have desired to utter here or elsewhere in St. Louis. I have no other message to make. I feel that Kentucky can afford to say this. We lie upon the border. We were called in olden times the heart of the Union. We gave Clay to try by compromise to save it from bloodshed, and when the horrid war did come, it ran as the plowshare, deep through nearly every family in that distracted State, and now we have made up our divisions. We hear nothing of the past there. We have turned our eyes to the future; our farmers are gathering wealth under that magnificent breast that gives the liquid milk under which we suck, and our citizens have made their strong arms brawny in the labor of love, and she is blossoming as the rose. We hear of hard times elsewhere, and sometimes in Kentucky you hear it. You hear it around the crowded and groaning table, amid all the evidences of comfort. She can afford to say we have no other choice; we desire no other thing said or done here than that which will unite the party, because the union of the party is the success of liberty in the country. When she looks backward and sees all the dire calamities of the division of this party; when she sees the unfortunate fruits of a quarrel amid its party; when she sees her Democratic brethren falling out among themselves, she comes with a simple message of union and fraternity. "Ye are brethren," is all she has got to utter. "Why will you not love one another, and turn your swords to a common enemy, and make all your fight against that enemy?" [Applause.] God knows it is enough to make all of us resolute, and to give us all that we can do. This is no common foe that we have to fight. This is no easy adversary that we have to meet. It is a party drunk with power, and strong with all the power of uncivil organization; a party that has carried in some degree the supposed gratitude of a country which it claims to have saved; that has possession of the purse and of the treasury, and unembarrassed by any conscientious scruples; that knows how to use both that purse, that sword, and all the power that that common government gives it. It is a party we cannot easily conquer.

Now, fellow-Democrats, all I desire to say, all that I am authorized to say—for I speak not only in my own name, but I speak in the name of the delegation of which I am an humble part, and of the great State which sends that delegation here—is, can we not, here among ourselves, leaving out all the animosities of the past, forgetting sectional lines, leaving behind us all unkind feeling, having no other object in view than the success of a party in whose success we honestly believe is involved the best interest of the country, come to some fraternal conclusion? And when that conclusion is reached, honestly and fairly, go into the battle to do all that men can do to make it victorious. [Applause.] I thank you for the compliment you have paid me. [Cheers and cries of "Go on!"]

Mr. BRECKINRIDGE: I am requested to say that the Hon. B. Gratz Brown, of Missouri, who was our candidate—and I choose the word expressly—our candidate, not merely the Liberal Republican, but the Democratic candidate for Vice-President four years ago, is in our midst. He never spoke except with strength—sometimes I thought, some years ago, not wisely, but he has learned better. [Laughter.] He is here and will address us if you so desire it.

Mr. DOOLITTLE, of Wisconsin: Please respond, or give us something of the views of the Liberals in this contest.

Loud calls for Gratz Brown brought that gentleman to the rostrum accompanied by a hearty round of applause.

SPEECH OF HON. B. GRATZ BROWN.

GENTLEMEN OF THE CONVENTION: I feel very thankful to you for this expression of kindness and of compliment, and I can say to you that I sympathize with you to-day heartily and cordially in all your efforts [applause] to get over difficulties, to adjust any minor differences that may exist among yourselves; to present a man to the nation worthy of the nation. and enable us all, Democrats and Liberals, to go forward to a crowning victory. [Cheers.]

The gentleman from Wisconsin (Mr. Doolittle) who preceded me had something to say about the debt of gratitude which the Liberals of this country were owing to the Democratic party. I believe that they recognize and acknowledge that debt. [Cheers.] And I believe that when the battle wears to the front you will find your banner borne as high and carried as far by the Liberal leaders [cheer] as by any Democrat. [Cheers.]

It is not my purpose, gentlemen, and it would be inappropriate if it were, that I should enter here upon any discussion of men or any discussion of platform. I take it that the two great fundamental principles which are to be settled in this canvass are putting this government into the hands of honest men [applause], and basing it upon free, liberal, universal principles. [Cheers.]

We want reform [cheers;] we want more than that. We want relief [cheers], and I have every confidence that the Democratic party, its leaders, its chieftains here assembled, will put forth a platform and put forth a candidate that will be synonymous with these ideas in the eyes of the country. [Cheers.]

Gentlemen, there are too many distinguished men here from abroad, that we would all be glad to hear, for me to intrude longer upon your time. [Cries of "Go on! go on!"] I have only to thank you for the kindness which has provoked this call, and to urge that some of them will come forward and let us hear from them. [Cheers.]

SPEECH OF SENATOR WALLACE.

Mr. Wallace, of Pennsylvania, was next called out, and spoke as follows:

GENTLEMEN OF THE CONVENTION: I thank you for the compliment that you have paid me, and through me the great old keystone commonwealth of the Union, in calling me to talk to you briefly, as I shall upon this occasion. I shall not attempt to detain you in presenting the issues that this Convention will present to the people of the country, but I will ask you to go with me briefly into the history of the recent past, and to inquire as to what these people who attempt to maintain their hold upon the government, their grasp upon the throats of the people, have been doing. They, at Cincinnati, in the vain hope that they could blind the people of the country to the character of the reform they would inaugurate, have passed a platform by their representative men, and selected candidates whose record is silent, whose characters are negative, in the hope that the people will accept negative characters and silent records as the pledge of well-doing in the future. Their ticket was born of antagonisms to the only strong candidate that the administration detested and denounced. It was skilfully accouched by those who manipulate the power and have blindly defended the measures of Gen. Grant. Its nursing mother will be a hated and a dying administration, and the first lessons it must learn will be the crooked and devious methods of Grantism. [Loud applause.] All the power of the national administration will be unscrupulously employed for its success, and if it be elected the reform that is inaugurated will be but a perpetuation of the reigning dynasty. To recount the disgraces of the past, to reproduce here the shameful record of the personal misgovernment of the past seven years, is but to produce a record of inevitable infamy in the future. Why, sirs, we have had an administration of the government that has discarded statesmanship and sought imbecility [applause]; that has ignored integrity in official trusts and yielded both patronage and place to the corrupt; that has held complicity with the gold gamblers and nurtured and petted the whisky ring [cheers]; that has stolidly winked at corrupt practices in the custom-houses; that has lost an Attorney-General because he could not refute the charges of the misuse of the public moneys; that has lost the Secretary of the Interior on unrefuted charges of corruption in that department; that has lost the Secretary of the Treasury, who was compelled to resign by grave charges of want of integrity and by public indignation; that has lost the Postmaster-

General, whose record and motives were unsatisfactory to a discriminating people, and that has lost a Secretary of War by bribery and corruption self-confessed, and that has lost a minister to Great Britain whose course has been unanimously declared to be indefensible and improper. Each and all of these are and they have been the staunchest supporters of the anomalous policy called Grantism, and it is to live and again misgovern us in the success of the ticket nominated at Cincinnati.

Why is it that in the platform which our adversaries enunciated at Cincinnati they forgot to pledge themselves to retrenchment, to reform, to economy in the administration of the government? What means this? Is this silence eloquent? Do they mean by this to approve the refusal of a Republican Senate to meet and agree to the retrenchment of a Democratic House? Is this what they mean by this eloquent silence in the Cincinnati platform? But I weary you. It would be useless for me to attempt to detain you longer from your dinner, the hour for which has arrived. Let us in this Convention, if we can, treat each other with tolerance, with harmony, with concord; and let us settle here, if we can, a ticket upon which the country can be a unit. Let us recognize that we have as well a Western and a central part of this country, as an Eastern and a Northern and a Southern one. [Applause.] Let us recognize the existence of twelve millions of people, among whom there are hundreds of thousands of Democrats, who live between the Mississippi and the Delaware. [Applause.] Let us remember that they exist. In the spirit of recognizing the interests of the whole country, let us endeavor to declare our principles and nominate our candidates. [Applause.]

At the close of Mr. Wallace's remarks the audience retired.

AFTERNOON SESSION—SECOND DAY.

The Convention reassembled at a quarter past two o'clock.

The CHAIR: The Sergeant-at-Arms will clear the aisle and see that order is preserved. The Committee on Platform, I am informed, is ready to report.

REPORT FROM THE COMMITTEE ON RESOLUTIONS.

Mr. MEREDITH, of Virginia: Mr. President and gentlemen of the Convention, the Committee on Resolutions have finally agreed upon their report. It is due to them to state that a great many resolutions were laid before them upon the subject likely to engage the attention of the Convention; that those resolutions have been read, examined, considered, and deliberately discussed, and they have finally agreed upon a report which they have instructed me to make to the Convention. As my voice is not strong, and not able to fill this hall, I have requested Gov. Dorsheimer to read the report for me, which he has kindly consented to do. [Applause.]

Gov. Dorsheimer read as follows:

THE PLATFORM.

We, the delegates of the Democratic party of the United States, in National Convention assembled, do hereby declare the adminstration of the Federal Government to be in great need of immediate reform [applause]; do hereby enjoin upon the nominees of this Convention and of the Democratic party in each State, a zealous effort and co-operation to this end, and do here appeal to our fellow-citizens of every form of political connection to undertake with us this first and most pressing patriotic duty for the Democracy of the whole country. We do here reaffirm our faith in the permanence of the Federal Union [applause], our devotion to the Constitution of the United States [applause], with its amendments universally accepted as a final settlement of the controversy that engendered the civil war [applause], and do here record our steadfast confidence in the perpetuity of republican self-government; in absolute acquiescence in the will of the majority, the vital principle of republics; [applause]; in the supremacy of the civil over the military [applause]; in the two-fold separation of church and state [applause], for the sake alike of civil and religious freedom; in the equality of all citizens before just laws of their own enactment [applause]; in the liberty of individual conduct unvexed by sumptuary laws [applause]; in the faithful education of the rising generation, that they may preserve, enjoy and transmit these best conditions of human happiness and hope. We behold the noblest products of a hundred years of changeful history. [Applause.] But while upholding the bond of our union and great charter of these our rights, it behooves a free people to practice also that eternal vigilance which is the price of liberty. [Applause.]

Reform is necessary to rebuild and establish in the hearts of the whole people the Union eleven years ago happily rescued from the danger of a secession of States, but now to be saved from a corrupt centralism, which, after inflicting upon ten States the rapacity of carpet-bag attorneys [applause], has honey-combed the offices of the Federal Government itself with incapacity, waste and fraud, infected States and municipalities with the contagion of misrule, and locked fast the prosperity of industrious people in the paralysis of hard times. [Applause.] Reform is necessary to establish a sound currency, restore the public credit and maintain the national honor. [Applause.] We denounce the failure for all these eleven years to make good the promise of the legal tender notes [applause], which are a changing standard of value in the hands of the people, and the non-payment of which is the disregard of the plighted faith of the nation. [Loud applause.]

We denounce the improvidence which in eleven years of peace has taken from the people in Federal taxes thirteen times the whole amount of the legal-tender notes [applause] and squandered four times their sum in useless expense without accumulating any reserve for their redemption. [Applause. A voice, "Bully!"] We denounce the financial imbecility and immorality of that party, which, during eleven years of peace, has made no advance toward resumption, no preparation for resumption, but instead has obstructed resumption by wasting our resources and exhausting all our surplus income, and while annually professing to intend a speedy return to specie payments, has annually enacted fresh hindrances thereto. [Applause.] As such hindrance we denounce the resumption clause of the act of 1875 [cheers,] and we here demand its repeal. [Cheers.] We demand a judicious system of preparation. [Voices, "Louder;

read it again."] We demand a judicious system of preparation by public economies, by official retrenchments, and by a wise finance, which shall enable the nation soon to assure the whole world of its perfect ability and its perfect readiness to meet any of its promises at the call of a creditor entitled to payment. [Cheers.]

We believe such a system, well-advised, and, above all, entrusted to competent hands for execution, creating at no time an artificial scarcity of currency, and at no time alarming the public mind into a withdrawal of that vast machinery of credit by which 95 per cent. of our business transactions are performed—a system open and public and inspiring general confidence—would from the day of its adoption bring healing on its wings to all our harassed industries, set in motion the wheels of commerce, manufactures and the mechanic arts, restore employment to labor, and renew in all its sources the prosperity of the people. [Cheers.]

Reform is necessary in the sum and mould of Federal taxation, to the end that capital may be set free from distress and labor lightly burdened. We denounce the present tariff levied upon nearly four thousand articles as a masterpiece of injustice, inequality and false pretence [cheers], which yields a dwindling and not a yearly rising revenue, has impoverished many industries to subsidize a few. It prohibits imports that might purchase the products of American labor; it has degraded American commerce from the first to an inferior rank upon the high seas; it has cut down the values of American manufactures at home and abroad; it has depleted the returns of American agriculture, an industry followed by half our people; it costs the people five times more than it produces to the Treasury, obstructs the process of production and wastes the fruits of labor; it promotes fraud, fosters smuggling, enriches dishonest officials, and bankrupts honest merchants. We demand that all custom-house taxation shall be only for revenue. [Cheers.] Reform is necessary in the scale of public expense, Federal, State and municipal. Our Federal taxation has swollen from sixty millions gold in 1860 to four hundred and fifty millions currency in 1870; our aggregate taxation from one hundred and fifty-four millions gold in 1860 to seven hundred and thirty millions currency in 1870—all in one decade; from less than five dollars per head to more than eighteen dollars per head. Since the peace the people have paid to their tax-gatherers more than thrice the sum of the national debt, and more than twice that sum for the Federal Government alone. We demand a rigorous frugality in every department and from every officer of the Government. [Cheers.]

Reform is necessary to put a stop to the profligate waste of public lands and their diversion from actual settlers by the party in power, which has squandered two hundred millions of acres upon railroads alone, and out of more than thrice that aggregate has disposed of less than a sixth directly to the tillers of the soil.

Reform is necessary to correct the omissions of a Republican Congress and the errors of our treaties and our diplomacy, which has stripped our fellow-citizens of foreign birth and kindred race, re-erasing the Atlantic from the shield of American citizenship, and has exposed our brethren of the Pacific coast to the incursions of a race not sprung from the same great parent stock, and in fact now by law denied citizenship through naturalization as being unaccustomed to the traditions of a progressive civilization, one exercised in liberty under equal laws; and we denounce the policy which thus discards the liberty-loving German and tolerates the revival of the Coolie trade in Mongolian women imported for immoral purposes, and Mongolian men held to perform servile labor contracts. [Applause.]

Reform is necessary and can never be effected but by making it the controlling issue of the election and lifting it above the two false issues with which the office-holding classes and the party in power seek to smother it.

First—The false issue with which they would enkindle sectarian strife in respect to the public schools [applause], of which the establishment and support belong exclusively to the several States [applause], and which the Democratic party has cherished from their foundation, and is resolved to maintain without partiality or preference for any class, sect or creed, and without contributions from the treasury to any. [Applause.]

Second — The false issue by which they seek to light anew the dying embers of sectional hate between kindred peoples once unnaturally estranged, but now reunited in one indivisible republic and a common destiny.

Reform is necessary in the civil service. Experience proves that efficient economical conduct of the government is not possible if its civil service be subject to change at every election, be a prize fought for at the ballot-box, be an approved reward of party zeal instead of posts of honor assigned for approved competency and held for fidelity in the public employ; that the dispensing of patronage should neither be a tax upon the time of our public men nor an instrument of their ambition. Here again, professions falsified in the performance attest that the party in power can work out no practical or salutary reform.

[Applause.] Reform is necessary even more in the higher grades of public service. President, Vice-President, judges, senators, representatives, cabinet officers—these and all others in authority are the people's servants. Their offices are not a private perquisite; they are a public trust. [Applause.] When the annals of this Republic show disgrace and censure of a Vice-President; a late Speaker of the House of Representatives marketing his rulings as a presiding officer [applause]; three Senators profiting secretly by their votes as law-makers; five chairmen of the leading committees of the late House of Representatives exposed in jobbery; a late Secretary of the Treasury forcing balances in the public accounts; a late Attorney-General misappropriating public funds; a Secretary of the Navy enriched and enriching his friends by a percentage levied off the profits of contractors with his department; an Ambassador to England censured in a dishonorable speculation; the President's Private Secretary barely escaping conviction upon trial for guilty complicity in frauds upon the revenue; a Secretary of War impeached for high crimes and misdemeanors [applause]—the demonstration is complete, that the first step in reform must be the people's choice of honest men from another party [applause], lest the disease of one political organization infect the body politic, and lest by making no change of men or parties, we get no change of measures and no real reform.

All these abuses, wrongs and crimes, the product of sixteen years' ascendency of the Republican party, create a necessity for reform, confessed by Republicans themselves; but their reformers are voted down in Convention [applause] and displaced from the cabinet. The party's mass of honest voters is powerless to resist the eighty thousand office-holders, its leaders and guides. Reform can only be had by a peaceful civic revolution. We demand a change of system, a change of administration [applause], a change of party [applause], that we may have a change of measures and of men. [Applause.]

Mr. BROWN, of Oregon: Mr. President—

Mr. DORSHEIMER: I will say that at the end of the resolution relating to the matter of the Mongolian importation there were two or three lines of language adopted by the committee which were written in lead pencil and which I was unable to read, and the Secretary, when I have closed, will supply that omission.

Mr. BROWN, of Oregon: We want that read now, Mr. President. I am on the committee myself, and I demand that that shall be read in conjunction with the other. [Cries of "No, no."]

GOV. DORSHEIMER: The resolution closes as follows: "We denounce the policy which thus discards the liberty-loving German and tolerates a revival of the Coolie trade in Mongolian women imported for immoral purposes, and Mongolian men held to servile labor contracts, and demand such modification of the treaty with the Chinese empire, or such legislation within constitutional limitations, as shall prevent further importation or immigration of the Mongolian race." [Cries of "Good!" "Bully!" and cheers.] Your committee have also had referred to them and recommend the adoption of the following resolutions:

Resolved, That this Convention, representing the Democratic party of the States, do cordially indorse the action of the present House of Representatives [applause] in reducing and curtailing the expenses of the Federal Government; in cutting down enormous salaries, extravagant appropriations, and in abolishing useless offices and places not required by the public necessities, and we shall trust to the firmness of the Democratic members of the House that no committee of conference and no misinterpretation of rules will be allowed to defeat these wholesome measures of economy demanded by the country. [Applause.]

Resolved, That the soldiers and sailors of the Republic, and the widows and orphans of those who have fallen in battle, have a just claim upon the care, protection and gratitude of their fellow-citizens. [Applause.]

The following dissent from the majority report was also presented by the Hon. Edward Avery, of Massachusetts:

The undersigned members of the Committee on Resolutions, most heartily indorsing the report of the committee with the exception hereinafter named, respectfully dissent from the following clause in that portion of the report relating to finance, viz: "We denounce the resumption clause of the act of 1875, and we here demand its repeal," as apparently inconsistent with the other portions of the report on that subject, and recommend that the report of the committee be amended by striking out the above clause; and we further respectfully ask that our dissent be recorded and reported to the Convention.

EDWARD AVERY, *Massachusetts.*
J. W. YATES, *New Jersey.*
D. K. HASTINGS, *Maine.*
WILLIAM DORSHEIMER, *New York.*
R. D. HUBBARD, *Connecticut.*

Gen. TOM EWING, of Ohio: At the request of several members of the Committee on Resolutions, I present a minority report as to one phase of the platform.

The undersigned members of the committee recommend that the following clause in the resolutions reported by the committee be stricken out: "As such hindrance we denounce the resumption clause of the act of 1875, and we here demand its repeal" [cheers], and they recommend that there be substituted for that clause the following: "The law for the resumption of specie payments on the first of January, 1879, having been enacted by the Republican party without deliberation in Congress or discussion before the people, and being both ineffectual to secure its object, and highly injurious to the business of the country, ought to be forthwith repealed." [Cheers.]

THOMAS EWING, *Ohio.*
D. W. VOORHEES, *Indiana.*
JOHN C. BROWN, *Tennessee.*
MALCOLM HAY, *Pennsylvania.*
H. H. TRIMBLE, *Iowa.*
JOHN J. DAVIS, *West Virginia.*
T. L. DAVIS, *Kansas.*
C. H. HARDIN, *Missouri.*

Mr. EWING: I therefore move that the clause referred to in the resolutions reported be stricken out and the resolution I have read inserted in its place.

Mr. EATON, of Kansas: I second the motion.

Mr. EWING: Gentlemen of the Convention—

Mr. COX: Mr. Speaker—

Mr. EWING: I have the floor.

Mr. COX: If the gentleman from Ohio intends to take the floor, I wouldn't take it from him.

Mr. EWING: Yes, sir; I have got it any way.

A DELEGATE from Michigan: The delegates in this part of the hall have not been able to distinguish the difference between the parts stricken out and the amendments to the platform. I request that that part of the platform be read again with the amendments.

The CHAIR: The request of the gentleman shall be complied with. The Secretary will read that part of the resolution sought to be stricken out.

The SECRETARY: I will read the passage stricken out, and then I will read the resolution:

"As such a hindrance we denounce the resumption clause of the act of 1875, and we demand its repeal."

Now I will read the whole resolution:

"We denounce the financial imbecility and immorality of that party which, during eleven years of peace, has made no advance towards resumption, no preparation for resumption, but instead has obstructed resumption by wasting our revenues and exhausting all our surplus income, and, while annually professing to intend a speedy return to specie payment, has annually enacted fresh hindrances thereto, and as such a hindrance we denounce the resumption clause of the act of 1875, and we demand its repeal."

The CHAIR: Now the substitute, or the amendment rather, will be read.

Mr. BROWN, of Oregon: I move to lay the report of the minority committee on the table. [Cries of "Good, good!"]

The CHAIR: The gentleman has not the floor yet.

Mr. BROWN: I withdraw the motion if I haven't the floor. [Laughter.]

The SECRETARY: I will read the resolution as it will stand if amended:

"We denounce the financial imbecility and immorality of that party which, during eleven years of peace, has made no advance toward resumption, but instead has obstructed resumption by wasting our resources and exhausting all our surplus income, and, while annually professing to intend a speedy return to specie payment, has annually enacted fresh hindrances thereto. The law for the resumption of specie payment on the first of January, 1879, having been enacted by the Republican party without deliberation in Congress or discussion before the people, and being both ineffectual to secure this object and highly injurious to the business of the country, should be forthwith repealed." [Applause.]

The CHAIR: The gentleman from Ohio (Mr. Ewing) has the floor now, and the Convention will please be silent.

Mr. EWING: Mr. Chairman and gentlemen of the Convention, I desire to briefly state the objections to the clause which we propose to have stricken out. It denounces one clause only of the specie resumption law. What clause is that? The clause fixing the time for the resumption of specie payment, leaving the rest of the act to stand unobjected to and by implication approved. But why does it object to that clause? Because it is destroying the business of the country in connection with the balance of the law? Not at all, but merely because it is a hindrance to specie payment, the fair inference being—at any rate, if not a fair one, an inference that will surely be drawn—that the objections of the national Democratic party to the specie resumption law is confined only to the date of resumption, and the objection to that is that that date is a hindrance to resumption, and the construction will be given, and with some degree of plausibility at least, that the Democratic party want resumption earlier than the date fixed. [Applause.] I object to that clause in the resolution because it has the effect—I will not say it was intended —to palter with the subject in a double sense, "keeping the word of promise to the ear to break it to the hope."

I said that by inference the balance of the law is approved, and it is a reasonable and a fair inference, if not a necessary one, and what does that committee say about it? It commits us to the issuing of gold bonds to take up the costless fractional currency.

It commits us to the reduction of the legal-tender currency by having bank paper take its place, thus increasing the power of an already dangerous monopoly—a monopoly that is thoroughly hated by the mass of the Democracy of this country. [Applause.] It commits us to the perpetuation of the national bank system, for if we have no objection to that law except the date of resumption, then we approve the provisions for the raising up of two or three thousand great monopolies to control the currency of this country in addition to the two thousand we already have. [Applause.] It leaves the Secretary of the Treasury with perhaps the power—I will not state it positively—but perhaps the power to issue gold interest bonds of the United States to buy up gold and lock it idly in the treasury waiting for the day of resumption that may be fixed—a policy to which the Democracy, my friends of the West, I am sure, are almost unanimously opposed. [Applause.]

What is this law which we thus, in our resolutions, by implication, approve? Who enacted it? Did it have a Democratic vote? Not one in the Senate or House. [Applause.] It is a purely Republican measure, and the sum of the financial villainies of the Republican party. [Cries of "Time, time," "Go on."]

Mr. WILLIAMS, of Indiana: I move that Gen. Ewing have his time extended fifteen minutes. [Cries of "No, no."]

Gen. Ewing stepped to the front of the platform amidst the most tumultuous applause.

Mr. COLLINS, of Massachusetts: We have a rule that no gentleman shall speak for more than five minutes. If objection be made his time cannot be extended. I object.

The CHAIR: The Chair holds that the point of order is well taken, unless the rule be reconsidered or set aside.

Mr. EATON, of Kansas: I move to reconsider the rule.

The CHAIR: There is a question pending, and no motion to introduce a new subject is in order.

Mr. DORSHEIMER: I have to ask the gentleman from Massachusetts [Hisses, cries of "Order," "Time," "Ewing"]—I have to ask that the gentleman from Massachusetts withdraw his objection and give Gen. Ewing an opportunity to speak. [Applause.]

Mr. KERNAN, of New York: Inasmuch as Mr. Ewing represents a portion of the committee, I think we should extend his time as moved, although we may not be able to make a precedent in favor of others who are not on the committee. I hope his time will be extended as it has been.

The CHAIR: The objection is withdrawn.

Mr. McLANE, of Maryland: I rise to a point of order. The point of order is that the Chair cannot entertain the motion of the gentleman from New York. The rules of the Convention are absolute. Nobody can reply to the gentleman from Ohio except in a five-minute speech. It is against the law of the Convention to enter a motion to have him heard more than five minutes.

The CHAIR: Will the gentleman from Maryland allow me to make a remark? The Chair was not aware of any objection.

Mr. McLANE: There was objection.

The CHAIR: The Chair did not hear it.

Mr. McLANE: It is the fault of the Chair—the objection was made in every direction. The noise in the galleries drown the objections.

The CHAIR: I recognize the gentleman from Ohio, and his right to proceed in the absence of objection, and I shall maintain that position. [Applause.]

Mr. McLANE: But objection *was* made. I appeal from the decision of the Chair, and call for a vote by States. The Chair had no right to give the floor to the gentleman, and I demand a vote.

A DELEGATE from Indiana: The rules were suspended, and Gen. Ewing's time extended fifteen minutes, and upon that motion I move the previous question.

The CHAIR: I could not receive a motion to suspend the rules while this business is pending. The gentleman from Maryland appeals from the decision of the Chair.

Gen. EWING: I am very much obliged to you for the kind spirit manifested, and will not ask the indulgence of the Convention further.

Mr. COX, of New York: I rise to a point of order.

Mr. MILLER, of Nebraska: Who has the floor?

The CHAIR: The gentleman from New York, Mr. Cox, has the floor on a point of order.

Mr. COX: My point of order was this: I was entitled, after Gen. Ewing spoke, to be recognized. I had no power to be upon that platform. My colleagues have rights that I have not.

The CHAIR: The gentleman is out of order.

Mr. COX, of New York: I will make my point. I propose to yield my time to Mr. Ewing. [Cheers.]

The CHAIR: The gentleman has no right to yield his time. He is out of order.

Mr. MILLER, of Nebraska: I rise to a question of privilege. I move that the galleries be cleared. [Cheers.]

The CHAIR: The gentleman from Nebraska moves that the galleries be cleared, and I wish to address myself to the galleries. We are not to be controlled or intimidated by outsiders, and unless we can have order, I will turn them out. [Cheers.]

Mr. DORSHEIMER, of New York: Mr. Chairman and gentlemen of the Convention, I do not propose to speak upon this matter at length. Five minutes is quite time enough for me. I propose here to make a straight issue between soft money and hard money. [Tremendous cheering.] By that we stand or we fall. [Cheers.] If you want soft money, give your votes to the resolution offered by the most distinguished advocate of soft money in the United States [cheers and hisses]; but if you want to leave to the hard-money men some chance to carry their States, then stand by the report of the committee [cheers], which was a compromise so great that a protest has been sent here signed by every one of the Eastern Democratic States, and to which I have put my own signature. [Cries of "Good," and cheers.] This is a middle ground which does leave some hope; but if you declare, in the language of the gentleman from Ohio (Gen. Ewing), for a repeal forthwith, then abandon all your hope. [Cheers.] I make this issue fair. [A voice, "You will get enough of it."] As I said, we will stand to that; and now, Mr. President, I demand a vote by the States. [Cheers, hisses and applause.]

Mr. Voorhees, of Indiana, took the stand.

Mr. BRECKINRIDGE, of Kentucky: I arise to a point of order. The distinguished gentleman on the other side did not rise from his seat before I did, but I arise that both of us may be heard for the purpose of moving the previous question. [Cries of "No, no," and confusion.]

Mr. VOORHEES: I will only occupy five minutes, and you had better let me do it.

Several delegates endeavored to get the floor amid great confusion.

The CHAIR: Gentlemen, you had better keep quiet; this conduct does not scare anybody and does not move anybody.

A DELEGATE from Kansas: I move that the galleries of this hall be cleared so that we may have order.

The CHAIR: It is moved by the gentleman from Kansas that the galleries be cleared. [Cries of "No, no."]

A DELEGATE from Massachusetts: I move to lay that motion on the table. [Cries of "Second the motion."]

The CHAIR: Does the gentleman withdraw the motion?

A DELEGATE: No, sir. I say it is absolutely disgraceful the conduct we are having in this Convention now, and I want it stopped, and for that purpose I insist upon my motion that the galleries be cleared now. [Cries of "No, no."]

Several delegates endeavored to get the floor amid great confusion.

Mr. SPAUNHORST, of Missouri: Mr. President, I arise to a point of order, and that is that Mr. Voorhees is entitled to the floor, having been recognized as such, and no motion is in order until order is restored.

The CHAIR: Of course; the Chair so rules. The gentleman from Indiana has the floor. [Cheers.]

REMARKS OF MR. VOORHEES.

Mr. VOORHEES: Gentlemen of the Convention, with your kind permission and silence I will take about five minutes, and no more. We had better be quiet and still in order to get through.

A DELEGATE: Mr. Chairman—

Mr. VOORHEES: I have the floor, and I serve notice on the gentleman that I expect to hold it. [Cheers.] The issue that is stated by the gentleman from New York is a false issue so far as this platform is concerned. There is no issue raised here as between hard money and soft money so-called. This platform to which the minority agree contains repeated stipulations that we are in favor, at as early a period as practical, of resumption of specie payment. [Cheers.] We are all in favor of that. I am in favor of a resumption of specie payment as soon as the true and healthful interests of this country will permit. [Cheers.] He who desires specie resumption at an earlier day than that desires it for some private and not from patriotic motives. [Cheers.]

A word or two, for I have but a short time, in regard to legislative resumption—a forced resumption of specie payment.

Men of New York sitting here before me, you have at this moment an act in favor of the resumption of specie payment on the 1st day of January, 1879, on your statute-books. That was enacted two years ago, and we are two per cent. further from a gold basis to-day than we were when it was enacted. That is what it has wrought in behalf of specie payment. [Cheers.] The Government currency is not as near unto a fair basis by two per cent. as it was before this miserable, bungling law was enacted upon your statute-book.

Again, gentlemen, I stand for a growth of the country into specie payment. I stand for that kind of specie payment that comes by a return of wealth and prosperity to all the sections. [Cries, "That's right."] We can all recall a time when our paper was worth but forty cents on the dollar in gold. It had grown to be worth ninety cents before the law was passed at all. It had appreciated fifty cents on the dollar before your favorite pet idea of forced resumption touched the question in the halls of Congress; it had, sir, by the natural laws of trade and by the laws of God's growth and prosperity returning to the country, appreciated fifty cents on the dollar in the course of eight years. Let us trust that the gap of only about ten or twelve per cent. remaining will be closed up by the same great laws in a very short time in the future. This idea that we must do this by law I utterly repudiate, not because I do not want, as soon as the business of the country will warrant, a return to specie payment, but because the healthful, right way to return to specie payment is to revive the industries. Let this question alone in the halls of Congress, and trust to God's laws to restore us in His own time.

My friends, something was said by the gentleman from New York about the effect on his State and other States. I stand here surrounded by ten States who have a right to be heard on this subject—West Virginia, Ohio, my own gallant Democratic State of Indiana [applause], Missouri, on whose bosom we are holding this Convention; Tennessee, that contains the Hermitage and the ashes of Jackson and Polk; Iowa and Kansas—are they not to be considered? do they amount to nothing? I will say, with all respect to the gentleman from New York who has just sat down, that we have followed the lead of New York for twelve long years, and each time to disaster [applause], and I, for one, assert the West, the mighty West, with its teeming population. I assert the power of this Mississippi Valley, with its mighty interests and its great resources. [Cries of "Time" and "Go on." Yes, I believe my time is up, and in good faith I should retire.

Mr. DORSHEIMER, of New York: Mr. Chairman—

The CHAIR: The gentleman from New York has the floor.

Mr. COX, of New York: Mr. President, I should like to inquire how often can a gentleman speak on one question?

The CHAIR: I don't know whether the gentleman proposes to speak. When the question arises the Chair will decide it.

Mr. COX: And I will make the point of order at the time.

Mr. DORSHEIMER: I claim the floor to be my right.

Mr. COX: You have had your speech once.

Mr. DORSHEIMER: And I yield the floor to Mr. Watterson, of Kentucky.

MR. WATTERSON'S REMARKS.

Mr. WATTERSON, of Kentucky: Gentlemen of the Convention, I presume that no reasonable member of this Convention would care to have his private business submitted to an excited and tumultuous body of this description. How is it, then, that reasonable men, who have made a most discriminating and representative selection of members of the committees to settle and decide the important business of the whole country, whose committee have come here after a whole night of careful deliberation, who have submitted a report by twenty-nine of your most representative members [applause]—how dare a man with his own theories to come here after all that and ask, in your excited and tumultuous condition, to reverse that report? Have we come here to deliberate, or have we come here to decide upon the important issue of this canvass by passion and theory? I don't care what the difference is between the majority and minority report; I do not want to know whether there is or is not a difference between them, I want to adopt the majority report [applause] because it is your act, and I do not want your delegated act reversed by eight of your number, who, failing to get satisfaction in the committee, come to open this dangerous question in this body. [Applause.] I don't believe that we shall grow wiser by discussing this question; I therefore move the previous question. [Applause.]

The CHAIR: Gentlemen of the Convention [confusion]— This noise will avail nothing; you cannot drive me out of propriety or position.

Mr. COX, of New York: Mr. President—[great confusion.]

The CHAIR: The Sergeant-at-Arms will report in the President's front.

Mr. Able came forward to the front of the President's stand.

The CHAIR (to the Sergeant-at-Arms): now hold yourself in readiness for a little while. I will have order.

Several voices: Mr. President—

The CHAIR: Gentlemen of the Convention, I have a communication from the Kansas delegation which claims my attention, and I want to call your attention to it.

Mr. COX, of New York: I rise to a point of order.

A DELEGATE from New Jersey: I rise, Mr. President—

The CHAIR: Mr. Cox has the floor. He rises to a point of order.

Mr. COX: Mr. President, this Convention does not understand the question.

The CHAIR: If the Convention will come to order I will state it.

Mr. COX: I want to rise to a point of order with all due respect to the Chair. I served with the Chair fifteen years ago in Congress.

The CHAIR: The gentleman is out of order. [Applause.] The question is on the previous question.

The DELEGATE from New Jersey who spoke last: I ask the gentleman from Kentucky (Mr. Watterson) if he will allow me five minutes on this question. He has a right to do it, inasmuch as he has moved the previous question. ["Object."]

The CHAIR: There is objection.

The same DELEGATE from New Jersey: Mr. Watterson is the only man who can object.

Mr. WATTERSON: I moved the previous question.

The CHAIR: Mr. Watterson objects.

The same DELEGATE: Then I ask for my right on this previous question. I call for a division of the question. The motion is to strike out and insert. I want the part which repeals that act stricken out and I want the other inserted. I want hard money. [Applause.]

The CHAIR: The question is upon the previous question now.

The motion was carried.

The CHAIR: The question now is upon the amendment offered by the gentleman from Ohio.

The New Jersey DELEGATE: My request is for a division of the question, which I have a right to. A division will bring the question up whether or not we ought to vote for soft or hard money.

The CHAIR: The gentleman's point is well taken.

Mr. WALLACE, of Pennsylvania: Mr. President, a point of order. My point of order is that the previous question has not yet been taken by this Convention. It requires a majority of this Convention to second the previous question and apply the gag. I demand a vote by States, in order that we may know whether the previous question be or be not seconded.

The CHAIR: It was the privilege of the gentleman from Pennsylvania to call for a vote by States, but he failed to do it.

Mr. COX: I call for a vote by States.

Mr. WALLACE: I second the demand for a vote by States.

Mr. DOOLITTLE: I propose to move an amendment to the minority clause before the vote is taken [cries of "Out of order]," and I desire to do it, and while my young friend from Kentucky or from any other State advises us—

The CHAIR: You are out of order.

Mr. DOOLITTLE: I wish to say my head is cool and level, and I know what I mean, and I know that victory or death is right here. [Applause.] I desire to be heard for five minutes upon my amendment. ["Object, object."]

The CHAIR: Objection is made, therefore the gentleman is out of order. The gentleman from New York calls for a vote by States.

Mr. COX: I am here endeavoring to carry out the rules as I understand them, and I raise this point of order.

The CHAIR: Call the roll.

Mr. COX: I insist upon my point of order.

Mr. DOOLITTLE: Before the roll is called I wish to offer my amendment.

Mr. COX: I want that Secretary to stop, and I want the delegates to leave the desk and go to their places. The rules of Congress require that to be done. I give you the authority of the rules of Congress that no man can stand around that desk as a delegate except in defiance of the rules of Congress, which you have adopted, and you know it, Mr. President, for you served there as long as I did.

The CHAIR: Gentlemen, the question now is upon the amendment offered by the gentleman from Ohio to the report made by the Committee on Platform.

Mr. DOOLITTLE: I move to amend that before a vote is taken—

The CHAIR: It is out of order.

Mr. DOOLITTLE: I want to offer my amendment.

The CHAIR: The main question is ordered and the gentleman is out of order.

Mr. DOOLITTLE: It is not yet ordered. . . . . I am told, although at the time I did not hear it, that the previous question had been ordered.

Mr. COX, of New York: Ordered and seconded.

Mr. DOOLITTLE: I wish to know further whether I am too late now to offer an amendment to Gen. Ewing's amendment, or the amendment of the minority of the committee. If I am not, I desire to read it now that it may be before the Convention.

The CHAIR: It will be out of order, the Chair regrets to say to the gentleman from Wisconsin (Mr. Doolittle), unless the Convention chooses to receive it by unanimous consent.

Mr. DOOLITTLE: Then by unanimous consent, gentlemen, I ask simply to read the amendment of Gen. Ewing.

Objection was made.

A DELEGATE from Massachusetts: Upon what are we voting?

The CHAIR: We are voting under the previous question.

The Massachusetts DELEGATE: The vote now is upon striking out the part of the majority report which repeals the resumption act. Therefore, if we vote in favor of that, this Convention will announce that it is not in favor of repealing the resumption act.

The CHAIR: A division of the question has been asked for, and it is upon striking out a portion of the original resolution or report.

Mr. WALLACE, of Pennsylvania: Pennsylvania asks leave to retire for consultation.

Mr. DOOLITTLE: I move that the Convention do now adjourn. [Cries of "No, no."]

The motion was lost.

Mr. DOOLITTLE: Then I will ask unanimous consent to read my amendment.

A DELEGATE from Arkansas: Has the Chair decided that the previous question is ordered?

The CHAIR: Yes, sir.

The Arkansas DELEGATE: Then I call for a vote on the question itself—the main question.

The CHAIR: The Chair has been trying to reach that point. Let the Clerk call the roll and not stop until I tell him to stop. [Laughter and confusion.] The question before the house is this: The minority report recommend the striking out of one of the resolutions of the majority of the Committee and to insert other matter. A division of the question is asked, and the question is first, whether the original report shall be amended by striking out any part of it. [Confusion.]

Mr. McLANE, of Maryland: There is so much disorder that we cannot tell what is going on. The lobby has been doing all the voting and all the cheering for the last half hour. We want to know what is going on, but we cannot hear anything, and I move, if it cannot be reached in any other way, that the galleries be cleared, much as I regret it. I want to try and see if we cannot have some order.

The CHAIR: The gentleman proposes that the galleries be cleared. Will the Sergeant-at-Arms detail one or two officers to the left and to the right and rear, to see that order is preserved?

A DELEGATE: Are we voting on the previous question or to strike out?

The CHAIR: To strike out.

A DELEGATE: I rise to a point of order. It appears that no member of this Convention—

Several DELEGATES: Mr. Speaker—

Mr. SPAUNHORST, of Missouri: Mr. Chairman, with a knowledge upon my part that this is one of the most momentous questions, and not generally understood [Cries of "Down! down!" much confusion], I therefore move that this Convention now adjourn until to-morrow morning at 10 o'clock. [Cries, "Call the roll."]

The CHAIR: The gentleman is out of order. The Clerk will call the roll.

Mr. DAVIS, of Kansas: I would ask if there had been a division of the motion made by Gen. Ewing? Are we putting the question whether the motion of Gen. Ewing shall prevail, or whether the question shall be divided?

The CHAIR: The question is whether we shall strike out a subsequent question as to insertion.

Mr. DAVIS: I say the motion to strike out is not in order, unless the motion to divide the motion is carried.

The CHAIR: The point is well taken.

Mr. DAVIS: Then I ask that the roll be not called now. I say we cannot take a vote on the nomination to strike out unless the house orders a division of the question.

The CHAIR: The original proposition, as coming from the Committee on Resolutions, will now be reported. The amendment proposed to be made thereto will also be reported, and then the question will be upon the amendment proposed.

Mr. DOOLITTLE: Can I then move to amend the amendment, or shall I do it now? I propose to do it at some time or other, and I wish the Chair to tell me when.

The CHAIR: It cannot be done until the previous question is exhausted.

Mr. DOOLITTLE: You mean after the proposition has been adopted?

The CHAIR: Yes, or defeated.

A DELEGATE: I move to reconsider the vote by which the previous question was ordered.

Mr. PORTER, of South Carolina: I desire to ask of this Convention that it vote intelligibly on the proposition. I understand, Mr. President, that the last motion made before this Convention was the motion of Mr. Watterson, the gentleman from Kentucky, who demanded the previous question.

The CHAIR: That was ordered.

Mr. PORTER: Sir?

The CHAIR: The previous question was ordered.

Mr. PORTER: Now I ask of the President of the Convention what the question is before the house?

The CHAIR: The Chair was going to explain, if the Convention will give the Chair an opportunity. The Clerk will read the original proposition and the amendment proposed thereto.

Mr. KERNAN, of New York: Mr. Chairman, one word. As I understand the question now, we are voting on that part of the minority report which proposes to strike out. Those who are in favor of the original report will vote aye. Am I right?

The CLERK (reading): "We denounce the financial imbecility—

Mr. BIRCH, of Tennessee: Mr. Chairman—

Another DELEGATE: Oh, well, sit down.

The CLERK: The gentleman will take his seat.

Mr. EATON: I desire to address the Chair and not the Clerk, and I take my orders from the Chair and not the Clerk. Now, the distinguished Senator from New York, in explaining his vote, gives me an idea that I desire to have explained by the Chair. It is extremely important that there should be no mistake.

The CHAIR: You are out of order.

Mr. EATON: Then, sir, I ask this. I ask the Chair what will be the effect of the vote if it be to strike out, and then there should be a failure to insert the amendment of the minority, I ask the Chair if that would not be to leave the law as it now is?

The CHAIR: It is so understood.

Mr. BIRCH: Then I ask, Mr. Chairman, if there is any parliamentary means by which we can get a fair and square vote upon the minority report, without being cheated—and I use the expression respectfully—by parliamentary legerdemain? [Applause. Voices, "Call the roll."]

The CLERK (beginning to read): "We denounce the financial imbecility and immorality of that party which, during eleven years of peace, has made no advance toward resumption, no preparation for resumption, but instead has obstructed resumption by wasting our resources and exhausted all our surplus income, and, while annually professing to intend a speedy return to specie payment, has annually enacted fresh hindrances thereto, and as such hindrance we denounce the resumption clause of the act of 1875, and we demand its repeal."

The CHAIR: Gentlemen, that is the original proposition. Now the amendment proposed by Gen. Ewing will be read.

Several DELEGATES: We cannot hear, and "Order."

The CHAIR: We must have profound silence to know what is going on. Let there be quiet. We are reading the resolutions now and it is very important.

The CLERK (reading): "The law for the resumption of specie payment on the first day of January, 1879, having been enacted by the Republican party without deliberation in Congress or discussion before the people, and both ineffectual to secure its objects and highly injurious to the business of the country, should be forthwith repealed."

Mr. HUTCHINS, of St. Louis: I rise for the purpose of making an inquiry.

The CHAIR: Nothing is in order.

Mr. HUTCHINS: I can be informed as to what effect my vote will have, so as to make sure. If this delegation votes aye, I understand that it, in effect, votes for the minority report. Does it or not? [A voice, "It does."] I want to hear from the Chair.

The CHAIR: Yes. If you vote aye you vote for the amendment.

Mr. HUTCHINS: Well, that is the minority report. If we vote no, we vote for the majority report in effect?

The CHAIR: Yes, sir.

Mr. HUTCHINS: Well, that is the first time the Convention has understood that much. I am much obliged to the Chair for the information.

The CHAIR: The Secretary will proceed to call the roll.

The Secretary proceeded to call the roll.

THE VOTE.

The vote on the motion to strike out and insert resulted as follows:

	Ayes.	Noes.
Alabama	....	20
Arkansas	....	12
California	....	12
Colorado	....	6
Connecticut	....	12
Delaware	....	6
Florida	....	8
Georgia	....	22
Illinois	18	22
Indiana	30	....
Iowa	5	17
Kansas	10	....
Kentucky	24	....
Louisiana	....	16
Maine	....	14
Maryland	....	16
Massachusetts	....	26
Michigan	5	17
Minnesota	....	10
Mississippi	....	16
Missouri	9	20
Nebraska	....	6
Nevada	....	6
New Hampshire	....	10
New Jersey	....	18
New York	....	70
North Carolina	....	20
Ohio	25	18
Oregon	....	6
Pennsylvania	58	....
Rhode Island	....	8
South Carolina	....	14
Tennessee	24	....
Texas	....	16
Vermont	10	....
Virginia	1	21
West Virginia	10	....
Wisconsin	....	20
Total	219	515

When New Jersey was called, the chairman of the delegation rose and said: I do not understand the ruling of the Chair as to the effect of this, and I ask the Chair to state it so that my delegation may vote intelligently. Does the Chair divide or refuse to divide the question?

The CHAIR: The question is upon the adoption of the minority report.

The DELEGATE from New Jersey: The Chair decided once it should be divided; has that decision been reversed?

The CHAIR: The point was made upon that, and the Chair corrected its decision upon that point.

The DELEGATE from New Jersey: Then New Jersey votes "No."

When Pennsylvania was called Mr. WALLACE said: Pennsylvania was instructed to cast her vote as a unit upon all questions of delegate and principle in this Convention, and casts her vote, 58 votes, "aye." [Applause.] And I want to inform the Convention that the vote stands 33 ayes and 23 noes in the delegation.

Mr. SPAUNHORST, of Missouri: I was not in when the Missouri delegation voted. I desire to vote "aye."

Mr. DOOLITTLE: While the clerks are figuring up the vote I can read this to the Convention. I have no doubt it will be unanimously adopted.

The CHAIR: The gentleman from Wisconsin asks the permission of the Convention to read a paper.

Mr. DOOLITTLE: I shall move to amend the majority report after the words declaring in favor or demanding the repeal of that clause of the resumption act, after the word "repeal," the following words: "That any law in place of the resumption law fixing the time for resumption for the payment or redemption of such legal-tender notes, shall provide that such retirement shall be so gradual and steady as not to disturb values, change the meaning of contracts, increase the burden of existing debts, destroy confidence, create alarm and uncertainty for the future, and thereby to paralyze industry and enterprise." Does anybody object to that? That is what we want in.

The Secretary announced the vote as follows:

AYES, 219; NOES, 550.

The announcement was received with cheers.

Mr. DOOLITTLE: I now move to amend the majority report by adding after the words which I have designated what I have read.

Mr. SMITH ELY, of New York: I rise to a point of order.

The CHAIR: The question is on the adoption of the report of the majority. There is a request made by a gentleman from the committee that a communication be read. Is there objection?

Objection was made.

Mr. DOOLITTLE: If I am recognized by the Chair, I move my amendment. I do not object.

The CHAIR: It is objected to.

Mr. DOOLITTLE: I do not object. I give way holding the floor to move my amendment, knowing that it will be unanimously carried.

The CHAIR: The gentleman is out of order, upon the ground that the previous question is not exhausted. Let the States be called upon the adoption of the report made by the majority of the committee.

The SECRETARY: Alabama!

Mr. DOOLITTLE: Mr. President, I desire to inquire for information. After this vote is taken, can I then move to amend—

DELEGATE from Arkansas: The previous question was not adopted on the report of the committee, but simply on the motion to strike out and insert.

The CHAIR: That reaches the main question. That has been discussed half an hour ago. Let the roll be called.

The SECRETARY: Alabama!

The CHAIRMAN of Alabama delegation: Alabama votes aye. [Applause.]

DELEGATE from Alabama. Is it not in order to—

The SECRETARY: Arkansas!

The CHAIR: The previous question commenced long ago upon the first proposition and it is not exhausted.

CHAIRMAN of Arkansas delegation: Arkansas votes aye. [Applause.]

The Secretary proceeded with the call of the roll with the following result:

	Ayes.	*Noes.*		*Ayes.*	*Noes.*
Alabama	20	....	Missouri	21	8
Arkansas	12	....	Nebraska	6	....
California	12	....	Nevada	6	....
Colorado	6	....	New Hampshire	10	....
Connecticut	12	....	New Jersey	18	....
Delaware	6	....	New York	70	....
Florida	8	....	North Carolina	20	....
Georgia	22	....	Ohio	21	20
Illinois	39	3	Oregon	6	....
Indiana	....	30	Pennsylvania	58	....
Iowa	18	4	Rhode Island	8	....
Kansas	4	6	South Carolina	14	....
Kentucky	24	....	Tennessee	24	....
Louisiana	16	....	Texas	16	....
Maine	14	....	Vermont	10	....
Maryland	16	....	Virginia	21	1
Massachusetts	26	....	West Virginia	....	10
Michigan	21	1	Wisconsin	20	....
Minnesota	10	....			
Mississippi	16	....	Total	651	83

Pending the call of the roll, when Indiana was called an Indiana delegate said:

The platform is so long, Mr. Chairman, that we do not understand it, and a portion of us are not prepared to vote on it.

The CHAIR: Proceed with the roll-call.

Mr. DAVIS, of Kansas: Being a member of the Committee, and having voted aye, I desire to make a statement of why I do it. The reason I voted aye in favor of the adoption of this report by the majority is this: I want to take the next best thing I can get for the Western States. If I can't get what I want exactly I will take the next best thing. I want harmony in this Convention and not discord and dissension. [Applause and hisses.]

Mr. EATON, of Kansas: I would ask where is the proper place for delegates in this Convention?

The CHAIR: In their seats.

Mr. EATON: Then I ask the delegates on the platform to take their seats.

Mr. WALKER, of Virginia: I move to make the report unanimous.

Mr. EATON: I rise to a point of order. I understand the delegate from Brooklyn still remains near the Chair.

The CHAIR: Please mention his name. I don't know him.

Mr. EATON: Mr. Jacobs. He is a delegate, and I wish him to take his seat with his delegation.

Mr. ALLEN, of Illinois: I desire, inasmuch as the Permanent Chairman of this Convention is from Illinois, to say that as he was on the Committee on Resolutions after he was chosen Permanent Chairman, the delegation from Illinois elected the Hon. S. S. Hays in his place on the Committee on Resolutions on yesterday afternoon, and I desire that fact recorded.

The CHAIR: It will be so ordered.

Mr. DOOLITTLE: There is another resolution which I wish to offer in connection with my amendment after the vote has been declared (reading): *Resolved*, That silver coin as well as gold—[cries of "Object."]

The CHAIR: Objection is made.

Mr. DOOLITTLE: I didn't hear it. [Laughter.] I would like to see the gentleman that objected. I want to appeal to him just to allow me to read it. I do not wish to take but a few minutes' time. [Cries of "Read."]

The CHAIR: The Secretary will report the vote upon the adoption or non-adoption of the report made by the Committee on Resolutions.

Mr. Bell, Secretary, announced the vote as follows:

Yeas, 651. [Applause.]

Mr. DORSHEIMER: Three cheers for the platform. [Hisses and applause.]

The SECRETARY: Noes, 83. [Applause.]

The CHAIR: The platform is adopted.

Mr. HUTCHINS, of Missouri: Mr. President—

Mr. DOOLITTLE: Mr. President—

The CHAIR: The gentleman from Wisconsin (Mr. Doolittle) has the floor.

Mr. DOOLITTLE: I now move to reconsider the vote by which the report was adopted, for the purpose of moving at the end of it and in addition to it what I am now about to read.

A DELEGATE from Arkansas: I move to lay the motion to reconsider on the table.

Mr. DOOLITTLE: I have a right to the floor. Will occupy but five minutes. (Reading):

Resolved, That silver coin as well as gold coin is legal-tender money ["Good"] by the Constitution ["Good" and applause]; that in its sound, normal condition there should be no money or currency but gold and silver coin and paper convertible on demand into coin; that we favor a gradual, certain and steady return to that condition; that as a most important step in that direction we favor the immediate restoration of the silver dollar, which has been for more than eighty years the unit of value or standard dollar of the republic, as legal tender, as it was before the act of February 12, 1873, and that immediate steps be taken to coin and to issue the same to meet the just demands of the Government and the people, and to restore the double standard of gold and silver upon a true adjustment of their relative value. And further,

Resolved, That any law in place of the resumption law, which we propose to repeal, providing for the payment or redemption of legal-tender notes, shall also provide that such retirement shall be so gradual and steady as not to disturb values, as not to change the honest meaning of contracts, as not to increase the burden of existing debts, as not to destroy confidence, create alarms and uncertainty for the future, and thereby paralyze industry and enterprise.

Those are the resolutions for which I move to reconsider the report for the purpose of moving them in addition.

Mr. BRECKINRIDGE, of Kentucky: I rise to a point of order. The point of order is that by the new rules adopted by this house all resolutions were to be referred without debate to the Committee on Resolutions, and that committee not having been discharged, those resolutions ought to go to that committee.

The CHAIR: The Chair will state, in answer to the gentleman from Kentucky, that the Convention is not in possession of the gentleman's resolutions. I understood him to be reading them as a part of his argument in the case.

Mr. DOOLITTLE: I will inquire of the Chair if I can move them in addition to the original report now, as additional resolutions?

The CHAIR: No; they are not in order.

Mr. DOOLITTLE: Then I make my motion to reconsider the vote adopting the report, for the purpose of allowing me to add these two resolutions as a part of the platform.

The CHAIR: The question is upon the motion to reconsider.

Mr. DOOLITTLE: I demand a vote by States. I am informed by gentlemen familiar with the rules of the House of Representatives that I am in order to move them now as independent resolutions to go with the platform; is that correct or not?

The CHAIR: The Chair overrules that view of the case.

Mr. DOOLITTLE: Then I stand on my motion to reconsider.

Mr. MCLANE: I rise to move that the motion to reconsider be laid upon the table.

The motion was unanimously agreed to.

Mr. HUTCHINS, of Missouri: Is it in order to move to make the vote unanimous by which the platform was adopted?

The CHAIR: Yes, sir.

Mr. HUTCHINS: I make that motion and yield the five minutes which I may be allowed to speak upon the motion, to the Hon. S. S. Cox, of New York.

The CHAIR: The motion is that the vote on the platform be made unanimous and that it be carried by acclamation.

Mr. HUTCHINS: In making that motion I have a right to speak five minutes, and I yield that five minutes to Mr. Cox and insist he has the right to use that five minutes.

The CHAIR: Objection is made.

Mr. COX: I claim the right to the floor for five minutes.

The CHAIR: Go on.

Mr. COX: I wish to say this: There is very little difference between the platform adopted—

Mr. BEEBE, of New York: A point of order. The motion to reconsider has been voted down; that is a finality upon that proposition.

Mr. COX: I only wish to say that after this Convention shall be through I pledge you—

A MOTION FOR NOMINATIONS.

Mr. McLANE, of Maryland: I move that the Convention now proceed to nominate candidates for President and Vice-President of the United States. [Cheers.]

The CHAIR: It is now moved that the Convention proceed to nominate candidates for the Presidency and Vice-Presidency of the United States. [Cheers.]

The motion prevailed.

THE NOMINATIONS.

The SECRETARY: Alabama.

DELEGATE from Arkansas: Is it proposed that we shall proceed to vote for nominees before any nominations are made? [Uproar.]

The CHAIR: The Convention will come to order.

The SECRETARY: The Chair desires the Secretary to read the rule in relation to making nominations [reading]: "The roll of States shall be called, and if a State has a candidate, he shall be presented to the Convention in a speech not longer than ten minutes." Alabama.

When Delaware was called, Mr. WHITELY mounted the platform and spoke as follows:

NOMINATION OF HON. THOS. F. BAYARD.

Mr. Chairman and fellow-Democrats — The Democracy of Delaware have instructed her delegation to put in nomination for the Presidency of the United States her distinguished citizen, the Hon. Thomas Francis Bayard. [Cheers.] Is it necessary, fellow-Democrats, for me to enumerate his claims upon you for that office? They are known, in our judgment, known and real and admitted by all Democrats of the Union. [Applause.] In the prime of his life, in the full vigor of his youthful manhood, drawing his Democracy from the Constitution, loyal to it, and to it above all other things, live and active in the protection of all the interests of all the sections of our country; a pledged friend to all reforms, civil service and others; a pledged enemy of and a foe to corruption in his own as in the Republican party. [Applause.] Talented; as honest in private life as in public, as God's glorious sun at noonday [applause]; he stands to-day before you and the country, a statesman worthy of the honor, confidence, and trust of any party or of any people.

In saying this, fellow-Democrats, I, of course, do not intend any comparison derogatory to the distinguished gentlemen who will be named hereafter. He is not above them, he is not below them, but he is their peer. [Cheers.] Entering the Senate seven short years ago, he has made his mark upon the senatorial scroll as high as any other man. [Cheers.] It is true he comes from a small State; but, my fellow-Democrats, while he belongs to Delaware, he belongs to the Union. [Cheers.] Then I say in his behalf and in behalf of the Democracy of Delaware, that the times demand his nomination. The reading, thinking, patriotic Democrats, who send you here, demand his nomination. Not Delaware alone, but the Union demands his nomination. Our country's danger demands his nomination; and permit me to say, you gentlemen who are friends of other candidates — success, success, which we are all after, demands his nomination. [Cheers.]

I leave him, therefore, fellow-Democrats, in your hands. All this I can say, that Delaware lies down upon that nomination, and means to fight it out on that line—if not all summer, during the sitting of this Convention. [Cheers.] But if you do nominate him, all I can say is, that you will have a gallant, worthy and brave standard-bearer; for, like the illustrious chevalier of France, from whom he takes his name, he is "without fear and without reproach." [Cheers.]

The call of the States proceeded until Indiana was reached.

NOMINATION OF HON. THOS. A. HENDRICKS.

Mr. WILLIAMS, of Indiana: Mr. President and gentlemen of the Convention—In the name and in behalf of the united Democracy of the State of Indiana, I put in nomination Gov. Thomas A. Hendricks, of Indiana, [loud and prolonged cheers] as your candidate for President of the United States. He is a man that is known to the whole nation. There is no spot or blemish upon his public or private character. He is presented as the unanimous choice of the Democracy of a Democratic State. He comes here backed by his delegation and by every Democrat in Indiana. There is no fire in his rear here. We believe that if he is our nominee we can carry the State of Indiana by from 12,000 to 20,000. [Cheers.]

You delegates in this Convention must determine for yourselves by your votes whether you want Indiana to remain Democratic or not. We propose to support the nominee of this Convention whoever he may be. There is no diversity among us on that subject, but we would like to have a man for our candidate that we know we can carry the State for. In conclusion, Mr. President, I desire to read the resolution that was adopted by the Democracy of the State at its last Convention, and with that, sir, I will close.

Resolved, That the people of Indiana recognize with pride and pleasure the eminent public services of Hon. Thos. A. Hendricks. In all public trusts he has been faithful to duty, and in his public and private life pure and without blemish. We therefore declare that he is our unanimous choice for the Presidency of the United States.

I now, Mr. President, give way to my friend from Illinois, Mr. Fuller.

Mr. FULLER, of Illinois: Mr. President and gentlemen of the Convention—Depressed under the weight of debt and taxation, universal corruption, general demoralization, and all the evils that inevitably flow from the persistent disregard of fundamental law in the long and uninterrupted retention of unlimited power in the same hands, the country demands a return to the principles and practice of the fathers of the Republic in this the hundredth year of its existence [applause], and the restoration of a wise and frugal government, that shall leave to every man the freest pursuit of his avocations or his pleasures, consistent with the rights of his neighbors, and shall not take from the mouth of labor the bread it has earned. Dissatisfied with bare respectability, which, though it may tend to retard, cannot stay the downward progress, the country turns to the Democratic Convention assembled, and asks this great party to place in nomination the next President of the United States. [Cheers.] That nominee must be intrinsically honest himself, that he may be the cause of honesty in others; capable himself, that he may be quick to discern and to appropriate the capacity of others as well as to exert his own; lofty in thought and pure in spirit, that it may be at once acknowledged that he may drag up drowning honor by the locks, raise governmental administration from the depths into which it has been plunged, and elevate and purify the moral tone of the nation. [Applause.] He must be a statesman of such breadth of mind and of such grasp of information as to be enabled to embrace the whole country within the compass of his judgment, and so to act that he will secure the greatest good to the greatest number, and so the good of all. Such a man, Mr. President and gentlemen of the Convention, is presented in the name of Thomas A. Hendricks, the gallant Governor of Indiana. [Great applause.] Endowed with that capacity for continuous effort, that tenacity of purpose, that simplicity of habit which characterized his hardy ancestry, who and whose fellows centuries ago wrested from the sea the land on which they lived; taught by an education, acquired by the use of the axe and the saw, the value of economy—economy which the world seems to spurn while it acknowledges and does homage to its fruits; schooled by thirty years of eminent and honorable practice at the bar and twenty-five of concurrent activity in high public stations; of stainless character, and with a record which needs no explanation, as it lies open to the sunlight without a blot to mar its purity [applause]; conversant with the wants of the entire country, in all its length and breadth, though particularly of those of the great West, in which his revolutionary sires were pioneers, and of that South, linked to it by a thousand ties of inter-communication, common interest and mutual affection; added to all, possessed of those qualities of heart that attract friendship and never disappoint it, Thomas A. Hendricks, as the Democratic standard-bearer, would realize the wishes of the people and would, at least, deserve success. [Applause.] And if deserved, what better leader to insure it? Here on the fertile plains of the West; here on the seat of empire, beneath that star which for so many years has led the way, and now shines fixed but resplendent above the valley of the Mississippi — here the decisive battle of the campaign is to be fought [applause], for here are to be waged those great contests which precede the main engagement and determine its results.

What better leader than he to meet the enemy at their first onset, drive back their wavering forces on the center, and mingle all in undistinguishable ruin? What better leader than he, who, believing odium incurred by the practice of virtue is glory and not odium, in the disastrous days snatched victory from defeat, and lighted up with the splendor of his achievements the darkness 'twixt the twilight of 1860 and the dawn of 1876? Already, in the expectation of his candidacy, hope elevates and joy brightens every crest in the consciousness of approaching victory; already thousands upon thousands are listening to catch the blast upon that bugle horn, well worth a million men. Already our opponents recoil at the suggestion of his name, for they know in that sign we can conquer.

Mr. President, on behalf of many delegates from Illinois; on behalf of thousands of Democratic voters of that State; on behalf, I believe, of myriads of my fellow-citizens of the West, the thundering tramp of whose feet, as they rush to the encounter, and the sound of whose voices as they rise in triumphant acclaim as they emerge from the smoke of battle, I even now seem to hear, I have the honor to second the nomination of Thomas A. Hendricks of Indiana.

Mr. WILLIAMS, of Indiana: I desire, with the permission of the Convention, that Gen. Campbell, of Tennessee, shall occupy five minutes of my time.

Gen. CAMPBELL, of Tennessee: Mr. President and gentlemen of the Convention—I am instructed by the delegates from the State of Tennessee, who received their authority from the largest Convention that ever assembled in that State, to second the nomination of the great and distinguished statesman of Indiana, the Hon. Thomas A. Hendricks. [Applause.] And I pledge the State of Tennessee that if this Convention, in its wisdom, shall see proper to approve the nomination which is made here to-day, that in November next we will carry him at the polls by a majority of fifty thousand votes. I would not be doing the great State of Tennessee justice, nor myself justice, or the other distinguished gentlemen whose names have been and will be presented to the Convention, if I did not say to you that all of them have many devoted followers and admirers in the grand old volunteer State. There are many there who would like to follow the lead of the great statesman-Governor of New York [applause], who has cleansed the Augean stables in his State, and driven the hydra-headed monster of corruption into exile.

There are many, very many in that State who would be glad to follow the distinguished soldier of the State of Pennsylvania [cheers], and it was when the black clouds of subjugation hovered over our heads that he was the first to produce a rift in the clouds, and to hold up the bow of promise to our people. It was he of whom our distinguished chairman once said he was like a sword wearing a jewel in its hilt. But there is one consideration that has more influence with Tennessee than any other, and that is the supreme consideration of success. [Applause.] We feel that we must conquer in the battle that is to be fought in November next, and in casting around among many of the distinguished men of the nation, whom Tennessee will follow, she is of the opinion that under the leadership of the great statesman of Indiana we are more certain to conquer than any other [cheers], and when we look at his character we find that his whole history is the very best and most eloquent sermon on political integrity and reform that was ever written by man. We find that his Democracy is as catholic as the Constitution itself. We find that he lives in a locality where there are no dissensions in his ranks. We find that his own people come up here in solid phalanx for him, like the Macedonian phalanx, with its lances all pointed outward, and move toward their friends. [Cheers.]

I thank you, gentlemen of the Convention, and give you now assurances of the hearty support that the State of Tennessee will give the distinguished statesman of Indiana in November next. [Applause.]

When New York was called there was a tremendous outburst of cheers, which subsided when it was discovered that she had been called out of order, before New Jersey.

The SECRETARY: The Secretary by mistake called New York instead of New Jersey.

NOMINATION OF HON. JOEL PARKER.

The State of New Jersey being called, Mr. Abbott, of New Jersey, took the stand and spoke as follows:

MR. CHAIRMAN AND GENTLEMEN OF THE CONVENTION: New Jersey is not so great in size as her mighty sister across the Hudson, but she is surely Democratic at all times [cries of "Good!"], and in this great fight which is to be waged against the Radical power at Washington, you need through this land the vote of New Jersey in the electoral college [cheers]; and we say this in New Jersey, that no matter what Democrat is presented to the people of this Union by this Convention, New Jersey Democrats know of no fealty to any man. [Cheers.] But, gentlemen of the Convention, we are deliberating in reference to this matter so as to select the man who can secure success not only in New Jersey, not only in New York, but through the entire Union. [Cries of "Good!"] We want not triumph in individual States, and we want at Washington no *haze*, but we want some honest Democrat. [Cheers.]

Now, we believe that although the State of New Jersey is not so great or mighty as some of her sisters in the Union, yet she can present to this Convention the name of a man that will sweep this country like a whirlwind from Maine to Florida, and from the Atlantic to the Pacific [cheers]; and, gentlemen of the Convention, the Democracy of that State come here through their delegates as a unit. [Cries of "Good!"] Every man in that State says, and I hereby, in obedience to the universal will of the Democracy of that State, nominate ex-Gov. Joel Parker, of New Jersey [cheers]—a man never beaten at the polls in his life; a man sixty years of age, and all that time from his earliest vote a Democrat. [Cheers.] His record, about which you have a right to know, as an available candidate, is this: His private and his public life is beyond and above reproach. He can look into the eye of his God Himself, feeling that there is no stain or shame that should make him blush [cheers] during the time that he has been Governor, and he has been honored with that nomination twice in his own State—an honor never given to any man twice elected there by the people.

He was during six years the Democratic Governor of New Jersey, and in one of them was the only Democratic Governor in the Union, and during that time wrote a record of which he can be proud. He stood by the Federal Government in the fight for the Union, and as long as there was armed rebellion in the land, New Jersey soldiers, under the direction of our Governor, were sent to the field. No man has ever heard from him aught but patriotic utterance; and the result was, that when other States were swept from Democratic moorings of patriotism, the wise, politic course of Joel Parker held New Jersey firm when all the rest of you were swept away. [Applause.] Now the question is, who can carry Pennsylvania ["Parker"], Connecticut, New Jersey, New York or Indiana? and, gentlemen, if I know aught of the Democracy in New York, if I see before me the enthusiastic friends of Gov. Tilden [cheers], let me ask them, will they say to this Convention, you cannot carry that State with Joel Parker? Will they do it? ["No, no."] Let me appeal to Pennsylvania, and ask Pennsylvania, who, in 1863, sent New Jersey regiments to aid your State when she was invaded? [Voices, "Parker and Seymour," and cheers.] Yes, and Joel Parker, within forty-eight hours from the time the cry came from Gov. Curtin, had his troops marching through the streets of Philadelphia. I ask you to go into the valley of the Cumberland, ye delegates from Pennsylvania, and tell them that the man nominated is the one who sent his troops to the front to save their homes and their families; tell them that that man, with a pure record, and a life above reproach, a loyal man, and one who stood by them in the hour of danger, and do you think Pennsylvania will desert him? ["No, no, never!" and a voice, "The war is over."] Yes, and on that I desire to say this, that when the war was over, Joel Parker, who stood by the Union as we all stand by it now, Gov. Parker was the first man to raise his voice to recognize the fact that when arms were laid down, it was that the South and every man in it should have the right to vote and send their representatives to Washington. [Cheers.] His last message at the end of his term in 1866, the first of January—his message then breathes only a proper spirit for a Democrat: "When your country is at war, know nothing except to win. When arms are laid down, take your brothers by the hand, and bury forever all animosities in the common good of the whole country."

Now, gentlemen of the Convention, I will not detain you longer, because my time is up; but I say this, that Joel Parker, if it be your pleasure to nominate him, can win this fight.

I say this, that there is not a single animosity or a single thing against which he would have to strive except the Republican party. There are no feelings against him. Upon him all could unite, and I believe that any Democrat who receives the nomination of this Convention, whoever he may be, will be the successful candidate in November, and for one little State, New Jersey, that nominates Joel Parker, will at least give him here nine electoral votes. ["Good!" and applause.]

NOMINATION OF GOV. TILDEN.

The Secretary called the State of New York.

The CHAIR: Gentlemen of the Convention, I have the honor to introduce to you Senator Kernan, of New York. [Long continued applause.]

Senator Kernan spoke as follows:

MR. PRESIDENT AND DELEGATES OF THE DEMOCRACY OF THE UNITED STATES: I desire to say to you that I rejoice and feel a pleasure in every word which has been said in commendation of the distinguished men who have been presented to you for your suffrages in this nominating Convention. [Applause.] They are my countrymen; they belong to the glorious party with which I act, and no man would repel with more indignation any word or insinuation to their detriment, and no man feels more pride in their glorious fame than I do. [Applause.] But, fellow-Democrats, while I appear before you to address my words, feeble though they may be, to your judgment, swayed by nothing but your love of country [applause], the election we are to have this fall rises far above the ordinary elections which we have. It is one, in my judgment, that touches the welfare and the prosperity of our people throughout the entire Union; it is not a mere question of whether honorable, honest and upright men shall be elected, but whether we shall select those men who are more sure to carry the election, that we may have reforms and changes which are essential to our prosperity and our happiness. [Applause.] Don't we need change and reforms, you warm-hearted men from the South, who have been trampled down under this Constitution [applause], and who have been wronged as no people ever have? Don't we need a restoration of proper administration, by which you men in those States shall be allowed to manage your own affairs, and shall be freed from plundering adventurers, who are eating up the substance of your people, and taking from you all real republican government? [Applause.] Don't we need change and reform, you men throughout this fertile and glorious West? Your industry does not get its just reward. Your labor goes without that which labor should always win. Your industry is paralyzed, and your capital even is too timid to aid enterprise. Don't we need it in my own section of the Union, with our closed factories, where our dispirited laborers seek in vain for that which shall give bread to their wives and children?

Oh, we need reforms that shall strike down taxation; which shall lighten our burden; which shall give us the prosperity that an economical and honest administration will give. We need reforms which shall bring back purity and honesty and economy in the administration of your public affairs. And, my fellow-Democrats, I appeal to your intelligence. The great issue which is in the minds of our people, the issue upon which this election will be lost or won, is that question of needed administrative reform—where we can get it. [Applause.] And in selecting our candidates, without any disrespect to others, we should select men who will command the entire confidence of our people, as much as we can, in reference to these questions of reform and economy and reduction of taxation. We all know that the Republican party resolved in 1868 and 1872, in language which we cannot excel, that they would give us reforms, and they would lighten the burdens of taxation. My friends, I know that any Democrat who comes into the administration will work out reforms, but if we are wise men we will take a man, if we find him, who has made reforms when in office. [Applause.] I have no disrespect for the Democrats who, in this Convention, can utter dissent to the good repute of any candidate named. I honor them all; I am addressing your judgment. I have said that if we had a man who had been so fortunate as to be placed in public position, who had laid his hand on dishonest officials, no matter to what party they belonged; who had rooted out abuses in the discharge of his duty; who had shown himself able and willing to bring down taxation and inaugurate reform—if we are wise men, and have such a man, it is no disparagement to any other candidate to say that this is the man that will command the confidence of men who have not been always with the Democracy, and make our claims strong, so that it will sweep all over this Union—a triumphant party vote.

Now, there is in the State whence I come it is familiar to you—a

Democrat who has the good fortune to be placed in the position where these qualities have been exemplified. There had grown up in our great Democratic city men who called themselves Democrats, who, under the guise of Democracy, dishonored our party by plundering the people whom they were bound to protect and serve. [Applause.] And citizens there, and the one I shall name, connected with others, and they overthrew these corruptionists in their own party, and they restored honesty and economy, and these men have flown to other lands, lest they be punished for their crimes. [Applause.]

He was selected as Governor of our State. He came into the office on the first day of January, 1875. The direct taxes taken from our tax-ridden people in the State of New York were over fifteen million dollars in the tax levy of 1874. [Applause.] He has been in office eighteen months, and the tax levy of the State of New York for the State Treasury for this year, 1876, is but eight million of dollars. [Cheers.] If you go among our farming people, among our men who find business coming down and their produce bringing low prices, you will find that they have faith in the man who has reduced taxation in the State of New York one-half in eighteen months [applause]; and you will hear the honest men throughout the country say that they want the man that will do at Washington what has been done in the State of New York. [Cheers.] Now, do not misunderstand me. We have other worthy men and good men in the State of New York who, if they had had the chance to have been elected, and had had a chance to have discovered the frauds in our State administration along our canals, which were thus depleting our people, would have done the work faithfully, I doubt not; but it so happened that Samuel J. Tilden [loud and continued cheers], but it so happened that the great Democratic party of the State of New York reaped this great benefit for our people, and this great honor for our party, because they elected Samuel J. Tilden. When they found in the State of New York he had been active in reforming abuses, it so happened that he was the man who by his measures—[cries of "Time, time," "Go on, go on."] I won't go on if anybody objects, but I ask only one minute. [Cries of "Go on," "Time," "Go on."]

I want to add one word, my friends, and it is this: I do not come here to vouch for my opinion, but I read from the resolutions passed by the Convention of the State of New York, with their two delegates from every Congressional district of our State—[a voice, "Three"] which is a part of the credentials which I laid before this Convention—I want to give you what the representatives of the Democracy of New York said in their judgment was the position of the gentleman I have named, after passing by their commendation of other things:

Resolved, That the Democratic party of New York, while committing to their delegates the duty of joining with the feelings of their fellow-Democrats in all the States in the momentous deliberations of the National Convention, declare their settled conviction that a return to the constitutional principles of frugal expenditure and the administrative purity of the founders of the republic is the first and most imperious necessity of the times.

This is the commanding issue now before the people of the Union, and they suggest, with respectful deference to their brethren of other States, and with cordial appreciation of other renowned Democratic statesmen, faithful like him to their political principles and public trust, that the nomination of Samuel J. Tilden to the office of President would insure the vote of the State of New York. [Cheers.]

Mr. Kelly, of New York, took the stand, amid cheers mingled with hisses.

A DELEGATE: Mr. Chairman, there seems to be some geese in the hall. I would like to have them removed. [Laughter.]

MR. KELLY: Mr. Chairman, I wish that I could convince myself in what has been said by the Senator from the State of New York in relation to the candidate that he has named to this Convention for its support. I, like him, am anxious—hopeful, prayerful—that we should regenerate this country from the thraldom which now—

A DELEGATE: Mr. Chairman, is the gentleman seconding the nomination made by the gentleman from New York? [Cries of "Kelly, Kelly!" and confusion.]

The CHAIR: Who can tell but what the gentleman has some other name to put in nomination? He has a right to speak in his own time.

A DELEGATE: Unless the gentleman is up there to second the nomination of Mr. Tilden, he is out of order.

The CHAIR: I have not understood for what purpose the gentleman has arisen yet. [Cries of "Kelly!" and confusion and hisses.]

MR. KELLY: Mr. Chairman, I was saying to you and to this Convention [more hisses] that I believe the candidate that can best meet the condition of things—[hisses.]

Mr. HUTCHINS, of Missouri: I move you, sir, that the President instruct the Sergeant-at-Arms to remove from this floor any gentleman who is not a delegate who seeks to interrupt the speaker. [Cheers.]

The CHAIR: The Chair will see that he is so instructed.

Mr. HUTCHINS: I will cast my vote for the gentleman against whom I know he is opposed, but I intend that he shall have fair play. [Cheers.]

Mr. DAVIS, of Kansas: I think it is a matter of very great propriety to scotch these vipers who hiss when gentlemen get up to speak.

The CHAIR: I hope the Sergeant-at-Arms will attend to those gentlemen who exercise their lungs in hissing.

Mr. KELLY: I was going to say to you, Mr. Chairman, and to the members of this Convention—[hisses.]

A DELEGATE from New York: It is the unanimous wish of the delegation from the State of New York that the gentleman be heard. [More hisses and confusion.]

Mr. WEED, of New York: I ask, in behalf of a majority of the delegation who are opposed in opinion to Mr. Kelly, that he should have a respectful hearing before this body. [More confusion and hisses.]

Mr. KERNAN, of New York: Mr. President, I appeal to every friend of the State of New York to give my colleague on the delegation a hearing. All good comes out of that, and no evil. [Cries of "Good!"] All I ask is, let every man talk before the nomination, and after the nomination let us all go in for the nominee. [Cheers.]

Mr. BRECKINRIDGE, of Kentucky: I rise and have a right to demand—

The CHAIR: Will the gentleman tell me what he wants?

Mr. BRECKINRIDGE: I did not hear the Chair.

The CHAIR: What is it the gentleman wishes to say?

Mr. BRECKINRIDGE: I desire to raise simply this point of order. I do not desire that the gentleman from New York shall not be heard; for, sir, I am for fair play and a free fight. [Cries of "Order!"]

The CHAIR: The gentleman has the floor, and will not be interrupted.

Mr. BRECKINRIDGE: The point of order I desire to make is this—[great confusion.]

Mr. KELLY [resuming]: Mr. Chairman, I believe the man to meet the exigency of the case is Thomas A. Hendricks, of Indiana [cheers], and while I believe so I feel convinced—

Mr. BRECKINRIDGE: Mr. Chairman, I have a right to state my point of order. It is a right I have as a delegate. [Cries of "Sit down" and "Kelly."]

The CHAIR: Make your point of order.

Mr. BRECKINRIDGE: The point of order I desire to make is for the Chair to decide whether the discussion on the merits of the candidates is in order; if so, whether other gentlemen can be heard besides the gentleman from New York; whether it shall be an open discussion for other gentlemen who choose to enter into it to take part in it. That is all I want. [Cries of "Kelly."] Is the point well taken?

Mr. KELLY: I believe I have the floor, Mr. Chairman, and in view—

The CHAIRMAN (to Mr. Breckinridge): You can be heard in reply.

Mr. KELLY: I believe that in view of the election that will take place in October next in Indiana and Ohio, that if that nomination were given to the Western people, we could save one or both of those States. [Cheers.] I believe, Mr. Chairman, that if you are beaten in those two States it is an utter impossibility to save New York. [Cheers and "That's so."] You gave the nomination for the Presidency in 1864 to the State of New Jersey, to a gentleman who did this country good service in the late war. The gentleman's connection was equally as great in the State of New York as it was in New Jersey. Now, gentlemen, you will recollect that that candidate was beaten. In 1868 you also favored New York's gallant son, Horatio Seymour, a man who is respected from Maine to California, wherever his name is mentioned; one whose long identity with the Democratic party makes him, in the mouths of the followers of that party, a household word. Again, in 1872, you gave the nomination to another New York gentleman. Both of these candidates were beaten, and you will recollect that in both and in all three cases the States of Indiana and Ohio were lost. Now you propose to repeat the errors that have been committed for the last twelve years [cheers] by again taking another New York man. ["No!" "No!"] It might appear to this Convention that I was only present here opposing Mr. Tilden's nomination. [A spectator in the gallery here proposed three cheers for Tilden.]

A DELEGATE: I rise to a point of order and ask that the Sergeant-at-Arms be instructed to expel the man who proposed the three cheers for Tilden. [Great confusion, and cries of "Put him out!" "No!" "No!"]

Several delegates rose to their feet and pointed to the man referred to, requesting Mr. Able, the Sergeant-at-Arms, to expel him, while others shouted "No!" "No!"

The Sergeant-at-Arms admonished the gentleman, but did not remove him.

Mr. KELLY: Members of this Convention, do not be guided by your passions, but by your reason; for if you are beaten in the coming canvass, it is the end, in my opinion, of the Democratic party. [Applause.] I believe sincerely that it will also result in the destruction of our Government. Isn't it, then, your duty to act cautiously and prudently? Do not be carried away by any affection that you may have for Samuel J. Tilden in this Convention. You may have cause to regret his nomination when you have made it, if you do make it. [Cries of "Tilden" and great confusion.] I was going to say that there are now sitting there in that New York delegation a very respectable minority who agree with me that it would be a fatal policy for the Democratic party to pursue at this time. [Renewed confusion.] Their mouths are stifled, their tongues are closed within their mouths. They can say nothing here in view of the action that was taken by a majority of that delegation. If they were allowed to speak here they would tell you that, sitting directly in front of me, there are seventeen delegates who are opposed to Mr. Tilden's nomination [applause;] not on personal or political grounds; not in malice; not in anything which would characterize our opinion as against our judgment, but because they believe in their hearts and souls that if this Convention nominate Mr. Tilden as their candidate for the Presidency they will regret it—[the last part of the sentence was lost in the confusion.] Mr. Chairman, I, as a member of that delegation, on the part of myself and them, protest against his nomination because we know and feel that disaster would come upon our great party if that thing be done. [Cries of "Time!"] Mr. Chairman, I hope that this Convention will reason upon this matter in cool judgment. I hope that they will look upon it as sensible men. Recollect what I have already said to the members of this Convention, that if we are beaten in the West in October, undoubtedly we will be beaten in the East.

Now, in conclusion, I thank the members of this Convention for the hearing they have given me. One word more, I warn you to recollect the words I have said—[the confusion and applause drowned the last part of the sentence.]

Mr. DOOLITTLE: By one of the rules of this house, I understand that persons upon the floor who are not members of the Convention, or in the gallery, if they make disturbance to interrupt a speaker, are out of order, and would be liable to be expelled from the chamber. I ask the President if that is the rule?

The CHAIR: The Chair would respond that such persons are not only out of order and liable to be removed, but I direct the Sergeant-at-Arms to remove them promptly. The Sergeant at-Arms finding any persons making any disturbance inside the chamber, is instructed to remove them from the hall. And I have further to say, and that will interest many, that the National Executive Committee are now considering the question, and that very seriously, whether they will issue any tickets to-morrow except to members of the Convention.

A DELEGATE: I have a point of order. There are several other gentlemen to be nominated in this Convention as candidates for President. Is it in order for any gentleman to rise on this floor to second that nomination, and thereby disparage the nominee, as has been done here?

The CHAIR: The Chair would respond that if the gentleman will read carefully the resolution which was adopted, he will find that it contains no such restriction.

THE CALL OF STATES CONTINUED.

Mr. FLOURNOY, of Virginia: Mr. President and gentlemen of the Convention—Virginia is not here in my person to disparage or to say aught against either of the distinguished men who are named in connection with the Presidency of the United States. As representing the Democratic party, Virginia desires, and the interest it takes in this great movement is, to place a tried, true and honest Democrat at the head of the government of these United States [applause]; and whoever this grand Convention, assembled from the North, from the South, from the East, from the West, shall name as its choice for President, will receive in November the vote of old

Virginia. We came here, our delegates, to inquire who it was that would most likely carry the majority of the electoral votes of the United States, and came here for the purpose and the determination to support the man that the Convention, in its wisdom, named and placed before the country. But, gentlemen, we have our opinions; and after an examination of the whole field, according to our best capacity, we have come to the conclusion that that wise, true, earnest, practical and successful reformer, Samuel J. Tilden, is the man. [Cheers.] I listened to-day to the reading of our platform with infinite interest and pleasure, and all through it, from the beginning to the end, rang reform! reform! reform! and honest constitutional administration of the government. [Cheers.] And it would seem to us, sir, that in this great movement of reform and the restoration of an honest constitutional administration of the government—that in moving to reform and leaving Samuel J. Tilden out, would be to act Hamlet with Hamlet out. [Laughter and applause.] The responsibility that is upon us who are assembled here is great almost beyond conception. In travelling from my home here I came across the whole of the original territory of the United States in 1776. The Mississippi river was its boundary. I stand now upon the western bank of the Father of Waters, in this grand city, with its half million of population, and in my mind's eye I look across to the Pacific, and this great country of ours is washed by the Pacific ocean. I look back to its early days and to the three millions of people. Now there are forty millions. The first century of our existence has passed away, and its trials and its triumphs have become historical; and the only humiliation we have at the end of the first century of our existence is that we find this government, grown as it has in population, spread as it has in territory, in the hands and in the possession of the spoiler. It is our duty to wrest it from the hands of the spoiler. It is our duty to snatch it from them and to place it in the hands of true, tried and honest men, who will bring the reform that we hear of in New York to Washington City, and spread its benign influences over all this land. And then, commencing the new century of our existence, we may see a country put upon a new track of honesty and constitutional administration that will give it a lease of life for ages yet to come; and, as it grows in power, as it increases in wealth and population, as it increases in territory, let its honest administration send forth a voice to the nations of the earth, and let the sons of liberty keep on in their struggle for a free government, and then let us make this country of ours the light-house of liberty to the world [cries of "Time! time!"]; and, sir, may this great Union endure until the last syllable of recorded time. [Cheers.]

Mr. HERNDON, of Texas: Mr. President and gentlemen of the Convention—In behalf of the Democratic State of Texas, occupying the most southwestern part of this Union—a State that once bore the burdens of the war to enjoy the smiles of peace as an independent sovereign power; a State that comes here with the States of this Union because she loved the system of government enjoyed by them, because she loved union and loved peace as she does to-day; a State whose people having once espoused a cause never faltered in its support—the people of that State have directed me, upon this occasion, in behalf of the Democracy, to second the nomination of Samuel J. Tilden, of New York [cheers], a statesman who stands in the first rank, who has inaugurated a policy in the great State of New York, that has borne the fruit of retrenchment, reform and honest government. [Cheers.] That policy which he has inaugurated has exercised an influence that has been felt all over this Union. It has pervaded the rank and file of the Democracy in every State, in every part of this great government, and his nomination upon the platform which you have adopted is a guarantee of success in November next. [Cheers.] We do not, in seconding this nomination, disparage the character, Democracy or statesmanship and ability of the gentlemen who have already been nominated, or who may hereafter be nominated. We profoundly respect them all, and although the gentleman whose nomination we now second may not be the successful candidate before this Convention, we will pledge our undivided support to whoever you may nominate. [Cheers.]

But I say to you that if you do place Samuel J. Tilden upon your platform, as the bearer of your standard, that for the State of Texas we pledge to you one hundred thousand majority in November next.

North Carolina was then called and there was no response.

NOMINATION OF HON. WM. ALLEN.

Ohio being next called, Mr. Ewing took the platform and said:

Gentlemen, a few moments ago a duty which had been assigned to another member of the delegation of my State, and which he was unexpectedly unable to perform, was assigned to me, of presenting from Ohio the name of one of our purest, best and most beloved citizens, and former statesman, William Allen [cheers,] the compeer of Webster, Clay, Benton and Wright. He brings from that earlier and better day of the republic, traditions and the spirit of personal and official purity which the times demand; and now, with a ripe and varied culture, a store of information, a clearness and vigor of intellect such as few able young men possess, he is one of the typical Democrats of the Western States. He is a Democrat at heart, a lover of the people, and beloved by the people. Never in the whole course of his official career has he forgotten that the Democratic party is the special representative and defender of the toiling masses against the exactions of the watchful, idle and rapacious few. His name would be a platform. His name would be a vast deal which the people of the Western States will be grieved to find left out of the platform of the Convention.

It would mean hostility to the whole series of finance measures of the Republican party, by which they have enormously increased the public burdens and enormously enriched that bonded aristocracy which has grown up out of the war. [Applause.] It would mean hostility to the act of 1873, by which, furtively, without a word of debate, the old standard silver dollar—which was made the standard of value by the act of George Washington of 1790, and which was the unit of measures and the legal tender for all amounts, however large, until 1873—was stricken out of the coinage laws, in order that the owners of the public debt might claim payment in a currency worth ten per cent. more than that standard dollar [applause], in order that the people of the United States should pay ten per cent. more to the gentlemen who get our bonds at fifty and sixty cents on the dollar, than they were entitled to by the very law in force under which the bonds were issued. [Applause.] His nomination would mean the absolute, immediate and unconditional repeal of the Republican resumption law. If it should be the pleasure of the Convention—which, of course, we are not very sanguine of [laughter]—to select him as its standard-bearer, and if those States are considered of any value in the impending contest, I may commend him to you by the statement that he would sweep them both (Ohio and Indiana) by a whirlwind of majority. [Great applause.]

NOMINATION OF GEN. HANCOCK.

The Secretary called the State of Pennsylvania.

Mr. WALLACE: Pennsylvania has a candidate by whom she means to stand. His name and his claims will be presented by the Hon. Mr. Clymer and two other gentlemen.

Mr. Clymer was introduced by the President, and said:

MR. PRESIDENT AND GENTLEMEN OF THE CONVENTION: I am charged by the delegation from the State of Pennsylvania, representing 325,000 Democrats, to present in their name, and by their authority, as their unanimous choice for the highest elective office on earth, the name of one born on their soil and dear to their hearts; the name of one whose character is the embodiment of all that is chivalrous in manhood and excellent in morals; the name of one who never drew his sword save in defence of his country's honor, or in obedience to her laws [applause]; the name of one who, in the hour of supreme victory, never forgot a common brotherhood; the name of one who, although the very exemplar of grim-visaged war, is yet the sincerest and lowliest devotee of the Constitution and the law; the name of one who, in the plenitude of military power, when dishonored, dismembered and dismantled States were placed in his absolute sway, declared that the liberty of the press, the habeas corpus, the right of trial by jury, the right of persons and of property must be maintained; the name of one whose fame and reputation are true to every American citizen of whatever race or color, party or creed—the name of Winfield Scott Hancock. [Loud cheers.]

We present it to you as the very shibboleth of victory. No man may doubt his honor; no man will dare to question his integrity. About him closes the affection of tens of thousands of men who sat with him by the camp-fire, who have gone with him through the shadow of death, and whom he has led into the clear sunlight of victory. And there are other tens of thousands who have never met him, save as foeman in battle-array, amid the roar of cannon and the blood and carnage of civil strife, who yet never breathe his name save in honor, and to whom he is endeared by his kindness, his justice, his mercy, and by his devotion to the Constitution and the law. His past record is his pledge for the future; we point to it with pride and rely upon it with unshaken faith. Standing here upon the banks of this mighty river, in this imperial centre, we ask the brethren from all the sections of the republic to unite with us in proclaiming him our nominee. [Applause.] His is no sectional fame; his will be no sectional support, and his will be no partisan victory. Good men everywhere, men who are devoted to the Constitution and the law, men who denounce fraud and corruption, men who are determined to give to the people of all the States the inestimable boon of home-rule and self-government, men who are determined to drive out from high places the thieves who have fattened upon the ill-gotten gains wrenched from citizen and soldier alike, men who are opposed to the infamous and corrupt military systems by which want, misery, suffering and almost universal bankruptcy are brought upon this land, will unite with us upon this son of ours [cheers]; and if they so unite, who may doubt the result?

Mr. Chairman, once in his career—history will record it as a fact—he saved his State, and through her the union of these States, at Gettysburg. If you nominate him in this Convention, history will record another fact, that he will rescue his State in November next, [cheers], and thus rescue the Federal Government from the degradation and misrule which now curses it. [Applause.]

Gen. Brent then appeared on the rostrum and addressed the Convention as follows:

MR. PRESIDENT AND GENTLEMEN OF THE CONVENTION: I would not have ventured to trouble this Convention if the delegation of the great State of Pennsylvania had not expressed their wish that something should be said in behalf of and in relation to their favorite son, who, in the State of Louisiana, made a civil record while he was exercising powers and functions not exceeded by any governor or government except that of the Sultan of Turkey or the Shah of Persia, and which government he exercised in the same spirit that George Washington, the father of his country, exhibited when, the war of the revolution being terminated, he sheathed his sword and delivered his commission to the civil authorities of the country. [Applause.] Therefore, gentlemen, human gratitude would be but an expression if a son of Louisiana should hear the name of Winfield Scott Hancock mentioned. We, in Louisiana and in the South, know Gen. Hancock as the great Union winner in war and in peace. [Cheers.] Along the fateful heights of Gettysburg, in the dark thickets of the Wilderness, we knew him standing in the van and fore front of the late war as the champion and embodiment of Columbia *victrix et benevolens*; and when peace came, and over this broad republic no flag was seen but the flag of our common country, we recognize him again as the representative of Columbia *victrix et benevolens* [cheers,] declaring to ten millions of his fellow-citizens that there still remain to them the civil birth-right and inheritance of the fathers—habeas corpus, trial by jury, protection to property in due course of law. Therefore, gentlemen, he has won us to the Union twice—by arms and in peace—and I cannot but think that the prosperity and safety of the country will be assured by him who has been illustrious in war and wise and generous in peace. [Cheers.]

Mr. SEXTON, of Texas: Mr. President and gentlemen—I come from a far-off State of this Union, and on the extreme Southwestern border, and I feel it my duty to say, and it is my pleasure to say, that there are a very considerable number of the people of that State who entertain the opinion that Pennsylvania's distinguished son, Gen. Winfield S. Hancock [cheers], is a pure patriot and a distinguished statesman, endowed by nature and by cultivation with ability and intelligence fully equal to discharge the high and responsible duties of President of the United States. [Cheers.] I should not have felt it my duty to say this much had I not been invited by the Pennsylvania delegation, and also because, while a very large majority of my fellow-delegates who represent the State of Texas entertain the opinion that another distinguished gentleman is the most available candidate whom we can present at this time for the consideration of the American people, there are a considerable number in Texas who think that Gen. Hancock is that man. [Cheers.] It is just and right to them, and to the sentiment which I represent for them, that this should be made known, and for the discharge of this duty I appear before you.

I have simply to say, as was said by the gentleman from Louisiana, that the ability of Gen. Hancock as a statesman has been tried in Texas by the severest of all ordeals—the ordeal of experience. It gives me pleasure to say this much, and to say if Gen. Hancock should be nominated by this Convention he will receive a most enthusiastic support. I know I speak the sentiment of Texas when I say this—that he will receive a most enthusiastic support from the whole of Texas. [Cheers.]

But, like my colleague who addressed you, I say further, that whoever may be nominated of the distinguished gentlemen whose names have been presented before you, you need have no doubt about the majority in Texas. We have 10,000 Democratic votes to give to the nominee of this Convention, and we only ask that those of you who come from the older and the greater States of this Union will present us a man who will be sure to win us success in November. [Cheers.]

After Wisconsin was called, Mr. Smith, of Wisconsin, said:

I was busy at the moment, and did not hear the name of Wisconsin called. As chairman of the delegation I have a word—only a word—to say, and I suppose I may say it, though we have not a candidate for President of the United States living within our borders, and what I wish to say—

A DELEGATE: I rise to a point of order.

MR. SMITH: No, sir, there is no point of order about it; what I shall say will have the merit of being the last that can be said upon the subject of nominations before this Convention, and if there is another gentleman in this assemblage who wants to call for order, let him do it now. If not, let him hold his peace for two minutes. Sir,

I represent a State—I represent, with my colleagues, a State in the valley of the great Mississippi river. bounded on the west by the Mississippi, the fifteenth State in point of population in these United States, and I knew it when it hadn't 20,000 people in it. We are not New York, but we are a colony of New York and of Germany [cheers] and of Ireland as well. The New Yorkers in Wisconsin, and the Germans in Wisconsin, and the Irishmen in Wisconsin, and the old Democratic voters who have stood by the Union and the flag of the Union and the Constitution, have instructed me to second the nomination of Samuel J. Tilden. [Cheers.] One other word and I have done. Not because we do not appreciate the high character of every one of the distinguished names that have been mentioned here —every one of whom I have the honor personally to know—and one or two equally distinguished who have not been mentioned at all; but it is because we believe that opportunity has enabled Samuel J. Tilden to rise like the great oak in the forest upon this forest of men. [Applause.] He can carry the State of Wisconsin; and if any man can carry the State of Wisconsin, he ought to carry any other State in this Union. [Applause and laughter.] Sir, we have suffered in common with the rest of the Democrats of this nation until we cannot tolerate this bickering about men; and I simply say here, that I do not like to see New York men come here, after the question was settled, and wash their dirty linen—[the rest of the sentence was inaudible, owing to the applause] I do not mean to say, Mr. President, that I have any opposition to these men personally, for I know that when men meet in National Convention they act just about as they do in County or State Conventions; but we go for Tilden because Mr Tilden has proved to the people of this country that he has ability, that he has courage, and that he has the power to crush corruption and corruptionists. [Great applause.]

Mr. DOOLITTLE: Gentlemen of the Convention, I agree with the chairman of our delegation that in the next election I believe we can carry Wisconsin for any one of the candidates who have been named in this Convention. [Applause.] But I am here to say but a single word. All the gentlemen named are my personal friends, and have been for many, many years; and I feel it now to be one of the most delicate and responsible duties that I have ever been called upon to perform, to state my views where it has to affect, so far as the views are worth anything, a question between friends. Mr. Tilden, of New York, and myself were associated many years ago in the Democratic party. With Mr. Hendricks, of Indiana, I have been associated for years, side by side in the Senate. I know both of them to be great men, able men, distinguished men. I know from sitting by the side of Mr. Hendricks that he is a perfectly honest, upright, able statesman, standing in the foremost rank of the statesmen of the United States. [Applause.] I have been through nine Presidential campaigns; I have been in five, aye six, National Conventions to nominate Presidents; and with all the experience that I have had in fighting one long political fight, I may say of thirty years—sometimes fighting with the Democratic party, when I believed it was right, and against it when I believed it was wrong; sometimes fighting with the Republican party, when I believed it right, and against it when I believed it wrong—knowing, as I believe I do, both the great parties of this country, inside and out, through and through, I believe that he have never yet, and no party has ever yet, been able to carry the Presidential election without carrying either one or two of the great central States of Pennsylvania, Ohio or Indiana. And, gentlemen, looking beyond this Convention coolly, planting now and here the campaign which we are to fight elsewhere—not in the excitement of the moment, not in the excitement of the hotels, not in the excitement of personal aspirations, but with that cool judgment with which a general lays down the campaign of a battle—I tell you that I do not believe you can carry even New York in November without carrying Indiana or Ohio in October. [Cheers.]

It does not depend upon us here; the battle would be already won; but there are millions of voters outside of St. Louis who are to have a voice in deciding this result; and I tell you that I know that it is in the platform which you shall form here, and the candidates that you nominate, upon which depends the question whether you can or not carry Indiana or Ohio or Pennsylvania in the October elections. Now, fellow-citizens, it is simply for that reason and no other that I believe—I feel assured—Mr. Hendricks will carry Indiana. [Applause.] And I say I am not sure that Mr. Tilden can carry Indiana. I am inclined to think he cannot. Now, judging from that alone, and upon that question alone, and because I love my country, and believe that now the only means of rescuing it is that the Democratic party should have a victory in November, that I give my preference to Mr. Hendricks, of Indiana. [Loud applause.] If these cheers would only elect a man, I would like to hear you cheer. What I want is: I want your votes, I want your judgment, I want your good sense, I want you to look over the field of battle. Understand me; I do not say that Gen. Hancock, of Pennsylvania, might not carry Indiana [applause]; I do not say that Mr. Parker, of New Jersey, would not carry Indiana [applause]. In relation to the candidates that are named, gentlemen, I wish the one who can carry the central States; and I tell you that whatever Democrat we nominate that will carry Indiana in the October election will carry New York in November. [Cheers.]

The Secretary then called the roll of the States for the first ballot, with the following result:

FIRST BALLOT.

STATES AND TERRITORIES.	TILDEN.	ALLEN.	THURMAN.	HENDRICKS.	BAYARD.	PARKER.	HANCOCK.	BROADHEAD.
Alabama	13	..	..	5	..	..	2	..
Arkansas	12	..	..	..	..	..	..	..
California	12	..	..	..	..	..	..	..
Colorado	..	..	..	6	..	..	..	..
Connecticut	12	..	..	..	..	..	..	..
Delaware	..	..	..	..	6	..	..	..
Florida	8	..	..	..	..	..	..	..
Georgia	5	..	..	..	16	..	1	..
Illinois	19	..	..	23	..	..	..	..
Indiana	..	..	..	30	..	..	..	..
Iowa	14	..	..	6	..	..	2	..
Kansas	..	..	..	10	..	..	..	..
Kentucky	24	..	..	..	..	..	..	..
Louisiana	9	..	..	..	2	..	5	..
Maine	14	..	..	..	..	..	..	..
Maryland	11	..	..	3	2	..	..	..
Massachusetts	26	..	..	..	..	..	..	..
Michigan	14	..	..	8	..	..	..	..
Minnesota	10	..	..	..	..	..	..	..
Mississippi	16	..	..	..	..	..	..	..
Missouri	..	..	..	14	..	..	..	16
Nebraska	6	..	..	..	..	..	..	..
Nevada	3	..	3	3	..	..	..	..
New Hampshire	10	..	..	..	..	..	..	..
New Jersey	..	..	..	..	..	18	..	..
New York	70	..	..	..	..	..	..	..
North Carolina	9	..	..	4	2	..	5	..
Ohio	..	44	..	..	..	..	..	..
Oregon	6	..	..	..	..	..	..	..
Pennsylvania	..	..	..	..	..	..	58	..
Rhode Island	8	..	..	..	..	..	..	..
South Carolina	14	..	..	..	..	..	..	..
Tennessee	..	..	..	24	..	..	..	..
Texas	10½	..	..	2½	1	..	2	..
Vermont	10	..	..	..	..	..	..	..
Virginia	17	..	..	1	4	..	..	..
West Virginia	..	10	..	..	..	..	..	..
Wisconsin	19	..	..	1	..	..	..	..
Total	404½	54	3	140½	33	18	75	16

Necessary to a choice 492

Mr. HUTCHINS, of Missouri: I desire to ask, on behalf of a portion of the Missouri delegation, if it is in order for that delegation to change its vote before the vote is announced? [Cries of "No, no!" and "Yes!"]

The CHAIR: The Chair rules that it is in order.

Mr. HUTCHINS: Well, we desire time in which to consult, in order to change our vote. Missouri asks to withdraw for five minutes in order to have a consultation.

The CHAIR: Missouri has leave to withdraw for consultation. [Cries of "No, no!" and confusion.]

Senator WALLACE, of Pennsylvania: I rise to a point of order. The only business in order is the announcement of the vote.

The CHAIR: The vote is not made up. The Chair rules that it is within the power and privilege of the Missouri delegation to withdraw for five minutes.

Mr. WALLACE: Then it follows that we may stay here all night.

The CHAIR: It is for the Convention to determine that.

A DELEGATE from Indiana: I move that when the vote is announced the Convention adjourn. [Cries of "No, no!"]

After consultation, Gen. Doniphan, of Missouri, announced that "Missouri changes her vote to sixteen for Tilden and fourteen for Hendricks." [Cheers.]

The CHAIR: The Clerk will announce the vote. Let there be attention.

The CLERK: Gentlemen, I would like to have quiet, if possible.

Whole number of votes cast.......... 738
Necessary to a choice.......... 492
S. J. Tilden received.......... 417½

[Cheers loud and long.]

Thos. A. Hendricks.......... 140½

[Slight cheering.]

Bayard.......... 33
Allen.......... 56
Hancock.......... 75

[A cheer.]

Parker.......... 18

The CHAIR: Gentlemen of the Convention, no one candidate having received two-thirds of the votes cast, no candidate is nominated. Let the roll be called again.

A DELEGATE: I move that the Convention adjourn.

The motion was not entertained by the Chair, and the Clerk proceeded to call the roll.

The roll was called with the following result:

SECOND BALLOT.

STATES AND TERRITORIES.	ALLEN.	TILDEN.	BAYARD.	HANCOCK.	HENDRICKS.	THURMAN.
Alabama	..	20	..	..	..	..
Arkansas	..	12	..	..	..	..
California	..	12	..	..	..	..
Colorado	..	6	..	..	..	..
Connecticut	..	12	..	..	..	..
Delaware	..	6	..	..	..	..
Florida	..	8	..	..	..	..
Georgia	..	22	..	..	..	..
Illinois	..	26	..	..	16	..
Indiana	..	..	..	..	30	..
Iowa	..	22	..	..	..	..
Kansas	..	2	..	..	8	..
Kentucky	..	24	..	..	..	..
Louisiana	..	16	..	..	..	..
Maine	..	14	..	..	..	..
Maryland	..	14	..	..	2	..
Massachusetts	..	26	..	..	..	..
Michigan	..	19	..	..	3	..
Minnesota	..	10	..	..	..	..
Mississippi	..	16	..	..	..	..
Missouri	..	30	..	..	..	..
Nebraska	..	6	..	..	..	..
Nevada	..	4	..	..	..	2
New Hampshire	..	10	..	..	..	..
New Jersey	..	18	..	..	..	..
New York	..	70	..	..	..	..
North Carolina	..	20	..	..	..	..
Ohio	44	..	..	..	..	..
Oregon	..	6	..	..	..	..
Pennsylvania	..	..	..	58	..	..
Rhode Island	..	8	..	..	..	..
South Carolina	..	14	..	..	..	..
Tennessee	..	..	..	..	24	..
Texas	..	16	..	..	..	..
Vermont	..	10	..	..	..	..
Virginia	..	17	4	..	1	..
West Virginia	10	..	..	..	..	..
Wisconsin	..	19	..	..	1	..
Total	54	535	4	58	85	2

Necessary to a choice.. 492

The announcement that Alabama cast her votes solid for Tilden was greeted with great applause.

The CHAIRMAN of the Colorado delegation: We think that the man receiving the majority of this Convention should receive our votes; we therefore change our vote from Hendricks to Tilden. [Great applause.]

Michigan asked to be passed, and was passed.

The CHAIRMAN of the New Jersey delegation: I ask to be passed for a moment, as the delegates desire to consult. The vote of New Jersey was to be cast for her distinguished son, and that we have done; we have had no consultation as to how we should cast our vote on the second ballot; therefore we ask to be passed.

Leave was granted.

New Jersey being called, the Chairman of the delegation announced eighteen votes for Joel Parker.

Mr. STOCKTON: There is no resolution of the delegation that affects the vote further than that the first ballot was to be cast for Joel Parker, with a direct understanding that even upon that, if it was insisted upon by the delegates, they had the right to cast their individual vote even then. It was not under any circumstances to extend further than the first ballot, and there are six of us who claim now the right to cast our individual votes for Samuel J. Tilden, of New York.

Mr. ABBOTT, of New Jersey: If I understand the rules of this Convention, it is for the chairman and the chairman alone in each delegation to announce what is the action of the delegation. And I say that the resolution passed by that delegation was that the chairman of the delegation cast the entire vote of New Jersey for Joel Parker and urge his nomination. I say it was not confined to one ballot or any number of ballots, and until there is a meeting of the delegation to rescind that rule I am bound by it to announce the vote, and I say here to-day that the entire people of the State of New Jersey want him, and these six gentlemen do not represent him.

Mr. STOCKTON: I rise and ask privilege for the New Jersey delegation to retire. I state to this Convention that the words of the resolution passed by our delegation, as stated by the chairman, permit each individual delegate to vote as he sees fit. With a respect for Gov. Parker, and an affection for him not exceeded by the chairman of this delegation — with such a respect for Gov. Parker, I believe that he desires the success of the Democratic party in the coming campaign. I feel it my duty to retire and have a meeting of this delegation, for the purpose of having properly recorded the votes of those gentlemen who agree with me, that to keep the vote which is manifest to the whole Convention, is nothing but a compliment, is not to help Gov. Parker, but to prevent, as far as our small vote does, a union of this Convention upon a candidate who could be selected.

Mr. ABBOTT: When the Senator asked to retire it is not the delegation. The delegation does not ask leave to retire. But I will say this, that so far as the success of the Democratic party is concerned, no man in New Jersey wants it better than Joel G. Parker; but knowing, as I do, the feeling of the people of that State, that they will support the nominee of this Convention, no matter who he is, I know this, that they would feel that it was treacherous to desert him at this hour in order to elect another man.

Mr. BRECKINRIDGE, of Kentucky: I rise to a point of order. Let these gentlemen settle their difficulties in their own committee-room, not here.

The CHAIR: The point of order is well taken. New Jersey casts 18 votes for Joel Parker.

Mr. FINCH, of Iowa: The Iowa delegation desire to change their vote to 20 for Tilden and 2 for Hancock. [Cheers.]

Mr. ALLEN, of Illinois: Illinois casts 24 votes for Tilden and 18 for Hendricks.

Gov. WOODSON, of Missouri: Missouri desires to change her vote to 20 votes for Samuel J. Tilden and 10 for Mr. Hendricks.

Mr. HARMON, of Virginia: Uninstructed West Virginia comes, and I appeal to this Convention, and the gentlemen of that delegation agree with me, that the vote of each delegate should be cast for himself. [Cries of "No!" "No!"] I demand my rights on this floor. I claim that the chairman is doing everything in violation of his right in casting my vote, and I insist upon it that he has no right to cast my vote. [Cries of "Sit down!" and confusion.]

The CHAIR. The gentleman from Virginia is out of order.

A DELEGATE from Virginia: I claim that the gentlemen of that delegation agreed that each member should cast his own vote. I ask, therefore, that we be heard. [Great confusion.]

The CHAIRMAN of the Nevada delegation: By authority of the Nevada delegation I am instructed to cast the entire vote of that State for Samuel J. Tilden. [Cheers.]

The CHAIR: Iowa casts 22 votes for Tilden solid.

Mr. ALLEN, of Illinois: Illinois casts 16 votes for Thomas A. Hendricks and 26 votes for Samuel J. Tilden.

Mr. HUTCHINS, of Missouri: Missouri wants to make a change, Mr. Chairman.

Mr. DONIPHAN, of Missouri: Missouri casts 28 votes for Tilden.

This announcement was greeted with great cheering, which finally culminated in the delegates and spectators rising and standing upon chairs and tables, throwing hats, fans and other articles into the air, continuing to cheer meantime with the most unbounded enthusiasm.

After quiet had been partially restored the Chairman called for Ohio. After the lapse of several minutes, during which there was general confusion, a delegate from Ohio, said, "Ohio wants to change her vote and casts 7 votes for Tilden." [Cheering.]

Another DELEGATE from Ohio: Mr. Chairman, we agreed to vote as a unit.

The DELEGATE first named: That is not so.

The second DELEGATE (excitedly): And there is no man in this delegation that has a right to cast the vote, save and except the chairman of this delegation. [Cheers.] They are bound to stand by their pledge.

The CHAIRMAN of the Texas delegation: The delegation from Texas will change its vote from 13 to 16 [cheering] for Samuel J. Tilden.

A DELEGATE from Missouri: I wish it distinctly understood by this Convention that there are five from the State of Missouri who do not vote for Tilden, but who still stand by Hendricks.

The CHAIR: The gentleman is out of order.

The same DELEGATE: Well, I only want to let you know, whether in or out of order.

The CHAIRMAN of the Louisiana delegation, when his State was called: Louisiana desires to change her vote. She votes for Tilden—all, except two are absent; but who, if present, would unite with us. [Three cheers for Louisiana.]

The CHAIR: The vote will now be announced.

Mr. WALLACE, of Pennsylvania: By order of my delegation I move to make the nomination of Mr. Tilden unanimous. [Applause and cries of "Announce the vote!"]

Mr. BELL, the Secretary: The whole number of votes cast—[cries of "Hush!" "Hush!"] 738. Necessary to a choice, 492. Of these Mr. Thurman received 2, Mr. Hancock 59, Bayard 11, Parker 18, Allen 54 [slight applause], Hendricks 60, Tilden 534. [Tremendous applause and cheers, which were kept up for several minutes.]

SEVERAL DELEGATES: I move to make the nomination unanimous.

THE NOMINATION MADE UNANIMOUS.

MR. WALLACE, of Pennsylvania: Pursuant to the order of the Pennsylvania delegation, I move to make the nomination of Mr. Tilden unanimous; and as the second State in the Union, although we should have preferred one born on our soil, still she will not slack one nerve nor weaken one effort for the success of the nominee of the Convention; and when the ides of November come, we feel assured that victory will crown our banner with success.

A DELEGATE from New Jersey: The New Jersey delegation desires to have the nomination of Mr. Tilden made unanimous. And I will tell the Convention this, that as we have stood by Joel Parker before this nomination was made, so, with the same energy and the same fire, we will stand by Samuel J. Tilden. [Loud cheers.] And although New Jersey has had no voice in the nominee, she will have nine votes in the Electoral College for Samuel J. Tilden.

A DELEGATE from Tennessee: In behalf of the delegation from Tennessee, whose votes have been cast against the voice of this Convention, Tennessee will give her electoral vote for Mr. Tilden.

A DELEGATE from Virginia: I am the man from Virginia who cast the one vote against Tilden. I move to make the nomination unanimous. I will take off my coat and work for him. [Loud cheers.]

The question was put, and Mr. Tilden was declared the unanimous choice of the Democratic party for President of the United States. [Tremendous applause.]

Mr. Paxton, of Ohio, moved that the Convention adjourn to 10 o'clock to-morrow morning.

The motion was carried and the Convention adjourned.

THIRD DAY.

ST. LOUIS, June 29th, 1876.

The Convention was called to order at 10:20 o'clock by the President, in the following words:

The Convention will please come to order. Gentlemen and delegates will please be seated. The Chair has the honor of presenting to the Convention Bishop Robertson, who will open the proceedings of the day with prayer.

THE PRAYER.

Let us pray. Almighty God, our Heavenly Father, the aid of those who need, the helper of those who flee to Thee for succor, we present ourselves before Thee now to implore Thy continued presence and blessing upon this vast assemblage, gathered from all parts of this land, to consult for the advancement of our liberties and for the continuance to us of good government. Our father's God and our God, we come to Thee as of old, to implore Thy preserving care still upon this land, whose infancy and sturdy youth Thou hast so greatly blessed. We would recall especially now in this anniversary year Thine abounding mercies, and our scant gratitude and unworthy use of them. May the greatness of Thy goodness quicken us to a national repentance; may the heavy hand of social and commercial adversity bring to us that wisdom and that recurrence to earlier virtues and principles which our years of prosperity did not accomplish. By Thy mighty hands stretched forth do Thou our Heavenly Father stay the progress of political vice and corruption; defeat the purposes of those who would use their trusts of government for schemes of personal advancement and emolument; give efficacy to the means adopted for thrusting from their misused offices those who have abused the confidence with which they were honored, and dishonored the offices with which they were invested. Respectfully do we ask Thy blessing upon the deliberations and further action of this Convention. May it remember that its highest office and wisdom will be to act in behalf of the enduring principles of which this great historical party has been evermore the representative, and for the people of whom it is but the servant and trustee. In all the consultations here, and in all the results hereafter, may the highest ends by the best means be sought. May those who act here be animated by a livelier memory of the worthies of the past whose places they now fill, and of the sacred traditions of the past, in whose light and by whose help they now work. May those older days, with their happy victories of peace, and of sound, constitutionally distributed authority and government, be more than fulfilled in our later times. Grant, too, our Heavenly Father, for the sake of the higher interests which are involved here, that moderation and a spirit of mutual conciliation may prevail. May personal prejudices yield to the common good. May the results which shall be reached here in the enunciation of great principles and in the choice of wise and worthy leaders supported and made effectual by labors after this body shall disperse, be greatly blessed in contributing to purify the state, to make permanent for our children and our children's children the blessed boon left us by the patriots of the past, of a pure, free constitutional government, with all the safeguards for political and civil morality, and with guarantees for religious liberty. All of which blessings, for ourselves, for our country, for our children, and for the generations yet to inhabit these broad lands, we ask of Thee, Almighty and merciful Father, for the sake of Thy Son Jesus Christ, our Lord and Saviour. Amen.

RATIFICATION.

Mr. WEBBER, of Michigan: Mr. President, I wish to offer a resolution.

The CHAIR: Will the gentleman from Michigan suspend for one moment until I make an announcement?

The SECRETARY: The chairmen of the delegations who have not sent to the Secretary a list of the names of delegates, with their post-office address, will please do so.

The CHAIR: Is it the pleasure of the Convention that dispatches addressed to its Chairman be read?

No objection being made, the Secretary read the following dispatches:

SEDALIA, MO.

To Gen. McClernand, President of the National Democratic Convention:

Sedalia fires one hundred guns for Tilden, and hoping Hendricks as Vice-President; and hurrah for Vest for Governor!

J. W. STEWART.

CINCINNATI, OHIO, June 28.

To Gen. McClernand, President of the National Democratic Convention:

Cincinnati nominated Hayes. Cincinnati has just fired two hundred guns on the approval of the platform and the nomination of Tilden.

(Signed) J. W. C. JOHNSON, *Mayor.*
ALEXANDER LAW,
H. C. BRECK,
JOHN E. DALE,
J. J. MILLER,
D. J. MALLORY,
And a hundred others.

JACKSON, MISS.

To Gen. E. C. Walthall, Chairman Mississippi Delegation:

The nomination of Tilden was received last night with great enthusiasm. One hundred guns fired pledges Mississippi to the Convention for the ticket by twenty-five thousand majority.

MOUNT VERNON, ILL.

To the President and Members of the National Democratic Convention:

Glory, hallelujah! at the good work you have done. The nomination of Tilden received with great enthusiasm.

MILWAUKEE, WIS.

To Hon. Alexander Mitchell:

The nomination of Tilden upon the platform adopted gives great satisfaction to all friends of reform.

WILLIAMS, *Daily News.*

GENEVA, N. Y.

To Senator Kernan:

The young Democracy indorses the choice of the Convention. Great enthusiasm over Tilden's nomination. [Applause.]

DETROIT, MICH.

To Hon. W. L. Webber, Chairman of the Michigan Delegation:

The nomination received at nine o'clock. All Detroit is out. Cannon, fireworks, music, cheers for Tilden.

NEWARK, N. J.

Great throng, fireworks, whole town in great enthusiasm. Essex club greets the New Jersey delegation and Tilden. [Applause.]

The SECRETARY: I cannot read it all.

A VOICE: All right, we understand the spirit. [Cheers.]

NEW YORK.

To Peter B. Olney, St. Louis, Lindell Hotel:

Tilden's nomination received with firing of guns and great enthusiasm.

WILLIS B. PAYNE. [Cheers.]

RICHMOND, VA.

To Judge John A. Meredith, Virginia Delegation:

The Conservative club sends their greeting of Tilden's nomination. [Cheers.]

PHILADELPHIA, June 28, 1876.

To the President of the National Democratic Convention:

We heartily congratulate the Convention on the wisdom of their work, and predict the ultimate triumph of the Democracy in November.

(Signed) THE AMERICAN CLUB,
Of Philadelphia.

NOMINATION FOR VICE-PRESIDENT.

The CHAIR: Gentlemen of the Convention, when the Covention adjourned last evening, it was proceeding in the execution of an order. Having nominated the Democratic candidate for President, under that order it remained for the Convention to proceed to nominate a candidate for Vice-President. That order remains now to be executed as the business in hand.

VOICES: Call the roll!

The Clerk proceeded with the roll-call, no State making a nomination until the call of Indiana, which was received with tumultuous cheers and waving of hats and handkerchiefs, and calls for "Hendricks."

The CHAIR: Come to order, gentlemen! Let us hear from Indiana.

Mr. DOOLITTLE: Mr. President—

The CHAIR: The gentleman from Wisconsin.

The CLERK: Indiana.

A DELEGATE: Mr. Chairman, the people of the Mississippi valley nominate Thomas A. Hendricks, of Indiana. [Cheers.]

Mr. McDONALD, of Indiana: Mr. Chairman, whenever we find ourselves brought face to face with a great responsibility, I know of no way of solving it, excepting we take counsel by our judgment and by our consciences. The mission of the delegation from Indiana in this Convention, so far at least as the name of Gov. Hendricks is concerned, was ended yesterday, when we had struggled from the time the canvass opened in this city until it closed last evening to place him before the country for the office which, as much as any man in all this broad land, he was qualified to fill. The Convention saw proper to decide otherwise, and so far as that decision is concerned we bow to the will of the Convention. [Cheers.] The Democracy of Indiana has never yet suffered its flag to trail in the dust; has never yet lowered its standard to the common enemy. Whether we shall be able to comply with the wishes of this large and most respectable assemblage of Democrats in what we may be able to do in our State in the coming election, is one of the questions of the future.

Mr. SLAYBACK, of Missouri: Mr. President, I rise to ask the gentleman a question— [Cries of "Object," "Sit down," &c.]

Mr. McDONALD: In the few words that I have to say—

The CHAIR: The gentleman is entitled to the floor.

Mr. McDONALD: I cannot admit of an interruption. Mr. President, I have already stated that the mission of the delegation of Indiana, so far as the name of Gov. Hendricks is concerned, ended on yesterday evening. We have no authority to say to this Convention that if it sees proper to place his name upon the ticket that he will accept it. Therefore, we do not propose to place ourselves in any false position upon that subject.

A DELEGATE: Illinois will.

Mr. McDONALD: When we say that, Mr. President, we do not say it because the office of Vice-President is beneath him. It has been held by men more distinguished than he, more known to history, and whose patriotism has illustrated some of the brightest pages of the history of our own party. For myself, Mr. President, I could only say that upon this question this Convention must take the responsibility— [Loud and prolonged cheering, and cries of "Hendricks," drowning all efforts on the part of the speaker to conclude his sentence.]

Mr. SPAUNHORST, of Missouri: Mr. President—

The CHAIR: Illinois has the floor.

Mr. SPAUNHORST: Mr. President, I ask that our distinguished citizen, ex-Gov. Woodson, of Missouri, be awarded the floor to respond to the call made in behalf of Mr. Hendricks. [Cheers, and cries of "Woodson."]

Mr. WOODSON, of Missouri: Mr. President, I feel extremely gratified on this occasion that we are told by the delegate from Indiana that the responsibility of placing Gov. Hendricks in nomination for the second office in the gift of the American people has devolved upon this Convention. [Cheers.] The Missouri delegation have instructed me, as the representative of this great State, to say that Missouri is a unit, and we believe the entire Democratic party of America will be a unit in the support of Tilden and Hendricks. [Cheers.] Gov. Hendricks has no truer friend from his own native State, or one who was willing to stand by him longer than I when his name was placed in nomination for the first office within the gift of this Convention, for I conceive that these offices are within the gift of this Convention. I stood by him, but, gentlemen, if I was disappointed in the realization of my expectation, if I felt my heart to weep for it, I this morning feel that I can rejoice when I remember that the distinguished reformer, the profound statesman, the honest man, Samuel J. Tilden, has been nominated by this Convention. [Applause.]

And now, gentlemen, let me say this: Place Samuel J. Tilden upon the ticket first, Thos. A. Hendricks next [applause], and then inscribe upon your banner under those names retrenchment and reform, honest administration, and from Maine to California our flag will float in triumph in November next. [Great applause.] I second the nomination of Gov. Hendricks. [Applause.]

Mr. WALLACE, of Pennsylvania: The Pennsylvania delegation (in obedience to the willingness of Indiana that this Convention take the responsibility of nominating Mr. Hendricks) give their support to that gentleman. [Great applause.] With the Governor of New York, Tilden, for President, and Hendricks, the Democratic Governor of Indiana, for Vice-President upon this ticket we will be triumphant in November. [Applause.] I arise, sir, to move that this Convention by acclamation declare Thos. A. Hendricks the nominee of this Convention for Vice-President of the United States. [Great applause and waving of hats, and cheers.]

Mr. STEADMAN, of Ohio: The delegation from the State of Ohio had thought of offering the name of one of her distinguished sons for Vice-President of the United States—the Hon. Henry B. Payne. We, however, decline to present his name, and second the nomination of Thos. A. Hendricks. [Applause.]

Gov. HARDIN, of Missouri: I send up a resolution to the Secretary, which I desire to have read.

The CHAIR: It is out of order, the question being upon the nomination. If the gentleman has anything to say upon that he will be in order.

GOV. HARDIN: I ask common consent to have the resolution read. [Cries of "Read! read!"]

The Secretary read as follows:

Resolved, That it is the duty of this Convention to select for Vice-President one who is the peer of him who has been nominated for the Presidency [applause]; and believing that Hon. Thos. A. Hendricks [great applause], of Indiana, is the full measure of this position, and also that in our judgment it is his duty to serve his country and his party in this position if nominated and elected, we therefore nominate him unanimously for that office.

A DELEGATE from Virginia: As the only man in the Virginia delegation who voted for Hendricks, from my district, I second the nomination of Indiana's distinguished son.

Gov. BROWN, of Tennessee: The delegation from Tennessee have from the beginning supported Thos. A. Hendricks for the first position upon this ticket. The Convention saw fit to choose another. We not only bow to that choice, but we pledge Tennessee to a majority for that selection of fifty thousand votes in November. But to enable us to do it we ask this Convention, by acclamation, to put upon that ticket, as the second choice of this Convention, Thos. A. Hendricks, of Indiana. [Loud applause.]

Mr. WALLACE, of Pennsylvania: I move that the rules be suspended, the call of the roll of States be suspended, and the vote taken by acclamation.

Gov. BROWN, of Tennessee: I second the motion.

The CHAIR: There is objection on the right. The call will proceed.

Mr. WALLACE: I move a suspension of the order of business, and I demand a vote upon that, in order that Thomas A. Hendricks may be nominated by acclamation. The motion is in order.

The CHAIR: I think the quickest way to reach the result will be to go on with the call.

Mr. ABBOTT, of New Jersey: I renew the motion of Senator Wallace, of Pennsylvania, that the rules be suspended, and that we vote by acclamation for the nomination of Thomas A. Hendricks. I will tell this Convention why. Thomas A. Hendricks is not the property of Indiana—he is the property of the Democracy of the United States. [Cheers.] Governor Hendricks—

The CHAIR: The gentleman from New Jersey will come to order. Senator Doolittle has the floor.

Mr. ABBOTT: I understood the gentleman recognized the gentleman from New Jersey. Am I correct?

The CHAIR: I recognized this gentleman on the right (Mr. Doolittle) first.

Mr. DOOLITTLE: Let me say to my friend—

Mr. ABBOTT: It is for the Chairman of the Convention to say whether I have the floor or not. I shall finish in a very few words. But I say there is no Democrat in the land that can refuse the nomination of the National Convention, and Thomas A. Hendricks, magnificent man as he is, would as soon think of committing suicide as to refuse the wish of the entire Democracy of the land. [Applause.] The Democracy of the country will do all they can for success, and as his name seems to be the choice of the country, I say to the Democracy of Indiana, you have no right to raise your voice against it, when the entire people of this Union want it; and I therefore insist upon the motion made by the Senator from Pennsylvania (Senator Wallace). [Cheers.]

The CHAIR: The question is upon the motion to dispense with the call of the roll upon the ballot for Vice-President.

The motion was lost, and the Secretary called the roll of the States on the ballot for the nomination of a candidate for the Vice-Presidency, with the following result:

BALLOT FOR VICE-PRESIDENT.

	Hendricks.
Alabama	20
Arkansas	12
California	12
Colorado	6
Connecticut	12
Delaware	6
Florida	8
Georgia	22
Illinois	42
Indiana	30
Iowa	22
Kansas	10
Kentucky	24
Louisiana	16
Maine	14
Maryland	16

Massachusetts	26
Michigan	22
Minnesota	10
Mississippi	16
Missouri	30
Nebraska	6
Nevada	6
New Hampshire	10
New Jersey	18
New York	70
North Carolina	20
Ohio	36
Oregon	6
Pennsylvania	58
Rhode Island	8
South Carolina	14
Tennessee	24
Texas	16
Vermont	10
Virginia	22
West Virginia	10
Wisconsin	20
Total	730

Ohio cast 8 votes blank.

The Clerk proceeded with the roll-call as far as Indiana.

MR. WILLIAMS, of Indiana: I ask that Indiana be passed for the present.

The Clerk proceeded with the call of the roll.

The following remarks were made by the chairmen of the various delegations in casting their votes:

Kentucky is proud of the privilege she has of casting her united vote—24 in number—for Thomas A. Hendricks. [Cheers.]

Mississippi casts her entire vote—16 in number—for Hendricks, and wishes she had 16 more to cast.

Pennsylvania, with the open hearts of all her Democracy, casts her 58 votes for Thomas A. Hendricks. [Cheers.]

Texas authorizes and instructs her delegation to cast her 16 votes solid for Thomas A. Hendricks, and we have 100,000 to give for Tilden and Hendricks in November next. [Cheers.]

South Carolina (the entire delegation in chorus) gives 24 votes for Hendricks. [Laughter and cheers.]

Upon the conclusion of the roll-call the Clerk again called Indiana.

Mr. WILLIAMS, of Indiana: Mr. President, I have but one word to say. [Confusion.]

The CHAIR: Gentlemen, be seated, be seated; Mr. Williams, of Indiana, has the floor.

Mr. WILLIAMS: The Indiana delegation are not authorized to say that Gov. Hendricks will accept this nomination. They are not authorized to say that he will accept it. [Cries of "Good, good!" and cheers.] We have no right to do so. But, sir, in view of this mighty demonstration, the delegation from Indiana acquiesces in the decision of this Convention. [Loud cheers and cries of "Good."]

VOICES: Announce the vote.

THE CHAIR: Order! The Secretary will announce the result of the vote. [Cries of "Vote, vote!"]

Mr. Bell, the Clerk, then announced the vote as follows: Total number of votes cast, 730.

The CHAIR: Eight blank?

Mr. BELL: Yes, sir, 738, of which Mr. Hendricks receives 730. [Tremendous cheers and waving of hats.]

The CHAIR: Mr. Hendricks having received the entire vote of the Convention for Vice-President, is therefore the nominee of this Convention for that office. [Tremendous cheering and loud cries for Voorhees and Kelly.]

ADDRESS OF MR. KELLY, OF NEW YORK.

Mr. Kelly, of New York, made his way upon the platform, amid loud cheers, and spoke as follows:

MR. CHAIRMAN AND GENTLEMEN OF THE CONVENTION: There is no man holding a seat in this Convention who has worked more strenuously against the nomination of Samuel J. Tilden than myself. I did it in the full belief that it was impossible for us to carry the election with an Eastern candidate. I gave my opinion to this Convention yesterday that this nomination should have gone to the Western States. The Convention has decided otherwise. I submit my opinion to the decision of this Convention [cheers], and now that Mr. Tilden is the candidate of our party, I promise you, and I tell you that I am capable of working [cheers], that there is no man in the Convention that will work harder for his election than myself.

In the conviction that I had upon this question, my mind ran toward that eloquent, that honest, that upright statesman of Indiana. [Applause.] I knew him twenty-two years ago in Congress. I have watched his course from that day to this. Is there an individual in this whole country that can assail the purity of that man's character? [Cries of "Not one" and applause.] The nominations of this Convention having been made, it therefore becomes the duty of every Democrat in this country to use his best endeavors and exertions to elect them. [Applause.] I believe if that be done there can be no doubt upon that question. We should now bury all our opinions [applause] that we entertain in favor of the candidates that were presented to this Convention. Let us now look to the objective point, and that is that if the Republican party's power should be perpetuated, all understand and easily comprehend what would be the misfortune to our country. How is it now under this administration? Our people everywhere unemployed, thousands of our business men running into bankruptcy, our commerce driven from the seas by the neglect of our national rulers—everything showing a tendency to destroy our business men. Is there any one here who will suppose for a moment that we can have any better condition of things if this Republican administration should be continued in power? They have selected two men. Now, let me say to you, gentlemen, that two swallows do not make a summer. [Laughter.] The party remains the same. It is corrupt in its tendencies, and it is due to the honesty, to the well-intentioned acts of our members of Congress, that the exposures of these individuals have been given to the world. Reform not only commenced in New York, but it was continued in Congress, and while we are perfectly willing to give all the credit to Gov. Tilden that he deserves in that respect, let us turn our eyes to the House of Representatives and say, "Well done, good and faithful servants, you have rendered a noble work to the party and to the people; accept your reward in the respect and admiration of a grateful country." Mr. Chairman, I will not continue my remarks any longer; but let me say before concluding that we appeal to the members of the Convention to bury their differences of opinion, bury their hates and their disappointments, and bury every prejudice that their minds entertained upon this subject.

Let them go home to their districts, and to their people, and say to them, those who differed with the gentlemen who made these nominations, "They were not our nominations, we preferred other men, we were beaten; other gentlemen were chosen. Why should we, then, continue to find fault? Why should we not then turn in and do everything that we can, as it is our duty to do, to elect these candidates of this Convention?" If this be done, Mr. President, there can be no question about the result; and that old Democratic party who founded this government, who made the people what they are, will once more be elevated to power; the flag which you have carried in many a fight will once more float in triumph over your head. [Cheers.] And you will have that self-assurance that you will have an honest government, an honest administration, and that the people will be once more happy and contented. [Loud applause.]

The CHAIR: Gentlemen of the Convention, Mr. Hanna, of Indiana.

MR. HANNA'S ADDRESS.

MR. PRESIDENT AND GENTLEMEN OF THE CONVENTION: I thank you for this expression of kindness towards Indiana, and I have reason to say that in the great contest that has been made, Indiana, I trust, has done nothing more here than what you would have expected her to do. But I take this occasion to say to the Convention, and especially our brethren of New York, that although this contest has been hard and bitter, Indiana says to you the tomahawk is now buried to rust forever. [Cheers.] Two among the greatest of all American citizens have been placed in nomination by this Convention. They are old and tried captains in the service. Let the old guard of Democracy now go to the front once more. This is a fight, my fellow-citizens, for constitutional government and reform. We take the standard in Indiana for our part of it. We raise it up to-day higher than Presidents; raise it so high that it may be seen by all States and received by all the people of the States; that, like the serpent of brass which Moses set up, it may give life and faith and hope and restitution to all who look upon it throughout this country.

"The wilderness of Shiraz and the bitter waters of Marah have long been our portion, but we go now to the land of Elam [laughter and applause], where at the promised twelve wells of water, and beneath the score and ten palm trees, we will spread at last the feast of our rejoicing and our restitution." [Cheers.]

THE TWO-THIRDS RULE.

Mr. WILLIAMS, of Indiana: I offer the following resolution:

The resolution was being taken to the platform by a page, when

Mr. MILLER, of Nebraska, said: I have a resolution which I will send to the Chair.

The Secretary read Mr. Williams' resolution as follows:

Resolved, That this Convention recommend to all future Democratic Conventions *not* to adopt the two-thirds rule in nominating candidates for President and Vice-President of the United States. [Cries of "No! no! no!"]

THE NEW COMMITTEE.

DELEGATE from Louisiana: I move that the roll of the States be now called, and a National Committee-man from each State be announced.

The CHAIR: That is the first business in order. The next business will be the resolution of the gentleman from Nebraska (Mr. Miller).

DELEGATE from Louisana: I have a resolution already on that subject which is ahead of that.

The CHAIR: Let the roll of the States be called upon the appointment of National Committee-men. After that these resolutions will be in order.

The SECRETARY [commencing to call the roll]: Alabama! [Uproar.] Gentlemen, please sit down. The Secretary desires to say to the gentlemen, please to send the name on a slip of paper with the post office address of the member of the Central Committee when each State is called. Alabama!

NATIONAL DEMOCRATIC COMMITTEE.

ALABAMA—Walter L. Bragg, of Montgomery.
ARKANSAS—John J. Sumter, of Hot Springs.
CALIFORNIA—F. McCoppin, of San Francisco.
COLORADO—B. M. Hughes, of Denver.
CONNECTICUT—Wm. H. Barnum, of Lime Rock.
DELAWARE—Harberson Hickman, of Lewes.
FLORIDA—Wilkinson McCall, of Jacksonville.
GEORGIA—Geo. T. Barnes, of Augusta.
ILLINOIS—Wm. C. Goudy, of Chicago.
INDIANA—Thomas Tolin, of Terre Haute.
IOWA—M. M. Ham, of Dubuque.

KANSAS—Isaac E. Eaton, of Leavenworth.
KENTUCKY—H. D. McHenry, of Hartford.
LOUISIANA—B. F. Jonas, of New Orleans.
MAINE—Edmund Wilson, of Thomaston.
MARYLAND—Outerbridge Horsey, of Burkettsville.
MASSACHUSETTS—Frederick O. Prince, of Boston.
MICHIGAN—Edward Kanter, of Detroit.
MINNESOTA—Wm. Lochran, of Minneapolis.
MISSISSIPPI—Ethal Barksdale, of Jackson.
MISSOURI—John G. Priest, of St. Louis.
NEBRASKA—Geo. L. Miller, of Omaha.
NEVADA—Robert P. Keating, of Gold Hill.
NEW HAMPSHIRE—Aaron W. Sulloway, of Franklin.
NEW JERSEY—Miles Ross, of New Brunswick.
NEW YORK—Abraham S. Hewitt, of New York City.
NORTH CAROLINA—M. V. Ransom, of Weldon.
OHIO—John D. Thompson, of Columbus.
OREGON—John Whitaker, of Pleasant Hill.
PENNSYLVANIA—Wm. L. Scott, Erie.
RHODE ISLAND—Nicholas Van Slyck.
SOUTH CAROLINA—James H. Rion, Waynesboro.
TENNESSEE—Wm. B. Bate, of Nashville.
TEXAS—F. C. Stockdale, of Indianola.
VERMONT—B. B. Smalley, of Burlington.
VIRGINIA—Robert A. Coghill, of New Glasgow.
WEST VIRGINIA—Alex. Campbell, of Bethany.
WISCONSIN—Wm. F. Vilas, of Madison.

THANKS TENDERED.

Senator MURPHY, of New York: I ask leave to introduce a resolution by request. I know that we and every delegate here have a grateful sense of the kindly manner in which we have been received by the citizens of St. Louis. The hospitalities which they have extended to us demand an expression of gratitude. I therefore present the following resolution:

Resolved, That the thanks of this Convention are hereby tendered to the Committee on Reception and the citizens of St. Louis for their generous, courteous and liberal hospitality to the Convention.

Resolved, That the Secretary communicate a copy of the foregoing resolution to the Chairman of the Committee on Reception. [Applause.]

COMMITTEE TO NOTIFY NOMINEES.

Mr. HANNA, of Indiana: I now move that a committee consisting of one from each State, to be chosen by the delegations, be appointed to convey to Gov. Hendricks the congratulations of the Convention.

The CHAIR: There was a resolution sent up by Gov. Brown, of Tennessee, to that effect before. The question will be the resolution of Senator Murphy, of New York.

The resolution was unanimously adopted.

The CHAIR: Gov. Brown, of Tennessee, offers the following resolution; let it be reported.

The Secretary read the resolution as follows:

Resolved, That a committee be appointed, consisting of the President of this Convention and one delegate of this Convention from each State, to visit the nominees of the Convention and inform them of their nomination.

Mr. MITCHELL, of Wisconsin: I suggest that the roll be called and the States name their delegates.

The resolution was adopted.

The CHAIR: Let the roll be called.

The Secretary proceeded to call the roll of States upon the appointment of the committee to notify Messrs. Tilden and Hendricks of their nomination, with the following result:

THE COMMITTEE ON NOTIFICATION.

ALABAMA—Francis S. Lyons.
ARKANSAS—B. D. Williams.
CALIFORNIA—Geo. H. Rogers.
COLORADO—Adair Wilson.
CONNECTICUT—W. B. Franklin.
DELAWARE—Gov. Saulsbury.
FLORIDA—J. D. Harris.
GEORGIA—Allen G. Fort.
ILLINOIS—Perry H. Smith.
INDIANA—Bayless W. Hanna.
IOWA—B. F. Montgomery.
KANSAS—Chas. W. Blair.
KENTUCKY—W. W. Bush.
LOUISIANA—Louis St. Martin.
MAINE—S. J. Anderson.
MARYLAND—Robt. T. Banks.
MASSACHUSETTS—Josiah G. Abbott.
MICHIGAN—H. J. Redfield.
MINNESOTA—J. N. Castle.
MISSISSIPPI—J. C. Prewett.
MISSOURI—Henry J. Spaunhorst.
NEBRASKA—G. B. Scofield.
NEVADA—R. P. Keating.
NEW HAMPSHIRE—Lafayette Hall.
NEW JERSEY—Patrick Henry.
NEW YORK—Henry C. Murphy.
NORTH CAROLINA—W. J. Green.
OHIO—Isaac C. Collins.
OREGON—Mark V. Brown.
PENNSYLVANIA—Hendrick B. Wright.
RHODE ISLAND—Wm. B. Beach.
SOUTH CAROLINA—M. P. O'Connell.
TENNESSEE—Thomas O'Connor.
TEXAS—Joseph E. Dwyer.
VERMONT—Jasper Rand.
VIRGINIA—S. C. Neale.
WEST VIRGINIA—G. D. Camden.
WISCONSIN—Joseph Rankin.

The following resolution, offered by Mr. Webber, of Michigan, was read:

Resolved, That it be recommended to future National Democratic Conventions, as the sense of the Democracy here in Convention assembled, that the so-called two-thirds rule be abolished as unwise and unnecessary, and that the States be requested to instruct their delegates to the National Democratic Convention to be held in 1880, whether it be desirable to continue the two-thirds rule longer in force in the National Convention, and that the National Committee insert such request in their call for the Convention.

Mr. BIRCH, of Tennessee: I move the adoption of that resolution.

The question was put amid great confusion.

The CHAIR: The adoption of the resolution has been moved. Let the gentlemen attend to it.

A DELEGATE: Mr. Chairman, I understand the resolution to be to rescind the two-thirds rule.

The CHAIR: Yes, sir.

A DELEGATE: Then I sincerely hope that the members of this Convention will think seriously before they adopt this resolution. I believe it is against the interests of the Democratic party, and contrary to a long method of proceeding in our Conventions.

The CHAIR: I will respond to the gentleman by stating that I did not intend to be understood as saying that this resolution abolishes that rule. This Convention has no power to control any subsequent Convention. It is simply a recommendation that it be dropped at the next Convention.

A DELEGATE: I ask that the resolution be read again.

The resolution was read.

Mr. BIRCH, of Tennessee: I move to lay that resolution on the table.

A DELEGATE: I demand the ayes and nays.

Voices: Call the roll.

The roll was called, and the vote resulted as follows:

LAYING ON TABLE MOTION TO SUSPEND TWO-THIRDS RULE.

	Aye.	Nay.
Alabama	20	......
Arkansas	......	12
California	12	......
Colorado	......	6
Connecticut	......	12
Delaware	......	12
Florida	8	......
Georgia	22	......
Illinois	16	26
Indiana	30	......
Iowa	7	15
Kansas	9	1
Kentucky	24	......
Louisiana	......	16
Maine	......	14
Maryland	......	16
Massachusetts	......	26
Michigan	......	22
Minnesota	......	10
Mississippi	......	16
Missouri	17	13
Nebraska	......	6
Nevada	5	1
New Hampshire	1	9
New Jersey	18	......
New York	......	70
North Carolina	20	......
Ohio	44	......
Oregon	2	4
Pennsylvania	58	......
Rhode Island	......	8
South Carolina	......	14
Tennessee	24	......
Texas	2	14
Vermont	......	10
Virginia	......	22
West Virginia	10	......
Wisconsin	10	10
Total	359	379

Pending the calling of the roll, the Chairman of the Kentucky delegation said: Kentucky, under her rule, voting as a unit, though divided in her own delegation, votes aye.

The CHAIRMAN: While casting up the vote the Chair, with permission of the Convention, will direct the Clerk to report the following resolution which is on the table:

The Secretary read as follows:

Resolved, That the thanks of this Convention are tendered to the Hon. John A. McClernand, of Illinois, for the able and impartial manner in which he has discharged the duties of presiding officer of this Convention.

Adopted unanimously.

At this point a large portrait of Mr. Tilden by Kurtz was placed behind the speaker amidst great applause.

Mr. Spaunhorst, of St. Louis, offered the following resolution, which one of the Secretaries proceeded to read:

Resolved, That this Convention recommend future National Democratic—

The voice of the Secretary not being sufficiently strong to make it audible all over the hall, there were repeated calls for "Bell."

The CHAIR: Until less noise is made it will take the lungs of a bellows to read anything.

Mr. Bell then took the resolution amidst cheers, and read in a stentorian voice as follows:

Resolved, That this Convention recommend future National Democratic Conventions to allow each Territory and the District of Columbia a vote each.

A DELEGATE: I move to lay the resolution on the table.

The motion was carried.

Mr. Riley, of Pennsylvania, offered the following resolution, which was adopted:

Resolved, That the Recording Secretary be requested to prepare the proceedings of this Convention to be printed in proper form, and that the National Committee cause a suitable number of copies to be distributed among the delegates of this Convention.

The CHAIR: Mr. Smalley, of Vermont, offers the following resolution, which the Clerk will read:

The Secretary read the resolution as follows:

Resolved, That the place for holding the next Convention be left to the decision of the National Committee, and that the basis of representation be the same as in the present Convention.

The resolution was adopted.

The CHAIR: The Chair will announce that the vote upon the question of laying upon the table the resolution in regard to the two-thirds rule is as follows: Whole number of votes cast, 738; of which the ayes are 359, nays 379; so the resolution does not lie upon the table. The question is now upon the adoption of the resolution.

Mr. WALLACE, of Pennsylvania: I rise to call for a division of the question by dividing the question, ending the first proposition at the word "abolished."

A DELEGATE from Missouri: I move the previous question upon the original resolution.

Mr. WALLACE: It is scarcely necessary for me to say a division of the question is in order either before or after the main question be ordered. I desire, Mr. President, simply to bring this Convention to a vote upon the naked question as to whether we are to have instructions from the States in regard to the abolition of the two-thirds rule, or whether this Convention is to instruct future Conventions as to their action.

The CHAIR: The gentleman from Pennsylvania demands a division of the question. The Clerk will read that portion upon which he calls a division.

The Clerk read as follows:

Resolved, That it be recommended to future Democratic National Conventions, as the sense of the Democracy here in Convention assembled, that the so-called two-thirds rule be abolished as unwise and unnecessary.

The resolution was adopted.

The Secretary read the second part, as follows:

Resolved, That the States be requested to instruct their delegates to the Democratic National Convention to be held in 1880, whether it be desirable to continue the two-thirds rule longer in force in National Conventions, and that the National Committee insert such request in the call for the next Convention.

The resolution was adopted.

Mr. McMichael, of Missouri, presented the following resolution, which was adopted:

Resolved, That we, as delegates, hereby pledge our individual and united support to the nominees of this Convention; esteeming it a positive duty to employ every honorable means for the success of the same in the November election.

Mr. MILLER, of Nebraska: I have a resolution to offer.

The CHAIR: Pass it up.

The resolution as read was as follows:

Resolved, That the thanks of this Convention are due and hereby tendered to Hon. N. M. Bell, for his efficient services as Reading Secretary. [Applause.]

Adopted.

The CHAIR: The Chair desires to announce that each delegation will take their banners with them when this Convention adjourns.

A DELEGATE: And bring them back victorious in November. [Applause.]

The Chair then announced that the committee appointed to wait upon Govs. Tilden and Hendricks, and notify them of their nomination, would meet at room 20, Lindell Hotel, immediately after the adjournment of the Convention; also that the new National Committee would hold a meeting upon the adjournment of the Convention, at the National Committee rooms.

Mr. Riley, of Nevada, offered the following resolution:

Resolved, That the thanks of this Convention be tendered to the President and Board of Directors of the Merchants' Exchange of St. Louis, for their liberality in presenting the use of their magnificent building for the deliberations of this Convention, and also to the citizens of St. Louis for their generous hospitality. [Cheers.]

The resolution was passed unanimously.

PRESENTATION TO THE RESIDENT COMMITTEE.

Mr. KERNAN, of New York: Mr. President, I am directed by the delegation from the State of New York, who have been greatly indebted to the Resident Committee in St. Louis, to present to that Committee, in token of our appreciation of their hospitality and efficiency, a portrait of Samuel J. Tilden which is above your chair. Permit me to say one word more, as I have your ear for a moment. I feel that we are now to go to work harmoniously and energetically to elect Tilden and Hendricks, and if we elect them I say to you I believe they will sweep over the country, and after the fourth of March they will sweep the carpet-baggers from the South and the thieves from the North. [Cheers.]

The CHAIR: What is the further pleasure of this Convention?

Mr. WILLIAMS, of Indiana: I move that this Convention do now adjourn.

The question was put and the motion carried, and at 12:30 P. M. the Convention adjourned *sine die.*

After the adjournment of the Convention, there were loud calls for Preston. In response Gen. Wm. Preston, of Kentucky, came upon the platform and spoke as follows:

I feel sensibly touched, gentlemen, by the call with which you have honored me, and it would be discourtesy on my part not to say something in acknowledgment of it. The words that I say shall be very brief, and I feel it the more because the tribute of this call is not given to me, for I hold no official position, and it is given to a powerless man. It is given, I suppose, simply by some partial friends with whom I have been united in former Democratic Conventions, and I see before me now the faces of men who have held great and important trusts in the party—Senators, Governors and magistrates—all united for the first time on the west bank of the Mississippi to send an honest man as President to the East. In this noble hall, in this beautiful building erected upon ground acquired by the splendid wisdom of Jefferson, in the acquisition of Louisiana, the people see for the first time assembled the representative men of that great Democratic party that he may be said to have founded, and who now come to protect the inheritance he obtained. They come under the leadership of their chiefs to select another chief. They come from the East, and by a united and harmonious action you have secured two nominees who, let me say, are not so much your choice as that of the people, for the names of Tilden and Hendricks were fastened in the hearts of the country before you assembled here. You are indeed true and faithful representatives of your party, and the reflex will go back, giving us an assurance of victory such as we have not had for twenty years.

We go for two purposes. We find the country torn and distracted, but the Southern people, among whom I was born, find that for twenty odd years no hand has been lifted that did not belong to the Democratic party, to help us, and that the Democratic party have held out the flask of oil to pour balm into our wounds, but that it has again and again been dashed to the earth by the remaining rancor of the Republican chiefs. I recognize at Cincinnati that there was a certain degree of concession in that body in still seeking the remembrances which were presented in the names of some of those candidates, but all men must feel that the true reform and amnesty party was never led by Mr. Blaine nor Gov. Morton, but is to be found under such names as Tilden and Hendricks. [Applause.] When he beheld the rights of Louisiana violated, and the South silenced as it were under it, the strongest hand and one of the noblest protests came from Tilden against the injustice of the act. There is no prouder cup in the history of the party. It fills us with hope, it elevates us to a nobler manhood, and we come with manful purpose and candidly say to you, that while we have nothing to remember in the past, we come in the hope of the future; that though the men who have so patiently sat here and awaited the developments that secured the nomination of two Northern candidates, peculiarly men of the South, that they came to preserve that silence so that the North may not hereafter have it said that the slightest dictation existed, as in the Seymour and Blair nomination, to the gentlemen of the North as to who they should prefer. We have waited till you indicated that; you have indicated it unmistakably, and now united we stand, with a platform of honest money and honest men. [Applause.] I must say one word more. Men in moments of temptation, and particularly of pecuniary distress, lose their nobility of soul under the temptations that are offered by way of relief. The South has preserved her heritage of self-respect, but she has been constantly accused of hostility to the Union. I hold that man to be an enemy to the people of America and this Union who seeks to sap its public pith or destroy the sanctity of a contract. [Applause.] I say that among the men that you will find faithful to that obligation, though poor, yet determined by every means in the world to give legitimate relief to labor in the hour of distress, is the impoverished South, and that you will find that they will adhere, in good and evil report, to the honest maxims of their fathers; and having selected in moments of tranquillity and calm the principles that command their judgment, that it is not for the storm to shake that tranquillity. We will pursue the science of politics amid sunshine and in storm, and stand by our principles till we fall at their base. [Applause.]

We have never given you a pledge we did not keep, and now seeing that it is accepted in that spirit and united on a platform after days of discussion here, I say that a new dawn is about to reach the Democracy of the Union. I say if you ask how long the Democracy have been out of power, that the future historian will write in a single sentence the whole story: "They were expelled from American power when the people lost their reason, and they returned to it when they recovered it." [Applause.] It is impossible for the minority, as the Democracy have been, to recover its place by weak counsels or timid action; you should always advance after you have fixed your line of battle. Do not apologize to the Republicans, but with free trade, honest money, reform, advance to the charge. If you think in moments of doubt you cannot go a step further, feel as you do in actual battle when you see the men advance—"only one step further for the love of God and of country," and you will carry everything. If you see them faint-hearted, with pencils calculating majorities, throw the pencils and the calculations to the earth and say, "We will count the arithmetic after we win the victory."

If you go in that spirit into the action, and, guided by the light of those principles, make no local modifications, but stand upon it, you will find the Democracy resuming a name long since abandoned—a name that, when I was a young Whig, struck terror to my heart—the name of the "unterrified." Let me then in this canvass behold the unterrified Democracy, and I will show you one that will redeem your country, and the people will say: "Lo! the wounded, exanimate Democracy, so long prostrate, has again risen in its might, and it *is* unterrified, inexpugnable—the Democracy of America and the world." [Cheers.]

Secretary Bell announced that delegates would find letters addressed to them, but uncalled for, at room No. 215, Board of Trade building.

APPENDIX.

ORGANIZATION

— OF THE —

NATIONAL DEMOCRATIC COMMITTEE.

St. Louis, June 29th, 1876.

The members of the National Democratic Committee appointed by the Convention met this day at the Exchange Building.

The following gentlemen were present:

ALABAMA	Walter L. Bragg	*Montgomery.*
ARKANSAS	John I. Sumter	*Hot Springs.*
CALIFORNIA	F. McCoppin	*San Francisco.*
COLORADO	B. M. Hughes	*Denver.*
CONNECTICUT	Wm. H. Barnum	*Lime Rock.*
DELAWARE	Harberson Hickman	*Lewes.*
FLORIDA	Wilkinson McCall	*Jacksonville.*
GEORGIA	Geo. T. Barnes	*Augusta.*
ILLINOIS	Wm. C. Goudy	*Chicago.*
INDIANA	Thomas Dowling	*Terre Haute.*
IOWA	M. M. Ham	*Dubuque.*
KANSAS	Isaac E. Eaton	*Leavenworth.*
KENTUCKY	H. D. McHenry	*Hartford.*
LOUISIANA	B. F. Jonas	*New Orleans.*
MAINE	Edmund Wilson	*Thomaston.*
MARYLAND	Outerbridge Horsey	*Burkettsville.*
MASSACHUSETTS	Frederick O. Prince	*Boston.*

MICHIGAN	Edward Kanter	*Detroit.*
MINNESOTA	Wm. Lochran	*Minneapolis.*
MISSISSIPPI	Ethal Barksdale	*Jackson.*
MISSOURI	John G. Priest	*St. Louis.*
NEBRASKA	Geo. L. Miller	*Omaha.*
NEVADA	Robert P. Keating	*Gold Hill.*
NEW HAMPSHIRE	Alvah W. Sulloway	*Franklin.*
NEW JERSEY	Miles Ross	*New Brunswick.*
NEW YORK	Abraham S. Hewitt	*New York City.*
NORTH CAROLINA	M. W. Ransom	*Weldon.*
OHIO	John D. Thompson	*Columbus.*
OREGON	John Whitaker	*Pleasant Hill.*
PENNSYLVANIA	Wm. L. Scott	*Erie.*
RHODE ISLAND	Nicholas Van Slyck	*Providence.*
SOUTH CAROLINA	James H. Rion	*Winnsboro.*
TENNESSEE	Wm. B. Bate	*Nashville.*
TEXAS	F. S. Stockdale	*Indianola.*
VERMONT	B. B. Smalley	*Burlington.*
VIRGINIA	Robert A. Coghill	*New Glasgow.*
WEST VIRGINIA	Alex. Campbell	*Bethany.*
WISCONSIN	Wm. F. Vilas	*Madison.*

On motion of Mr. John G. Thompson, of Ohio, Abraham S. Hewitt, of New York, was appointed Chairman of the Committee by acclamation.

On motion of Mr. M. M. Ham, of Iowa, Frederick O. Prince, of Massachusetts, was appointed Secretary and Treasurer of the Committee by acclamation.

Mr. John G. Priest, of Missouri, moved that an Executive Committee be appointed, to consist of the Chairman, Secretary, and nine others to be named by the Chair, and the following were appointed:

HON. JOHN G. PRIEST, of Missouri.
" M. M. HAM, of Iowa.
" GEORGE L. MILLER, of Nebraska.
" WM. H. BARNUM, of Connecticut.
" M. W. RANSOM, of North Carolina.
" JOHN G. THOMPSON, of Ohio.
" WM. L. SCOTT, of Pennsylvania.
" MILES ROSS, of New Jersey.
" WILLIAM B. BATE, of Tennessee.

It was voted that five members of the Executive Committee constitute a quorum.

On motion, the Committee adjourned to meet in New York on the 2d day of August, 1876.

GEN. JNO. A. McCLERNAND'S ADDRESS.

Governor Tilden:—The Democratic National Convention lately assembled at St. Louis, though come and gone, is worthily survived by its work, which may fairly claim candid scrutiny and approval.

The Convention itself was large in numbers, august in character, and patriotic in sentiment. It counted 738 delegates, representing 38 States, forming an ocean-bound Republic. It met in a rising and hospitable city enthroned upon the banks of the Mississippi, and nobly typifying the growing grandeur of the mighty valley of that river.

It met, too, under grave circumstances—at a time when the sharp cry of distress was heard in every part of the land; when the Constitution had ceased to be reverenced and faithfully obeyed by rash and infatuate rulers; when the civil authority was exposed to fresh encroachments from the military; when "hate" was rung as the watchword and the "bloody shirt" was flaunted as the banner of a sectional and aggressive party; when trade restrictions embarrassed commerce and impoverished the revenues; when hard money—the immemorial money of mankind—was dishonored and virtually banished by vicious legislation from accustomed circulation; when public waste and extravagance had long been a ruling and ruinous vice; when peculation and corruption were tainting and sapping the very foundations of government and society; when a ponderous public debt was grinding the over-strained energies of the people; when insatiate taxation was devouring their scanty substance and imperilling the public credit and faith; when gaunt famine, as the consequence of involuntary idleness, was dogging the heels of the laboring classes; when, in fact, the country, in its whole extent, was writhing and pining in extremity.

Yes, it was under these solemn circumstances that the Convention met, profoundly impressed with its responsibilities. It had but one feeling and a common purpose—to deliver the country from its peril, to bring the Government back to its constitutional moorings, to restore the States to their proper Federal relations and the people of the States to their old-time brotherhood, to raise up industry and labor from their despairing prostration and to renew their wonted hopes and rewards, to retrench public expenditures, to reduce taxation, to improve the currency, to punish and prevent official infidelity, to reform abuses—in short, to build up again the ancient glory of the Union—the Union, one, inseparable and perpetual.

Preliminary to these ends, the Convention, in its wisdom, made a declaration of principles and policy, to be observed by its members and the Democratic party, as a touchstone of political faith—a declaration as sound in promise as it is eloquent and graceful in expression. Next it proceeded to choose tried, true, able and experienced statesmen to incarnate its great argument, and to champion the same against all opposers and dangers; and finally, according to usage, it appointed a Committee to wait upon the eminent persons so chosen, and formally to notify them of their choice.

In conclusion, I have only to add that that Committee is here, in person, ready to perform this grateful service, and accordingly I have the honor and pleasure, as its Chairman, now to place in the hands of its Secretary a communication to be read and delivered by him to you as its act.

Mr. J. D. Harris, of Florida, the Secretary of the Committee, then read and delivered to Gov. Tilden the following address, signed by the members of the Committee.

COMMITTEE'S ADDRESS TO GOV. TILDEN.

NEW YORK CITY, July 11th, 1876.

GOV. SAMUEL J. TILDEN:

SIR:—The undersigned, a Committee of the National Democratic Convention which met at the city of St. Louis, Mo., on the 27th ult., consisting of its President and of one Delegate from each State of the Federal Union, have been intrusted with the pleasant duty of waiting upon and informing you of your nomination by that body as the candidate of the Democratic party for the Presidency of the United States at the ensuing election.

It is a source of great satisfaction to us, who but reflect the opinions of the members of the Convention, that a gentleman entertaining and boldly advocating, as you do and have done, those great measures of national and State reform, which are an absolute necessity for the restoration of the national honor, prosperity and credit, should have been selected as our standard-bearer in the approaching contest. Your name is identified with the all-absorbing question of reform, reduction of taxes, and the maintenance of the rights of the laboring masses.

The Democracy, in designating you as their chosen leader, do not feel that they are relying merely upon your pledges or promises of what you will do in the event of your election; your record of the past is our guarantee of your future course.

"Having been faithful over a few things, we will make you a ruler over many things."

Accompanying this letter of notification, we also present you with the declaration of principles adopted by the Convention. We have no doubt you will recognize in this declaration measures of political policy which immediately concern the happiness and welfare of the entire people of this country, and we feel that your election to the Presidency will be a guarantee of their success, and that it will be as much your pleasure to enforce and maintain them, if elected, as it was ours to give them the stamp of national representative approbation and approval in their adoption. Entertaining the hope that you will signify to us your acceptance of the nomination which we have tendered you, and that you concur with the Convention in their declaration of principles, we are, dear sir,

Your very obedient servants,

JOHN A. McCLERNAND, Chairman.

F. S. LYONS, Alabama.
B. D. WILLIAMS, Arkansas.
GEO. H. ROGERS, California.
ADAIR WILSON, Colorado.
W. B. FRANKLIN, Connecticut.
Gov. SAULSBURY, Delaware.
J. D. HARRIS, Florida.
ALLEN FORT, Georgia.
PERRY H. SMITH, Illinois.
BAYLESS W. HANNA, Indiana.
B. F. MONTGOMERY, Iowa.
CHAS. W. BLAIR, Kansas.
W. W. BUSH, Kentucky.
LOUIS ST. MARTIN, Louisiana.
SAMUEL J. ANDERSON, Maine.
J. G. ABBOTT, Massachusetts.
H. J. REDFIELD, Michigan.
J. N. CASTLE, Minnesota.
ROBERT T. BANKS, Maryland.
WADE HAMPTON, Jr., Mississippi.
H. J. SPAUNHORST, Missouri.
G. B. SCOFIELD, Nebraska.
R. P. KEATING, Nevada.
L. HALL, New Hampshire.
P. H. LAVERTY, New Jersey.
H. C. MURPHY, New York.
WHARTON J. GREEN, North Carolina.
ISAAC C. COLLINS, Ohio.
MAT. V. BROWN, Oregon.
HENDRICK B. WRIGHT, Pennsylvania
W. B. BEACH, Rhode Island.
M. P. O'CONNOR, South Carolina.
THOMAS O'CONNOR, Tennessee.
JOSEPH E. DWYER, Texas.
JASPER RAND, } Vermont.
B. B. SMALLEY, }
S. C. NEALE, Virginia.
G. D. CAMDEN, West Virginia.
JOS. RANKIN, Wisconsin.

GOV. TILDEN'S LETTER OF ACCEPTANCE.

ALBANY, July 31st, 1876.

GENTLEMEN:—When I had the honor to receive a personal delivery of your letter on behalf of the Democratic National Convention held on the 28th of June, at St. Louis, advising me of my nomination as the candidate of the constituency represented by that body for the office of President of the United States, I answered that, at my earliest convenience, and in conformity with usage, I would prepare and transmit to you a formal acceptance. I now avail myself of the first interval in unavoidable occupations to fulfill that engagement.

The Convention, before making its nominations, adopted a Declaration of Principles, which, as a whole, seems to me a wise exposition of the necessities of our country, and of the reforms needed to bring back the Government to its true functions, to restore purity of administration, and to renew the prosperity of the people. But some of these reforms are so urgent that they claim more than a passing approval.

REFORM IN PUBLIC EXPENSE.

The necessity of a reform "in the scale of public expense—Federal, State and Municipal"—and "in the modes of Federal taxation," justifies all the prominence given to it in the Declaration of the St. Louis Convention.

The present depression in all the business and industries of the people, which is depriving labor of its employment, and carrying want into so many homes, has its principal cause in excessive governmental consumption. Under the illusions of a specious prosperity, engendered by the false policies of the Federal Government, a waste of capital has been going on ever since the peace of 1865, which could only end in universal disaster.

The Federal taxes of the last eleven years reach the gigantic sum of 4,500 millions. Local taxation has amounted to two-thirds as much more. The vast aggregate is not less than 7,500 millions.

This enormous taxation followed a civil conflict that had greatly impaired our aggregate wealth, and had made a prompt reduction of expenses indispensable.

It was aggravated by most unscientific and ill-adjusted methods of taxation, that increased the sacrifices of the people far beyond the receipts of the treasury.

It was aggravated, moreover, by a financial policy which tended to diminish the energy, skill and economy of production, and the frugality of private consumption, and induced miscalculation in business and an unremunerative use of capital and labor.

Even in prosperous times, the daily wants of industrious communities press closely upon their daily earnings. The margin of possible national savings is at best but a small percentage of national earnings. Yet now for these eleven years governmental consumption has been a larger proportion of the national earnings than the whole people can possibly save even in prosperous times for all new investments.

The consequence of these errors is now a present public calamity. But they were never doubtful, never invisible. They were necessary and inevitable, and were foreseen and depicted when the waves of that fictitious prosperity ran highest. In a speech made by me on the 24th of September, 1868, it was said of these taxes:

> They bear heavily upon every man's income, upon every industry and every business in the country, and year by year they are destined to press still more heavily, unless we arrest the system that gives rise to them. It was comparatively easy, when values were doubling under repeated issues of legal-tender paper money, to pay these taxes out of the froth of our growing and apparent wealth; but when values recede and sink towards their natural scale, the tax-gatherer takes from us not only our income, not only our profits, but also a portion of our capital. * * * I do not wish to exaggerate or alarm; I simply say that we cannot afford the costly and ruinous policy of the Radical majority of Congress. We cannot afford that policy towards the South. We cannot afford the magnificent and oppressive centralism into which our Government is being converted. We cannot afford the present magnificent scale of taxation.

To the Secretary of the Treasury I said, early in 1865:

> There is no royal road for a government more than for an individual or a corporation. What you want to do now is to cut down your expenses and live within your income. I would give all the legerdemain of finance and financiering—I would give the whole of it—for the old homely maxim, "Live within your income."

This reform will be resisted at every step, but it must be pressed persistently. We see to-day the immediate representatives of the people in one branch of Congress, while struggling to reduce expenditures, compelled to confront the menace of the Senate and Executive, that unless the objectionable appropriations be consented to, the operations of the Government thereunder shall suffer detriment or cease. In my judgment, an amendment of the Constitution ought to be devised, separating into distinct bills the appropriations for the various departments of the public service, and excluding from each bill all appropriations for other objects, and all independent legislation. In that way alone can the revisory power of each of the two houses and of the Executive be preserved and exempted from the moral duress which often compels assent to objectionable appropriations rather than stop the wheels of government.

THE SOUTH.

An accessory cause enhancing the distress in business is to be found in the systematic and insupportable misgovernment imposed on the States of the South. Besides the ordinary effects of ignorant and dishonest administration, it has inflicted upon them enormous issues of fraudulent bonds, the scanty avails of which were wasted or stolen, and the existence of which is a public discredit, tending to bankruptcy or repudiation. Taxes, generally oppressive, in some instances have confiscated the entire income of property, and totally destroyed its marketable value. It is impossible that these evils should not react upon the prosperity of the whole country.

The nobler motives of humanity concur with the material interests of all in requiring that every obstacle be removed, to a complete and durable reconciliation between kindred populations once unnaturally estranged, on the basis recognized by the St. Louis platform, of the "Constitution of the United States, with its amendments universally accepted as a final settlement of the controversies which engendered civil war."

But, in aid of a result so beneficent, the moral influence of every good citizen, as well as every governmental authority, ought to be exerted, not alone to maintain their just equality before the law, but likewise to establish a cordial fraternity and good will among citizens, whatever their race or color, who are now united in the one destiny of a common self-government. If the duty shall be assigned to me, I should not fail to exercise the powers with which the laws and the Constitution of our country clothe its chief magistrate, to protect all its citizens, whatever their former condition, in every political and personal right.

CURRENCY REFORM.

"Reform is necessary," declares the St. Louis Convention, "to establish a sound currency, restore the public credit and maintain the national honor;" and it goes on to "demand a judicious system of preparation by public economies, by official retrenchments, and by wise finances, which shall enable the nation soon to assure the whole world of its perfect ability and its perfect readiness to meet any of its promises at the call of the creditor entitled to payment."

The object demanded by the Convention is a resumption of specie payments on the legal-tender notes of the United States. That would not only "restore the public credit" and "maintain the national honor," but it would "establish a sound currency" for the people.

The methods by which this object is to be pursued, and the means by which it is to be maintained, are disclosed by what the Convention demanded for the future, and by what it denounced in the past.

BANK NOTE RESUMPTION.

Resumption of specie payments by the Government of the United States on its legal-tender notes would establish specie payments by all the banks, on all their notes. The official statement, made on the 12th of May, shows that the amount of the bank notes was 300 millions, less 20 millions held by themselves. Against these 280 millions of notes, the banks held 141 millions of legal-tender notes, or a little more than fifty per cent. of their amount. But they also held on deposit in the Federal Treasury, as security for these notes, bonds of the United States, worth in gold about 360 millions, available and current in all the foreign money markets. In resuming, the banks, even if it were possible for all their notes to be presented for payment, would have 500 millions of specie funds to pay 280 millions of notes, without contracting their loans to their customers, or calling on any private debtor for payment. Suspended banks, undertaking to resume, have usually been obliged to collect from needy borrowers the means to redeem excessive issues and to provide reserves. A vague idea of distress is, therefore, often associated with the process of resumption. But the conditions which caused distress in those former instances do not now exist.

The Government has only to make good its own promises, and the banks can take care of themselves without distressing anybody. The Government is, therefore, the sole delinquent.

LEGAL-TENDER RESUMPTION.

The amount of legal-tender notes of the United States now outstanding is less than 370 millions of dollars, besides 34 millions of dollars of fractional currency. How shall the Government make these notes at all times as good as specie?

It has to provide, in reference to the mass which would be kept in use by the wants of business, a central reservoir of coin, adequate to the adjustment of the temporary fluctuations of international balances, and as a guaranty against transient drains artificially created by panic or by speculation.

It has also to provide for the payment in coin of such fractional currency as may be presented for redemption, and such inconsiderable portions of the legal tenders as individuals may, from time to time, desire to convert for special use, or in order to lay by in coin their little stores of money.

RESUMPTION NOT DIFFICULT.

To make the coin now in the treasury available for the objects of this reserve, to gradually strengthen and enlarge that reserve, and to provide for such other exceptional demands for coin as may arise, does not seem to me a work of difficulty. If wisely planned and discreetly pursued, it ought not to cost any sacrifice to the business of the country. It should tend, on the contrary, to a revival of hope and confidence. The coin in the treasury on the 30th of June, including what is held against coin certificates, amounted to nearly 74 millions. The current of precious metals which has flowed out of our country for eleven years, from July 1, 1865, to June 30, 1876, averaging nearly 76 millions a year, was 832 millions in the whole period, of which 617 millions were the product of our own mines.

To amass the requisite quantity, by intercepting from the current flowing out of the country, and by acquiring from the stocks which exist abroad without disturbing the equilibrium of foreign money markets, is a result to be easily worked out by practical knowledge and judgment.

With respect to whatever surplus of legal tenders the wants of business may fail to keep in use, and which, in order to save interest, will be returned for redemption, they can either be paid or they can be funded. Whether they continue as currency, or be absorbed into the vast mass of securities held as investments, is merely a question of the rate of interest they draw. Even if they were to remain in their present form, and the Government were to agree to pay on them a rate of interest, making them desirable as investments, they would cease to circulate and take their place with government, state, municipal, and other corporate and private bonds, of which thousands of millions exist among us. In the perfect ease with which they can be changed from currency into investments lies the only danger to be guarded against in the adoption of general measures intended to remove a clearly ascertained surplus; that is, the withdrawal of any which are not a permanent excess beyond the wants of business. Even more mischievous would be any measure which affects the public imagination with the fear of an apprehended scarcity. In a community where credit is so much used, fluctuations of values and vicissitudes in business are largely caused by the temporary beliefs of men, even before those beliefs can conform to ascertained realities.

AMOUNT OF NECESSARY CURRENCY.

The amount of the necessary currency, at a given time, cannot be determined arbitrarily, and should not be assumed on conjecture. That amount is subject to both permanent and temporary changes. An enlargement of it, which seemed to be durable, happened at the beginning of the civil war by a substituted use of currency in place of individual credits. It varies with certain states of business. It fluctuates, with considerable regularity, at different seasons of the year. In the autumn, for instance, when buyers of grain and other agricultural products begin their operations, they usually need to borrow capital or circulating credits by which to make their purchases, and want these funds in currency capable of being distributed in small sums among numerous sellers. The additional need of currency at such times is five or more per cent. of the whole volume, and, if a surplus beyond what is required for ordinary use does not happen to have been on hand at the money centers, a scarcity of currency ensues, and also a stringency in the loan market.

It was in reference to such experience that, in a discussion of this subject, in my annual message to the New York Legislature, of January 5, 1875, the suggestion was made that "The Federal Government is bound to redeem every portion of its issues which the public do not wish to use. Having assumed to monopolize the supply of currency, and enacted exclusions against everybody else, it is bound to furnish all which the wants of business require." * * * * * "The system should passively allow the volume of circulating credits to ebb and flow, according to the ever-changing wants of business. It should imitate as closely as possible the natural laws of trade, which it has superseded by artificial contrivances." And in a similar discussion, in my message of January 4, 1876, it was said that resumption should be effected "by such measures as would keep the aggregate amount of the currency self-adjusting during all the process without creating at any time an artificial scarcity, and without exciting the public imagination with alarms which impair confidence, contract the whole large machinery of credit, and disturb the natural operations of business."

MEANS OF RESUMPTION.

"Public economies, official retrenchments and wise finance" are the means which the St. Louis Convention indicates as provision for reserves and redemption.

The best resource is a reduction of the expenses of the Government below its income; for that imposes no new charge on the people.

If, however, the improvidence and waste which have conducted us to a period of falling revenues oblige us to supplement the results of economies and retrenchment by some resort to loans, we should not hesitate. The Government ought not to speculate on its own dishonor, in order to save interest on its broken promises, which it still compels private dealers to accept at a fictitious par. The highest national honor is not only right, but would prove profitable. Of the public debt, 985 millions bear interest at 6 per cent. in gold, and 712 millions at 5 per cent. in gold. The average interest is 5.58 per cent.

A financial policy which should secure the highest credit, wisely availed of, ought gradually to obtain a reduction of one per cent. in the interest on most of the loans. A saving of one per cent. on the average would be 17 millions a year in gold. That saving regularly invested at four and a half per cent. would, in less than thirty-eight years, extinguish the principal. The whole 1,700 millions of bonded debt might be paid by this saving alone, without cost to the people.

PROPER TIME FOR RESUMPTION.

The proper time for resumption is the time when wise preparations shall have ripened into a perfect ability to accomplish the object with a certainty and ease that will inspire confidence and encourage the reviving of business. The earliest time in which such a result can be brought about is the best. Even when the preparations shall have been matured, the exact date would have to be chosen with reference to the then existing state of trade and credit operations in our own country, the course of foreign commerce, and the condition of the exchanges with other nations. The specific measures and the actual date are matters of detail having reference to ever-changing conditions. They belong to the domain of practical administrative statesmanship. The captain of a steamer, about starting from New York to Liverpool, does not assemble a council over his ocean chart, and fix an angle by which to lash the rudder for the whole voyage. A human intelligence must be at the helm to discern the shifting forces of the waters and the winds. A human hand must be on the helm to feel the elements day by day, and guide to a mastery over them.

PREPARATIONS FOR RESUMPTION.

Such preparations are everything. Without them, a legislative command fixing a day, an official promise fixing a day, are shams. They are worse—they are a snare and a delusion to all who trust them. They destroy all confidence among thoughtful men, whose judgment will at last sway public opinion. An attempt to act on such a command, or such a promise, without preparation, would end in a new suspension. It would be a fresh calamity, prolific of confusion, distrust and distress.

THE ACT OF JANUARY 14TH, 1875.

The Act of Congress of the 14th of January, 1875, enacted that on and after the 1st of January, 1879, the Secretary of the Treasury shall redeem in coin the legal-tender notes of the United States on presentation at the office of the Assistant Treasurer in the City of New York. It authorizes the Secretary "to prepare and provide for" such resumption of specie payments by the use of any surplus revenues not otherwise appropriated, and by issuing, in his discretion, certain classes of bonds.

More than one and a half of the four years have passed. Congress and the President have continued ever since to unite in acts which have legislated out of existence every possible surplus applicable to this purpose.

The coin in the treasury claimed to belong to the Government, had on the 30th of June fallen to less than forty-five millions of dollars, as against fifty-nine millions on the 1st of January, 1875, and the availability of a part of that sum is said to be questionable. The revenues are falling faster than appropriations and expenditures are reduced, leaving the treasury with diminishing resources. The Secretary has done nothing under his power to issue bonds.

The legislative command, the official promise, fixing a day for resumption, have thus far been barren. No practical preparations towards resumption have been made. There has been no progress. There have been steps backward.

There is no necromancy in the operations of government. The homely maxims of every-day life are the best standards of its conduct. A debtor who should promise to pay a loan out of surplus income, yet be seen every day spending all he could lay his hands on in riotous living, would lose all character for honesty and veracity. His offer of a new promise, or his profession as to the value of the old promise, would alike provoke derision.

RESUMPTION PLAN OF THE ST. LOUIS PLATFORM.

The St. Louis platform denounces the failure for eleven years to make good the promise of the legal tender notes. It denounces the omission to accumulate "any reserve for their redemption." It denounces the conduct "which, during eleven years of peace, has made no advances towards resumption, no preparations for resumption, but instead has obstructed resumption, by wasting our resources and exhausting all our surplus income, and, while professing to intend a speedy return to specie payments, has annually enacted fresh hindrances thereto." And having first denounced the barrenness of the promise of a day of resumption, it next denounces that barren promise as a "hindrance" to resumption. It then demands its repeal, and also demands the establishment of "a judicious system of preparation" for resumption. It cannot be doubted that the substitution of a "system of preparation," without the promise of a day, for the worthless promise of a day without "a system of preparation" would be the gain of the substance of resumption in exchange for its shadow.

Nor is the denunciation unmerited of that improvidence which, in the eleven years since the peace, has consumed 4,500 millions of dollars, and yet could not afford to give the people a sound and stable currency. Two and a half per cent. on the expenditures of these eleven years, or even less, would have provided all the additional coin needful to resumption.

RELIEF OF BUSINESS DISTRESS.

The distress now felt by the people in all their business and industries, though it has its principal cause in the enormous waste of capital occasioned by the false policies of our Government, has been greatly aggravated by the mismanagement of the currency. Uncertainty is the prolific parent of mischiefs in all business. Never were its evils more felt than now. Men do nothing, because they are unable to make any calculations on which they can safely rely. They undertake nothing, because they fear a loss in everything they would attempt. They stop and wait. The merchant dares not buy for the future consumption of his customers. The manufacturer dares not make fabrics which may not refund his outlay. He shuts his factory and discharges his workmen. Capitalists cannot lend on security they consider unsafe, and their funds lie almost without interest. Men of enterprise who have credit or security to pledge will not borrow. Consumption has fallen below the natural limits of a reasonable economy. Prices of many things are under their range in frugal, specie-paying times before the civil war. Vast masses of currency lie in the banks unused. A year and a half ago the legal tenders were at their largest volume, and the twelve millions since retired have been replaced by fresh issues of fifteen millions of bank notes. In the meantime the banks have been surrendering about four millions a month, because they cannot find a profitable use for so many of their notes.

The public mind will no longer accept shams. It has suffered enough from illusions. An insincere policy increases distrust. An unstable policy increases uncertainty. The people need to know that the Government is moving in the direction of ultimate safety and prosperity, and that it is doing so through prudent, safe and conservative methods, which will be sure to inflict no new sacrifice on the business of the country. Then the inspiration of new hope and well-founded confidence will hasten the restoring processes of nature, and prosperity will begin to return.

The St. Louis Convention concludes its expression in regard to the currency by a declaration of its convictions as to the practical results of the system of preparations it demands. It says: "We believe such a system, well devised, and above all, intrusted to competent hands for execution, creating at no time an artificial scarcity of currency, and at no time alarming the public mind into a withdrawal of that vast machinery of credit by which ninety-five per cent. of all business transactions are performed—a system open, public, and inspiring general confidence—would, from the day of its adoption, bring healing on its wings to all our harassed industries, set in motion the wheels of commerce, manufactures and the mechanic arts, restore employment to labor, and renew in all its natural sources the prosperity of the people."

The Government of the United States, in my opinion, can advance to a resumption of specie payments on its legal-tender notes by gradual and safe processes tending to relieve the present business distress. If charged by the people with the administration of the Executive office, I should deem it a duty so to exercise the powers with which it has been or may be invested by Congress as best and soonest to conduct the country to that beneficent result.

CIVIL SERVICE REFORM.

The Convention justly affirms that reform is necessary in the civil service, necessary to its purification, necessary to its economy and its efficiency, necessary in order that the ordinary employment of the public business may not be "a prize fought for at the ballot-box, a brief reward of party zeal, instead of posts of honor assigned for proved competency, and held for fidelity in the public employ." The Convention wisely added that "reform is necessary even more in the higher grades of the public service. President, Vice-President, Judges, Senators, Representatives, Cabinet Officers, these and all others in authority are the people's servants. Their offices are not a private perquisite, they are a public trust."

Two evils infest the official service of the Federal Government.

One is the prevalent and demoralizing notion that the public service exists not for the business and benefit of the whole people, but for the interest of the office-holders, who are in truth but the servants of the people. Under the influence of this pernicious error public employments have been multiplied; the numbers of those gathered into the ranks of office-holders have been steadily increased beyond any possible requirement of the public business, while inefficiency, peculation, fraud, and malversation of the public funds, from the high places of power to the lowest, have overspread the whole service like a leprosy.

The other evil is the organization of the official class into a body of political mercenaries, governing the caucuses and dictating the nominations of their own party, and attempting to carry the elections of the people by undue influence, and by immense corruption funds systematically collected from the salaries or fees of office-holders. The official class in other countries, sometimes by its own weight, and sometimes in alliance with the army, has been able to rule the unorganized masses, even under universal suffrage. Here it has already grown into a gigantic power, capable of stifling the inspirations of a sound public opinion, and of resisting an easy change of administration, until misgovernment becomes intolerable, and public spirit has been stung to the pitch of a civic revolution.

The first step in reform is the elevation of the standard by which the appointing power selects agents to execute official trusts. Next in importance is a conscientious fidelity in the exercise of the authority to hold to account and displace untrustworthy or incapable subordinates. The public interest in an honest, skillful performance of official trust must not be sacrificed to the usufruct of the incumbents.

After these immediate steps, which will insure the exhibition of better examples, we may wisely go on to the abolition of unnecessary offices, and, finally, to the patient, careful organization of a better civil service system, under the tests, wherever practicable, of proved competency and fidelity.

While much may be accomplished by these methods, it might encourage delusive expectations if I withheld here the expression of my conviction that no reform of the civil service in this country will be complete and permanent until its chief magistrate is constitutionally disqualified for re-election; experience having repeatedly exposed the futility of self-imposed restrictions by candidates or incumbents. Through this solemnity only can he be effectually delivered from his greatest temptation to misuse the power and patronage with which the Executive is necessarily charged.

CONCLUSION.

Educated in the belief that it is the first duty of a citizen of the republic to take his fair allotment of care and trouble in public affairs, I have for forty years, as a private citizen, fulfilled that duty. Though occupied in an unusual degree during all that period with the concerns of government, I have never acquired the habit of official life. When, a year and a half ago, I entered upon my present trust, it was in order to consummate reforms to which I had already devoted several of the best years of my life. Knowing as I do, therefore, from fresh experience, how great the difference is between gliding through an official routine and working out a reform of systems and policies, it is impossible for me to contemplate what needs to be done in the Federal Administration without an anxious sense of the difficulties of the undertaking. If summoned by the suffrages of my countrymen to attempt this work, I shall endeavor, with God's help, to be the efficient instrument of their will.

SAMUEL J. TILDEN.

To Gen. JOHN A. MCCLERNAND, Chairman, Gen. W. B. FRANKLIN, Hon. J. J. ABBOTT, Hon. H. J. SPAUNHORST, Hon. H. J. REDFIELD, Hon. F. S. LYONS, and others, Committee, &c.

ADDRESS TO GOV. HENDRICKS.

NEW YORK CITY, July 11th, 1876.

GOV. THOMAS A. HENDRICKS:

SIR:—The undersigned, a Committee composed of the President of the National Democratic Convention which met at St. Louis the 27th ult., and one Delegate from each State, have been intrusted with the agreeable duty of waiting upon and notifying you of your nomination by that body as the Democratic candidate for the Vice-Presidency of the United States.

Your unanimous nomination by that Convention to the distinguished position of the party's candidate for the second office in the gift of the people assures us that you will accept the candidacy.

Your long life of public service, and the purity and integrity with which you have invariably discharged the official duties intrusted to you, commend you especially to the favorable consideration of our great party.

We also present you a declaration of the principles adopted by the late Convention, and which are designed for the governing action of the party in its future course.

(13)

Hoping that these will meet your co-operation and concurrence, we, in the desire and earnest expectation that you will notify us of your acceptance of the nomination tendered, beg leave to renew our assurances of regard, &c.

Your very obedient servants,

JOHN A. McCLERNAND, Chairman.

F. S. LYONS, Alabama.
B. D. WILLIAMS, Arkansas.
GEO. H. ROGERS, California.
ADAIR WILSON, Colorado.
W. B. FRANKLIN, Connecticut.
Gov. SAULSBURY, Delaware.
J. D. HARRIS, Florida.
ALLEN FORT, Georgia.
PERRY H. SMITH, Illinois.
BAYLESS W. HANNA, Indiana.
B. F. MONTGOMERY, Iowa.
CHAS. W. BLAIR, Kansas.
W. W. BUSH, Kentucky.
LOUIS ST. MARTIN, Louisiana.
SAMUEL J. ANDERSON, Maine.
J. G. ABBOTT, Massachusetts.
H. J. REDFIELD, Michigan.
J. N. CASTLE, Minnesota.
ROBERT T. BANKS, Maryland.
WADE HAMPTON, Jr., Mississippi.
H. J. SPAUNHORST, Missouri.
GILBERT B. SCOFIELD, Nebraska.
R. P. KEATING, Nevada.
L. HALL, New Hampshire.
P. H. LAVERTY, New Jersey.
HENRY C. MURPHY, New York.
WHARTON J. GREEN, North Carolina.
ISAAC C. COLLINS, Ohio.
MAT. V. BROWN, Oregon.
HENDRICK B. WRIGHT, Pennsylvania
W. B. BEACH, Rhode Island.
M. P. O'CONNOR, South Carolina.
THOMAS O'CONNOR, Tennessee.
JOSEPH E. DWYER, Texas.
JASPER RAND, } Vermont.
B. B. SMALLEY, }
S. C. NEALE, Virginia.
G. D. CAMDEN, West Virginia.
JOS. RANKIN, Wisconsin.

GOV. HENDRICKS' LETTER OF ACCEPTANCE.

INDIANAPOLIS, July 24, 1876.

GENTLEMEN:—I have the honor to acknowledge the receipt of your communication, in which you have formally notified me of my nomination by the National Democratic Convention at St. Louis, as their candidate for the office of Vice-President of the United States. It is a nomination which I had neither expected nor desired; and yet I recognize and appreciate the high honor done me by the Convention. The choice of such a body, pronounced with such unusual unanimity, and accompanied with so generous an expression of esteem and confidence, ought to outweigh all merely personal desires and preferences of my own. It is with this feeling, and I trust also from a deep sense of public duty, that I now accept the nomination, and shall abide the judgment of my countrymen.

It would have been impossible for me to accept the nomination if I could not heartily indorse the platform of the Convention. I am gratified, therefore, to be able unequivocally to declare that I agree in the principles, approve the policies, and sympathize with the purposes enunciated in that platform.

The institutions of our country have been sorely tried by the exigencies of civil war, and, since the peace, by a selfish and corrupt management of public affairs, which has shamed us before civilized mankind. By unwise and partial legislation every industry and interest of the people have been made to suffer; and in the executive departments of the Government, dishonesty, rapacity and venality have debauched the public service. Men known to be unworthy have been promoted, while others have been degraded for fidelity to official duty. Public office has been made the means of private profit, and the country has been offended to see a class of men, who boast the friendship of the sworn protectors of the State, amassing fortunes by defrauding the public treasury and by corrupting the servants of the people. In such a crisis of the history of the country I rejoice that the Convention at St. Louis has so nobly raised the standard of reform. Nothing can be well with us or with our affairs until the public conscience, shocked by the enormous evils and abuses which prevail, shall have demanded and compelled an unsparing reformation of our National Administration, "in its head and in its members." In such a reformation the removal of a single officer, even the President, is comparatively a trifling matter, if the system which he represents, and which has fostered him as he has fostered it, is suffered to remain. The President alone must not be made the scapegoat for the enormities of the system which infest the public service, and threatens the destruction of our institutions. In some respects I hold that the present Executive has been the victim rather than the author of that vicious system. Congressional and party leaders have been stronger than the President. No one man could have created it, and the removal of no one man can amend it. It is thoroughly corrupt, and must be swept remorselessly away by the selection of a government composed of elements entirely new, and pledged to radical reform.

REFORMS NEEDED.

The first work of reform must evidently be the restoration of the normal operation of the Constitution of the United States, with all its amendments. The necessities of war cannot be pleaded in a time of peace; the right of local self-government as guaranteed by the Constitution of the Union must be everywhere restored, and the centralized (almost personal) imperialism which has been practiced must be abandoned, or the first principles of the republic will be lost.

Our financial system of expedients must be reformed. Gold and silver are the real standard of values, and our national currency will not be a perfect medium of exchange until it shall be convertible at the pleasure of the holders. As I have heretofore said, no one desires a return to specie payments more earnestly than I do; but I do not believe that it will or can be reached in harmony with the interests of the people by artificial measures for the contraction of the currency, any more than I believe that wealth or permanent prosperity can be created by an inflation of the currency. The laws of finance cannot be disregarded with impunity. The financial policy of the Government, if indeed it deserves the name of policy at all, has been in disregard of those laws, and therefore has disturbed commercial and business confidence, as well as hindered a return to specie payments. One feature of that policy was the resumption clause of the act of 1875, which has embarrassed the country by the anticipation of a compulsory resumption for which no preparation has been made, and without any assurance that it would be practicable. The repeal of that clause is necessary, that the natural operation of financial laws may be restored, that the business of the country may be relieved from its disturbing and depressing influence, and that a return to specie payments may be facilitated by the substitution of wiser or more prudent legislation, which shall mainly rely on a judicious system of public economies and official retrenchments, and, above all, on the promotion of prosperity in all the industries of the people.

I do not understand the repeal of the resumption clause of the act of 1875 to be a backward step in our return to specie payments, but the recovery of a false step; and although the repeal may, for a time, be prevented, yet the determination of the Democratic party on this subject has now been distinctly declared. There should be no hindrances put in the way of a return to specie payments. "As such a hindrance," says the platform of the St. Louis Convention, "we denounce the resumption clause of the act of 1875, and demand its repeal."

I thoroughly believe that by public economy, by official retrenchments, and by wise finance, enabling us to accumulate the precious metals, resumption at an early period is possible, without producing an "artificial scarcity of currency" or disturbing public or commercial credit; and that these reforms, together with the restoration of pure government, will restore general confidence, encourage the useful investment of capital, furnish employment to labor, and relieve the country from the "paralysis of hard times."

OUR INDUSTRIES.

With the industries of the people there have been frequent interferences. Our platform truly says that many industries have been impoverished to subsidize a few. Our commerce has been degraded to an inferior position on the high seas; manufactures have been diminished; agriculture has been embarrassed, and the distress of the industrial classes demands that these things shall be reformed.

The burdens of the people must also be lightened by a great change in our system of public expenses. The profligate expenditures which increased taxation from five dollars per capita in 1860 to eighteen dollars in 1870, tells its own story of our need of fiscal reform.

Our treaties with foreign powers should also be revised and amended, in so far as they leave citizens of foreign birth in any particular less secure in any country on earth than they would be if they had been born on our own soil; and the iniquitous coolie system which, through the agency of wealthy companies, imports Chinese bondsmen, establishes a species of slavery, and interferes with the just rewards of labor on our Pacific coast, should be utterly abolished.

In the reform of our civil service I most heartily indorse that section of the platform which declares that the civil service ought not to be "subject to change at every election," and that it ought not to be made "the brief reward of party zeal," but ought to be awarded for proved competency and held for fidelity in the public employ. I hope never again to see the cruel and remorseless proscription for political opinions which has disgraced the administration of the last eight years. Bad as the civil service now is, as all know, it has some men of tried integrity and proved ability. Such men, and such men only, should be retained in office; but no man should be retained on any consideration who has prostituted his office to the purpose of partisan intimidation or compulsion, or who has furnished money to corrupt the elections. This is done and has been done in almost every country of the land. It is a blight upon the morals of the country, and ought to be reformed.

OUR SCHOOLS.

Of sectional contentions, and in respect to our common schools, I have only this to say: That in my judgment, the man or party that would involve our schools in political or sectarian controversy is an enemy to the schools. The common schools are safer under the protecting care of all the people than under the control of any party or sect. They must be neither sectarian nor partisan, and there must be neither division nor misappropriation of the funds for their support. Likewise I regard the man who would arouse or foster sectional animosities and antagonisms among his countrymen as a dangerous enemy to his country. All the people must be made to feel and know that once more there is established a purpose and policy under which all citizens of every condition, race and color, will be secure in the enjoyment of whatever rights the Constitution and laws declare or recognize; and that in controversies that may arise the Government is not a partisan, but, within its constitutional authority, the just and powerful guardian of the rights and safety of all. The strife between the sections and between races will cease as soon as the power for evil is taken away from a party that makes political gain out of scenes of violence and bloodshed, and the constitutional authority is placed in the hands of men whose political welfare requires that peace and good order shall be preserved everywhere.

GOV. TILDEN.

It will be seen, gentlemen, that I am in entire accord with the platform of the Convention by which I have been nominated as a candidate for the office of Vice-President of the United States. Permit me, in conclusion, to express my satisfaction at being associated with a candidate for the Presidency who is first among his equals as a representative of the spirit and of the achievements of reform. In his official career as the Executive of the great State of New York, he has, in a comparatively short period, reformed the public service and reduced the public burdens, so as to have earned at once the gratitude of his State and the admiration of the country. The people know him to be thoroughly in earnest; he has shown himself to be possessed of powers and qualities which fit him, in an eminent degree, for the great work of reformation which this country now needs; and if he shall be chosen by the people to the high office of President of the United States, I believe that the day of his inauguration will be the beginning of a new era of peace, purity and prosperity in all departments of our Government.

I am, gentlemen, your obedient servant,

THOMAS A. HENDRICKS.

To the Hon. JOHN A. McCLERNAND, Chairman, and others, of the Committee of the National Democratic Convention.

www.ingramcontent.com/pod-product-compliance
Lightning Source LLC
LaVergne TN
LVHW010742120826
845150LV00009B/1406

9781425517311